Bringing Up
Baby Bilingual

Bringing Up Baby Bilingual

Jane Merrill

Facts On File Publications
New York, New York ● Bicester, England

Bringing Up Baby Bilingual

**Library of Congress Cataloging in
Publication Data**

Merrill, Jane.
    Bringing up baby bilingual.

    1. Language acquisition.
2. Bilingualism.   I. Title.
P118.M44   1984   404'.2   83-11532
ISBN 0-87196-717-0

Published by Facts On File, Inc.
      460 Park Avenue South
      New York, N.Y. 10016

Printed in the United States of America
10 9 8 7 6 5 4 3 2 1

In memory of
R. Thomas Merrill

. . . I want to beg you . . . to be patient toward all that is unsolved in your heart and to try to love the *questions themselves* like locked rooms and like books that are written in a very foreign tongue. . . . *Live* the question now. Perhaps you will then gradually, without noticing it, live along some distant day into the answer.

Rilke
Letters to a Young Poet

Contents

Introduction

Most of the languages spoken in the world are heard in the United States and Canada. Throughout North America, pockets of native Americans cling to their tribal tongues. Navajo is one of the official languages of New Mexico. In cities, Haitians speak Creole when they get together to party and have fun. The Cajuns of Louisiana gather at their favorite bars in the evening and sing in their Acadian French. In every large American city, sizable communities of Estonians, Poles, Hungarians and other Eastern European groups are present and fill their neighborhoods with non-English conversations, newspapers and books. The new language of the shrimping boats of Biloxi, Mississippi is Vietnamese.

We Americans are proud of these immigrant roots, yet we view citizenship as an English-language activity. Benjamin Franklin and other founding fathers spoke European languages as a matter of course, but after we turned away from Europe, official Americans were only too happy to have a great ocean separate us from the polyglot Continent. This isolation, together with the decline of classical education, has made us somewhat blind to the realities of international politics, economics and culture that are inherently multilingual. As living in isolation becomes more and more impossible, we are at last waking up to the importance of speaking other nations' languages. In the past 20 years, the federal government has spent millions of dollars to support the teaching of Asian and Third-World languages. Washington recognizes that always to translate the information exchanged with other nations into English is to rely on palaver of the worst sort. As foreign policy moves from dominating to understanding, expertise in *their* tongue takes on a premium.

For this book I have interviewed and corresponded with hundreds of families who speak dozens of languages, from Icelandic to Japanese, in their American homes. They vary in religiousness, self-consciousness and literariness. Whether they are fresh off the boat or preparing to return in retirement to a native land, what works for one family basically works for all. The families I used are pioneers. Just as in pioneer America parents passed on to their children many skills, so in these families parents have let or are letting language flow—opening their mouths, not shutting them, on the native language, or the language acquired by systematic study. They have overcome the strange fear, common in the United States, that multilingualism is a Pandora's box, an inadmissible quirk. True, a common language has facilitated the development of this powerful nation. But how completely false it is that a common language requires the sacrifice of a mother tongue, or licenses deafness to the rest of the linguistic world. The choice need not be between mother tongue and English. With a lot of care and a little effort you can raise a child who speaks and reads two languages excellently.

A language you have studied or can recall is a skill you can pass on to your child more specifically than any other. As Rilke says in the quotation that begins this book: Live, if you can, the question now, and try to love the questions themselves. In all probability the extra language will enhance your children's social life, better prepare them for a job and give them a synoptic perspective on languages and cultures. It will also whiz a kid through a college entrance exam! Start using your second language tomorrow, whether you have the terrific vocabulary you consider ideal or just a basic level of knowledge. You have years in which to cross the ocean of language, but you must launch the ship! This book not only shows you that bilingualism can be achieved, but that the result is a child *in touch* with the world as it really is.

A Note on Languages Highlighted

Spanish, Italian, German and French are the four largest minority languages in America. In the last census, 10.6 million Americans reported a Spanish-language background, 2.9 million an Italian, 2.7 million a German and 1.9 million a French. Other languages fall below the million mark, although several Asian languages are growing rapidly. Still, the four major languages are those most often taught in grammar and high schools and schools of higher learning. Because of the numbers of speakers and the educational focus on these four languages, they are the top four languages for bilingual child-rearing in this country. Accordingly, in the chapters that follow I refer to them often, especially in discussions of learning materials. They will stand as examples for language-learning in general.

The choice was difficult and, despite the logic of the four, arbitrary. On the one hand, I wanted to emphasize active groups struggling to maintain their language and culture. Often the smaller minorities—say, Estonians or Yiddish-speaking Jews—are struggling harder. On the other, because my program is designed to give your children a skill they will find useful in the adult world, Japanese (to take a salient example) would probably be of more use than Estonian. The justification for the basic slant toward the four major languages is that ultimately, for most people in America, they are the easiest to raise children to speak.

But the principles of the book apply to all languages. If you live in New Bedford, Astoria, Detroit or San Francisco, you may be able to learn Portuguese, Greek, Arabic or Chinese more readily than Spanish, Italian, German or French. The resources—or friends, festive occasions, street life, sometimes published materials—are there, "in place." Family situation, neighborhood and your attitude, not statistics, make the context in which you will raise your child bilingual.

1
Confessions of a Mother of Bilinguals

People are often asked what five books they would take on a lifeboat to a desert island. My children *are* on a desert island, in a manner of speaking; an island of French language in an English sea. They are there by their mother's design, the result of a cradle-wish I made over them, that they might learn a second language from babyhood.

I decided to raise my children speaking a second language because two languages are better than one. Let us count the ways. Travel is inestimably more fun if you speak the language of the natives. When you speak a foreign language, opportunities open up in your career and for friendships. And reading books from another literary tradition refines the mind and delights the spirit. By starting young, my children will be able to read books in French with the same facility as they do books in English. In high school they will be stars, in college superstars, in at least one subject. In their careers they will be on an inside track. In Europe, successful people are usually bilingual or multilingual. The dynamics of world economy will reward bilingual Americans greatly in the future, as we become more competitive in world markets. What more enduring skill can I give my children than an additional language? They are growing up one-up.

They are also growing up citizens of the world. I am very concerned that though, by chance, my children roam one neighborhood they should not be blind to the wider reality of a world that is dauntingly large and incredibly diverse. Speaking a second language brings home daily the plurality and interconnectedness of the world at large. Finally, I am raising them bilingual for the pure interest of the task and because it takes up some unfinished business of my own.

My travels as a Navy brat took me to an American base near Paris in the late 1950s. My brother, Tom, and I could not attend a French school, for local school authorities frowned on extensive absences for students, and our parents wanted us to be able to travel. So we went instead to the American military school. There a sixth-grade teacher, Jim Yeannakopoulos, beckoned us into French culture. He taught us French songs, took us to parties at a French orphanage and featured the great bicycle race, the Tour de France, in both geography and math.

My brother and I had ulterior reasons for learning French. Tom wanted to gain permission to explore Paris and its environs *sans* parents. And I longed to understand the captions on the *gravures,* the colorful broadsheets of royalty and explorers, fruits and birds, that I was collecting like baseball cards. We shared two other goals. We wanted to order good things in restaurants instead of relying on our mother's tenuous, if fetching, comprehension of the menu. She was strong on *soupe du jour* but ran the risk of getting a platter of *haricots* instead of *entrecôte.* We also longed to get off the bicycles that sped us from the American compound through the tiny French village to the open road, and plant our feet firmly in conversation with the French kids.

Sundays, my family often visited Madame Jadot, the expatriate widow of a Belgian officer who had died shortly after World War II. These visits spanned most of the day. While she served vodka and raw oysters, Tom and I were left very much to our own devices. With two other children, we played foursquare and shuttlecock in the courtyard of the building for most of the day, until our laughter rose in the evening air and we could no longer see to play. At the end of those sundays, when I was 11 and 12, French rolled off my tongue in waves—with nowhere to go. That early exposure to French did not make me fluent, but it made me language-keen.

My brother eventually managed to become a professor of French. But for us both, as for many who love to learn languages informally, college foreign-language courses were frustrating. Over-air conditioned, fluorescent-lit language labs—space-age contexts for language learning—are lonely and boring compared with conversing with living people. It is so discouraging to write a passionate essay about surrealist hero-ines, or leprosy in nineteenth-century poetry, and receive a poor grade for forgetting commas, or because the essay wasn't *triée* (structured in three parts). By the time I graduated from Wellesley College I spoke four languages, but commanded a French that wasn't schoolgirl-perfect enough to permit me to go on a junior year to Paris. Yet I held to my dream of living the language someday, and, at 28, mid-marriage but before bearing children, went to Paris for a wonderful year. I found a congenial job in the Seventeenth *Arrondissement* and a cold-water garret in the Seventh, drove around on a spanking new white motor scooter, became enamored of antique earrings, made French friends, read next to nothing and at last had a foreign-language experience on the order of what I am giving my twins.

I did not implement the plan for my children immediately. For their first year, it remained a wish upon a star. Then the remark of a psychoanalyst friend provoked me. He gave me the same counsel about raising the twins bilingually that he had given (and which I had happily ignored) about breast-feeding past infanthood: DON'T. (Bilingual child-rearing *is* like breast-feeding: It is giving a child a tender gift. It costs you nothing and fits in beautifully with everyday life.)

I consulted a child psychiatrist, Dr. Luis Marcos, who is him-self bilingual. Dr. Marcos gave a green light to the "artificial" bilingual experiment. He asserted that if a parent feels com-fortable with and positive, not fearful, about "adopting" a lan-guage, his or her level of fluency is of little issue. Dr. Marcos cautioned only that a parent should be ready to abandon the foreign language if the child seems very troubled later at talking "different."

Despite an inchoate longing to prove my psychiatrist friend wrong, I still held back. With the twins at the babbling stage, I told myself it was too soon. Then I met the Schwartzmans, a Japanese mother and a Yiddish-speaking, Jewish-American father. They interested me particularly because their sons' trilingualism was deliberately constructed, as our children's bilingualism would be.

The father, although he had spoken Yiddish since childhood, had no contact with other Yiddish speakers. Mr. Schwartzman put me on the spot: "If you are seriously interested in bringing your children up in more than one language, what are you waiting for?" I bemoaned my restricted vocabulary, barren especially in the area of household objects and activities where small children substantially operate. He shoved aside my doubt: "I keep a dictionary by my bed. You can do the same."

When I walked in the door after visiting the Schwartzmans, I inaugurated the bilingual plan, greeting the twins with *"Bonjour, les bébés!"* Emma and Burton were 18 months old when my exclusive language with them became French. My husband, Chris, continued to use English, both with the children, and in conversations with me. I was elated to be realizing a dream. So many things one plans for children before having them become difficult or impossible once the children are present. Many ideas become irrelevant in the rush of life. Will you really have a viola da gamba quartet together, or build a log cabin or animate a marionette theater? Will your diverse interests converge in collecting American Indian artifacts, or in white-water rafting? Will you be willing to sacrifice and deflect from the paths of your jobs and avocations to engage yourselves in worthwhile projects with your children? As relatively late parents, in our 30s, Chris and I had many interests and pastimes already set. Our careers had claims on us. Yet we wanted to "handcraft" our parenting, and not merely conform mindlessly to the status quo. I was sure our children would become language-rich anyway in English from living in an English-speaking land. Moreover, I intuited, I was sure I could give the children time for French. After all, it would require only the translation of normal speaking time.

You must become conditioned to speaking a foreign language with the baby before it feels natural. How silly it felt at first to speak a foreign language to toddlers! At 18 months, they were already babbling and speaking a few words in English. At the onset, Emma and Burton answered my French in English. I saw what a bore and travail that would be as a continuing pattern, and so spent a lot of time rewarding their early French words, weaving them into phrases, and sometimes, with a smile of complicity, pretending not to understand the English word when the French was on the tip of their tongues. Even if the child has contact with many other adult and young speakers of his first language, if one is consistent about using his second language in direct conversation with the child, the passive knowledge will shift to active.

Within a few months, the children were answering me in French, and the reverse—that is, English dialogue—would have seemed odd. The twins' speech quickly advanced from being a porphyry, of English mass-encrusted with French words and phrases, to two distinct language skeins. Before they ever spoke French, when given the definite article, they could point to the right object in a pair. When they wanted to nurse, they asked for *du lait*. Their repective security objects were *mon oreiller* and *ma couverture*. They will never have to memorize the genders!

I often reflect that my French is the last part of me to wake up in the morning. The children speak to me in French which, reinforced now (they are six) by their other sources of learning, may in a few years outdistance my proficiency. We go to a new environment like wildlife preserve, a dairy or the Fulton Street fish market, and I had better remember my dictionary, or missing French vocabulary will tie my tongue. Sometimes the mere thought of wording an explanation of a mechanical process or scientific principle in French makes me pass the buck to their father. But must not words be carefully chosen for dialogues with the young even in one's native language? And isn't it fun to discover with the children that hijackers in French are "pirates of the air?"

French is like a saddle to which I have become accustomed. There's the pleasure of the exercise, like a ballet dancer who walks wearing weights on her feet. Dictionaries are no longer heavy, dry tomes, but friends who offer me the terms I most want to know. From reading children's books with them and listening to French children's songs I have a host of shared nursery heritage with the twins that is a very helpful baggage. If you restore your house you enjoy it more because of the work you have put into it; this is how I feel about life lived in two languages. My maternal grandmother, Emma, kept her Latin grammar and readers on the bedside table, alongside her prayer books and the *New York Times* daily crossword puzzle. She applied herself to language study because the intellectual work had its own satisfaction. As only those who are interested in informal home bilingualism will understand—let my other readers howl and hoot—I feel how flat and routine relating to my children would be without the added language and culture. One thing more. The parent/coach realizes from the beginning that his pupil will soon show superior mastery. This, too, eases the effort. Someday, you remind yourself, your child will be weaned from you as the absolute source of the second language, and will, indeed, bring the language into the family from other sources.

I recognize that living bilingually places an extra demand on my children. I prod them to sort out words from one language to the other, but refrain from correcting their grammatical mistakes. I try to tone down their occasional quibbles over gender or the pronunciation of a word. Similarly, I encourage them to attend to a speaker's meaning, not to try to recut and sew the cloth of another person's thought.

Every mother teaches a child on her knees, but speaking French probably accentuates the instructional element in our mother–child relationship. When they are doing artwork, if I don't teach them that to rubber-stamp is *tamponner,* who will? When I see how they like to type their names on the typewriter, one ambitious dip into the dictionary equips me with the words for "key" and "keyboard," which they are sure to hear the next time they have a go at the machine. Unconsciously, the children and I may compensate for this pedagogy with a lot of spontaneity and nonverbal sharing. Arts and crafts activities and picnics happen extravagantly *à l'improviste.* Perhaps our dancing to records and cuddling up in blankets and pillows to read are balm for the effort a second language may cost us.

The children's French habit with me is watertight. They know my bath time is for luxurious unwinding. I space out mentally. At my more permissive, I let them sail their boats and float their Fisher-Price figures in the tub while I lie submerged. Although I'm willing to create some wave action with the strokes of a hand or position my knees as atolls, I don't want to lift my lids to acknowledge the tubside players. Yet whether alone or together, their bathtub talk is entirely in French. Burton, who is fonder of water play, tells himself long stories and sends orders to his fleet. We are in *foreign* waters. As ethologists say about ducklings with surrogate mothers, the twins are "imprinted" with water play in French.

The family at a distance from their language's culture is forever coining or guessing at words. If only we could mail-order from a Quebec supermarket, much of this homegrown French could be dispensed with. As it is, when dictionary and friends fail us, we give things our own descriptive names. Wheat germ is termed *grains de germes de blé*. We call the card game Old Maid *Vieille Fille,* and have no idea whether the same game is played outside North America.

Staying in the French context is so important that I choose to invent words, talk around the missing word, rather than resort to an English equivalent. The English word only serves to puncture a hole in the French context. Until I find expert opinion, our new porch swing is a *siège de réflexion*. These neologisms, a family patois, are a lesser sin than Franglais.

To start a small child on the bilingual path, you must have confidence enough to march to your own drumbeat. There are controlling moments, times when a child speaks back to you in English and you gentle the conversation back into the foreign language. If you fear being draconic, visit a bilingual family and see how naturally the give-and-take occurs, how joyously the children take part. Why? Because the second language is one of emotional identification for them. If it is not native to you, your identification will in fact be less than theirs.

When you want to praise your child, or respond to an accident or misdemeanor, your first impulse—especially early in the home bilingual program—will be to use English. Your emotional responses must never take precedence over language learning. In *Teacher*, Sylvia Ashton-Warner describes that Maori children learn to read those words with an emotional content for them before others. My children have had very few spankings, but when they have been punished it has been in French. I learned the words for threatening a *fessée*, and how to say "Go to the corner this instant" in plenty of time to use them, and to talk about *bobos* (ouches), Band-Aids and mosquito bites in French as well. I set out to speak to the twins *entirely* in French, and later, to converse with them entirely in French. The foreign language is not, with us, a sometime thing.

You are going to feel the need to keep your child's foreign-language world watertight. A young child's use of the second language waxes and wanes according to the degree of exposure, which you want to keep at a maximum. After an early visit to their grandparents, my children returned excited over the new place, friends and goings on, but forgetful of their French. The following visit, we rendezvous-ed with their grandparents on the turnpike. When I gathered the twins for goodbyes, like the mother of Red Riding Hood, I had messages. I told them to keep faith with our private language and to use the other one mindfully. "When people visit the house," I told them, "say, 'Hello, I'm Emma,' 'Hello, I'm Burton' in French. There are several French records in your suitcase. Listen to them from time to time so you don't forget.

Today, the search for roots has engendered a new reason for learning multiple languages; to connect with one's whole identity—because our ethnic origins help us to identify ourselves. Seeing my children and me chat with one another in French, and with the world in English, strangers sometimes approach us to comment. I tend to say we are a "French-speaking family," in order to minimize the "experimental" aspect of raising Emma and Burton bilingual. And so, when the twins were six, though indifferent genealogists, we touched base with our Huguenot heritage in La Rochelle. There is rarely anything casual, nearly always something soulful and earnest, about the remarks of house painters, check-out clerks, police officers, young people and college professors who wish *their* parents or grandparents had taught them their ethnic languages instead of letting them die of neglect.

When one or both parents speak a non-English language natively, or have the language strongly in the family, if they do not teach it to their children, they are cutting them off from their roots. It is fun to cook and eat the food of our various ancestors, learn about their customs, maybe even celebrate their traditional holidays. Our roots remain with us in a real way when we continue religious and cultural traditions, but without the language a heritage struggles to survive. More than any other activity, language irrigates the soil of culture, and turns it into a rich loam in which the individual thrives, along with the group.

French is a commitment in the life of my family. It would be an enormous dislocation if for weeks or months no one spoke it with the children. It seems impossible to me now that they could ever forget French. They would not be themselves without it, yet it doesn't come automatically to us. Similarly, the link with one's ethnic heritage is not strong for a family in the United States unless they make the effort to preserve the recessive tongue.

The wonderful aspect of bilingual child-rearing, discipline though it be, is that it meshes with, yet does not add burdens to, an already busy life. You may commit yourself to a physical-fitness program and then catch the flu; or you might decide as a family to raise all your summer vegetables, but simply can't find the time to separate and weed. But the language commitment can be satisfied in different ways at different times. Sometimes you should make a big effort to drive your child to the nearest other family with bilingual children for a language fest. Other times, because you monitor your child's progress, you want to meet—say—her budding interest in sewing with an appropriate foreign-language book on the subject. An example of your commitment all along is your investment in books and records. You will resist, as I have, buying English books; instead, scout out secondhand books in the foreign language, and find a reliable foreign bookseller. You should be ready with a first book of geography a season *before* your child becomes fascinated by his toy globe.

The twins nearly always bring me books from their library that I have read before in French (no matter what the book's original language). If they ask for *The Poky Little Puppy*, it is a translation they really want to hear. Hence I launch into *Le Petit Chiot brun et blanc*, or some other improvised conceit. Our bond is French enough that I am happy to do so. Classics in English like *The Wind in the Willows* and *Charlotte's Web* are read aloud by the twins' father, not by me—unless I lay my hands on a French translation. I keep two dozen classics about English-speaking children, such as *Mary Poppins, Stuart Little* and *A Cricket in Times Square*, in French, for interspersing with picture books, now that Emma and Burton are growing older.

The rewards of perseverance are daily. One day, when she was almost four, Emma asked me in French, "*Maman*, when I am an adult, can I leave for France?" "Certainly," I answered. She said, "Thank you, *Maman*. I need to see people who know only French."

I suspect that sensitivity to and love for language are especially apt to develop when a child lives in two languages, and is semi-consciously comparing one to the other. Emma took out construction paper, markers and white glue, and did a painting of glue swirls on a midnight blue paper drawn with orange loops. Then she tore off the corners and glued them at the center. "Je fais un collage avec beaucoup de colle, un collage collé," she said with delight. ("I'm making a collage with a lot of glue, a glued glue drawing.") She has also, while stretched out in front of the fire, cocked her head up to say, "Me? Oh, I'm watching the fire and understanding more of its language."

Bilingual children may be unusually attuned to verbalizing the definition of words. We saw a picture of a baby in a hammock in a nursery book. "I know what a hammock is," volunteered Burton, nearly four, in French. "You take a blanket, climb a tree, make a knot—no, two knots—and go inside."

The children summon their most fluent French for different subjects. Emma takes some of her giant steps with reference to beautiful clothes and dressing up. The sight of a new flower-girl mannequin in a bridal shop set off a monologue about womanhood, an unprecedented spurt of French at three years and seven months. "When I am an adult, I'm going to marry Burton," said Emma, swooning over the gowns. But mightn't Burton like to be best man, I suggested, and carry the ring? She retorted: "Then I am going to marry a papa man who takes care of animals at the zoo. I invite you to the wedding, *Maman.* Everyone is going to dance."

Contrarily, many of Burton's language leaps are made when he thinks about cars and trucks, just as his first reading was of car-model names. Playing with Lego is a time for relaxed language, as opposed to language that endeavors to convey a message. When I passed by his Lego garage, Burton, just past three and a half, plunged into French speech markedly more complex than the usual, in order to let me in on his construction.

Children in their late threes are lovable for their emotiveness, the extent to which they exteriorize many of their feelings and problems. During the same month that Emma secured my promise of a trip to France someday, Burton was sorting out the implications of the two languages as well. He told me he wanted French people who come to the house to learn English—and English people to learn French. The beginning of a utopia!

That night, Burton asked me what an Erector set in his big Richard Scarry word book was called in French. I didn't know, I replied, and asked him to bring me the French version. He brought it, found the same page and we read *"jeu de construction."* Burton understood a big word in French such as this instantly, but he still had trouble getting his mouth around it. Then, after reading the rest of the double-page spread and showing certain objects to Emma, he remarked that he would like to put the books together. That way we could speak French and English at the same time. Off he went for *le scotch* (French for all kinds of adhesive tape), and after laying the back covers side by side, bound them together. The result did not please him entirely, but he carefully flexed the conjoined sides of the new "book" a number of times before deciding that each worked better separately. What effort to relate the languages could be more concrete?

The children often translate important communiqués into French or English for the benefit of one or the other parent. Both parents may understand both languages, but it is axiomatic to Emma and Burton that a different language be associated with each. They know they can lapse into English with me and be understood, yet I will not respond in kind. Emma, slightly the more advanced in language development, does this as a pleasantry from time to time. I look mildly puzzled: why has she broken our code? She continues, with a look of mischief, *en français*.

They were four before they seemed to realize that I speak English too. Many Fridays a neighbor's little boy comes to play. Naturally, I speak English when speaking directly to Tony (although his mother likes having Tony come home with a few French words too). After Tony left, one Friday, Burton asked me, "Mommy, do you speak English?" Even at five they have an insouciance about which language they are hearing or speaking. They saw *Argent de Poche* (*Small Change*), François Truffaut's film, in an audience of American children, and reported wrongly to their father that the film was in English. I heard this interchange when they were nearly four: Emma: "Daddy, how do you say 'bathrobe' in English?" "Emma, that *is* English." Emma: "*Oh, donc, Maman. Comment dit-on 'bathrobe' en français?*"

Translating for a third party bestows authority on a child. The child feels proud, in charge. With our home's bilingualism, the children have many chances to teach Mommy and Daddy. Burton: "*Emma ne m'aime pas.*" (Emma doesn't like me.) Mother: "*Emma taquine.*" (Emma is teasing.) Emma: "*En anglais, Maman, on dit 'teasing.'*"

A second illustration shows how methodical the children are about such translations. After Burton told some peanut-butter jokes—statements about peanut butter as though it were a child, not a thing—Emma said to me, "*Il est rigole. Tu sais ce que ça veut dire? Qu'il donne des drôles histoires.*" (He is a joker. You know what that means? That he tells funny stories.)

Although the children keep their language as pure as they can in conversation, in private they fluctuate. Particularly when alone with books, dolls and trucks, they often take the net of separation down at will, bouncing their thoughts from one side of the verbal court to the other. As he colored at four and a half, Burton noted that "This house is crunched, or you could say in French that it's *écrasé*." One day in February I listened to the tail-end of Emma's reading aloud a picture book to herself. After she closed the book, her singsong talk ran as follows:

"*Maman*, you are the most, the most. *Le la le lapin*, Bugs Bunny, *se cache dans un trou*. A little baby. *Une touterelle*. A little book. *Un drapeau. Petit vers, haricot vert, vers, vert*." The cascade and patchwork of language reminds me of Colette's daughter, Bel Gazou. During World War I, the four year old chattered in the window-blacked house for half an hour in English (learned from Nursie-Dear) and in French before sleep. Wrote Colette: "English chatter, statements in dialect, interrupted songs, improvisations on a beloved theme, 'Come, Christmas, come', variations of fables, and 'Madelon, Madelon . . .' between words, between songs, there is laughter."

Bilingual children develop a keen sense of audience too. They become adept at reportage from one language to another. They exercise the storytelling faculty powerfully in the situation where they tell one parent thus-and-so happened, translating from the other language. Everything is the art of storytelling when Burton and Emma tell Daddy in English about the farm they visited, essentially, in French. It is funny to hear, but right to the children, extensive English embedded in an overall French speech. To give the briefest example, Emma, at four, said: "*Jean a essayé d'enlever mes lunettes mais je les ai gardé.' Et Valerie m'a dit—anglais—*'Don't look at him.' *Donc je ne l'ai pas regardé. 'Good for you!' elle a crié*. Silly John." (John tried to take off my glasses but I kept them. And Valerie said to me—English—'Don't look at him.' So I didn't look at him . . . .")

Emma has begun to critique my French. She has learned young that a parent's wisdom is finite, that Mommy (in our case) can be wrong. She makes gentle corrections of my use of genders and my pronunciation. Under a French-Canadian roomer's tutelage, at three they dropped a false elision in *en haut* (upstairs), and reminded me to do so as well. Another French-speaking babysitter shuddered when the children articulated the "p" in *sirop*. They raced up to my home office, eager for me to set her straight. Alas, *Maman* ceded to the native speaker.

2
Family Portraits

Si les murs pouvaient parler!
—French-Canadian proverb

Certain traits characterize nearly all families who raise their children bilingually with success. They have an inner security, a sense of family destiny about this special gift. Their enthusiasm makes even what is hard seem easy, and every member of the family (even the mother or father who doesn't speak the extra language) lends support and feels involved. The bilingualism forms an extra bond. The family enjoys rituals, jokes and warm, intimate occasions in abundance. The families in this chapter tend to be families with a strong personality. They don't give up on the second language when the child reaches school age, and they try multiple approaches at every age and stage of their child's development.

I have divided a number of bilingual families into three categories, for the purpose of looking at them: (1) the family for whom the second language comes utterly naturally, (2) the family where one parent joins the other in speaking that parent's native tongue and (3) the family where one or both parents simply choose to raise the children bilingually (the situation you have read about in the last chapter, describing my twins). The most salient difference among families, you see, is the relationship of the *parents* to the extra language. In all the families, even ethnic families ensconced in an ethnic American community, ingenuity and a high level of involvement in the philosophy of learning are required. But no matter whether you give birth to the "gift of language" naturally, or adopt it, you and your child will love it just as much!

Naturally Speaking

Spanish/English. Maria Torres, a social worker in Brooklyn, New York, uses her English, Spanish and "a street mix" in her social-work job in the *barrio*. It was her mother who, through the power of love, incorporated Spanish into her children's achievement-oriented lives, giving them the bilingual advantage.

The Torres family, an Hispanic family with an international extended family, are not atypical of their multi-ethnic Brooklyn neighborhood. Mr. and Mrs. Torres' brothers and sisters have married into Jewish, Italian and French, as well as Hispanic families. Various of the aunts and uncles are passing on Yiddish, Italian and French to their individual families, in homes where Spanish is spoken too. On the day I interviewed Maria Torres, she was celebrating Jewish Purim with one branch of her family.

Mrs. Torres, Maria's mother, came to the mainland from Puerto Rico first at age four, then again at nine, and has not been back since. She didn't finish high school but can read and write English well. Mr. Torres came to New York at 17. He picked up the language easily through his job as a machinist; having worked for the same company for 29 years, he is now plant foreman. There are four Torres children, two girls and two boys, with nine years' difference between oldest and youngest; all are New York-born.

Their neighborhood was mostly Italian and Jewish when the family moved in. Mrs. Torres didn't have anyone to talk to, so she learned English of necessity. She started her children off in English as well as Spanish, speaking both languages at home. Today the parents' first impulse is to communicate in Spanish, while the children sometimes translate their thoughts *into* Spanish. When they are in public, depending on who "leads" with which language, a conversation among family members can go either way.

Maria, the oldest child, is Youth Employment Director for their Williamsburg neighborhood. Like her sister and the elder brother, Maria qualified for her government job in part due to her bilingualism.

As a child, Maria went to parochial school. She resented being made to take speech class in elementary school. "A lot of us born here," she says, "didn't want to be lumped with the immigrants. We spoke with no more accent than our Italian friends, but our names were Spanish. I now can detect my accent, but I'm not ashamed of it." Many people in the school spoke something besides English. Maria recalls no problems from other students about being bilingual. She thinks, though, that the teachers were overzealous in pressuring children of Puerto Rican background to use no Spanish. "Unnecessary," she says, "since we were all reasonably capable of keeping the two languages straight."

The Torres children acquired English early through the conscious effort of their parents. Although the parents actually spoke more Spanish than English at home, and the children heard Spanish in large enough doses to grasp its subtleties, English got excellent billing. Maria says, "The Puerto Ricans were just beginning to immigrate in large numbers. They came with one dream—they were proud of their American citizenship and wanted to be Americans all the way."

At 13, Maria decided she did not want to speak Spanish or associate herself with Spanish culture. At that same point, in 1969, her mother made up her mind not to let the Spanish culture—or language—go. Mrs. Torres recalls, "I wanted the kids and myself to learn English well, but I was also proud of the Spanish culture and wanted to make sure the kids had both, and lost neither." As Maria began high school, it appeared she might lose her Hispanic heritage. Seeing situations in the neighborhood and in the family where from one generation to the next people preserved nothing of their past, Mrs. Torres was jolted into concern and action. "She began hitting us with Spanish, telling stories and history, playing up the culture," says Maria.

For example, on January 6, Mrs. Torres sat her children down and explained how Epiphany, not Christmas, was gift-giving day in Puerto Rico. The younger children were charmed by the tradition of putting water and grass under their beds for the Three Kings to feed their camels and refresh themselves on their long journey.

In the Torres household, although the father spoke Spanish to the children, he came home from work late. It was more the mother's presence and determination that kept the family bilingual, in the face of the children's strong urge to "be American." And it was the girls who became more interested in reading and writing Spanish as well as English. "If you ask my mother which of her children are fluent in Spanish she says 'My two daughters,' " says Maria. Mrs. Torres laughs and explains: "That's because the girls are in the house. Boys are in Little League, in this and that. The girls had outside interests, yes, but did more with me at home—cooking, listening to Spanish music, reading fiction I had around, and liked too." The second son picked up Spanish well too, benefiting from the fact that Mrs. Torres has more leisure these days for talking with her youngest after school. His siblings are helping increase his Spanish fluency as well.

Sometimes, when with another bilingual, the family falls into a linguistic mix. Maria says, "When I'm talking with a Spanish monolingual, I realize, from his stunned expression, that I'm speaking English, and reprogram myself to speak only Spanish. That's one of the pitfalls. It's natural in my *barrio* to use five words English, two Spanish, three English, eight Spanish, but it really throws off people who speak only one or the other." When dealing with the neighborhood, Maria finds young people understand and speak the "street mix," but she makes an effort to speak Spanish consistently at home.

Once a source of embarrassment, being bilingual has for Maria and her brothers and sisters become a source of pride. "Maybe I didn't think having two languages was so terrific growing up," says Maria, "sometimes it was very conflicting; but I do now. It makes me feel I'm more interesting to other people. It makes me more effective in my job. It also sets my family apart in a way that makes us feel very secure."

Polish/English. The Moscickis, Polish immigrants, both spent time in concentration camps, and met in Sweden following World War II. They lived in Sweden for seven years, during which their first two daughters were born. In 1952, the family immigrated to the United States, settling in Detroit, where they had relatives. The three girls grew up learning Polish before English and—here the Moscickis' language story blazes with success—all now speak, read and write Polish as grown women while holding challenging jobs in the English-speaking world.

Detroit's Polish community is large and active. A Polish festival is held at the Hart Plaza every August. The nearby city of Hamtramck, a community founded by Poles, has Polish restaurants, bookstores and cultural shops. The *Polish Daily News* is published weekly in the Detroit area, and two radio stations, WCAR and WPON, broadcast Polish programs. Involvement with various cultural organizations such as the Polish Youth Organization (the Polish Scouts) gave the Moscicki children the opportunity to learn the language after school and at summer camps, with others brought up in the same cultural heritage, as well as at home. Constantly having Polish-speaking visitors in the home, and speaking and listening to them, also helped reinforce the second language.

Many families begin speaking their ethnic language with their first-born but, as more English enters the home, lose their resolve with the second or third child, who is therefore less fluent. By contrast, the Moscickis persisted. When a daughter talked to the parents in English, they claimed they didn't understand what she was saying. Says Wanda, the youngest, "I used to get angry at them because I knew they *did* understand, but now I am grateful that they did that." The home abounded in books and other reading materials sent by relatives from Poland, which were important in developing literacy skills without any formal instruction.

What earthly good does Polish do a hospital pharmacist in Michigan? According to Wanda, being bilingual nourishes her whole life: "Speaking the language of my minority has always been very rewarding to me. In cultural organizations I learned Polish folk songs, traditions, history and legends, in addition to what was passed on at home. Most of my closest friends to this day are other bilingual individuals with the same cultural background, whom I got to know during childhood. I have also met people and traveled to places that I might never have seen otherwise. When I visited Poland in 1969, I had no difficulty communicating with relatives and other people I met. I firmly believe that being bilingual makes learning additional languages that much easier. In school, I learned Spanish quickly, and well enough to use it when called upon in my job."

Russian/English. Our first two family portraits were of newcomers, the children of recent immigrants. However, families with no recollections of a home country, American born and bred, can elect to accentuate the language of their heritage too— no matter that it was learned in Newark, New Jersey or Toledo, Ohio. The families of Nadia and Dimitri Rakoff are Russian Orthodox. Both families left Russia for political reasons, though at different times. On Dimitri's side, they were White Army officers who left Russia after the Revolution in the 1920s to gather forces in a free country. First they went to Bulgaria, then France, Luxembourg and Belgium, living out of suitcases; and because they never thought of themselves as being other than Russian, they gave lessons in Russian and Russian history. Wherever they settled they built churches.

The children of these people, Dimitri's parents, learned French and German in European schools, but remained adamantly Russian and passed this on to their children. Dimitri came to America from Luxembourg when he was 11, speaking French, Russian and some English. But Russian was his first tongue, the language spoken at home, in church and with friends in the Russian community.

Nadia's side of the family lived in the Soviet Union until World War II, when they were taken as slave laborers by the Germans for work in Germany. At the end of the war these people, displaced persons, wanted to stay in the West. Nadia's family was in the American sector of Germany and in 1951 they were able to come to America. Seeing themselves as political refugees, they did not in their hearts leave Russia, but only the USSR, so Nadia's family too kept the mother tongue and culture alive.

Dimitri and Nadia were, at 13, both enrolled in a Russian-American church-run high school in New York City. The school, organized in a dual curriculum, taught Russian history, language, religion and culture on the same level as the English studies. It was natural and expected that both families should rear their children in the Russian style. Nadia's and Dimitri's three children (two sons and a daughter) started speaking Russian in infancy, and spoke no other language until school age. English was introduced to them not by their parents but by school, American neighbors and other children.

In order to keep their ethnic language the *first* language, the Rakoffs do the following:

1. Speak only Russian to the children, no matter what the subject, unless they have an "American" guest.

2. Begin teaching Russian reading, writing and grammar to their children at home, *before* they are enrolled in American kindergarten.

3. Try to keep their children within the Russian culture through observation of holiday customs, church attendance and summer camps.

4. Urge the children when they play and socialize among themselves (and with other Russian-speaking friends) to speak only Russian.

The Rakoffs find they gain support from other bilingual families—albeit of totally different national backgrounds. Very helpful, Dimitri and Nadia believe, is the fact that they live in a mixed neighborhood. Many children in the neighborhood and at the school are of Asian extraction, and their parents insist on their going to Korean, Chinese or Japanese evening or Saturday schools, motivated by the same burning desire for their children to grow up bilingual as are the Rakoffs. What's more, the Rakoffs claim that people outside the ethnic community tend to be supportive, not censorious. Says Mrs. Rakoff, "Passersby are often very appreciative of bilingual, well-bred children—especially passersby who also speak a second language."

"When the children grumble," says Mrs. Rakoff, "it mostly has to do with 'time wasted' when they could be outside play-

ing with others. I tend to think: 'We all went through that.'
When I told my mother, when I was in fifth grade in American
public school, that I did not need Russian anymore, she only
stepped up Russian lessons for me with a different teacher. We
point out to the children that we are Russian, that we will be
that way even though we are also American citizens, and that
they are obliged to learn, speak, know and cherish their language. Rebellion will still come in different forms at different
ages and stages. The best I can do is keep to my path or be an
anchor for them in theirs. We hope when our children grow
up they will be able to find spouses who, if not Russian-speaking, at least will try to learn and keep up our traditions."

Russian, as Mrs. Rakoff explains, is functional in the children's social lives. "Most of our friends are in the same boat.
Some take the easy way out and speak English to their children
at home and then the children are no longer bilingual but retain
only a small and domestic vocabulary of highly accented Russian. Others preserve the Russian and forget the church. Those
children learn languages as a hobby as they take up astronomy
or stamp collecting. In getting older and marrying they may
not think of Russian as important idealistically, as we do, but
at least they will have the skill. Still others of our friends and
acquaintances push and fight to preserve our language, be it
for political or religious motives, and with their American-born
children speak fluent and perfect Russian."

Without Russian the children would feel like outsiders. If
they could not speak Russian, they would not be able to communicate with their own grandparents. "Our problem with
grandparents is not opposition to bilingualism, but grumbling
we have not done and are not doing enough," Nadia stresses.

Japanese/Yiddish. With fathers taking a more active role in
child-tending, it is often a toss-up in the bilingual/bicultural
family which of the parents' languages will be passed on. Already, some families pass on *two* ethnic languages in addition
to English, something they are able to do because of the father's

greater participation in life at home. In the case of the Schwartzmans, those two languages could not be more different. When
his American-born father, Frederick Schwartzman, walks
Harry to the Park Avenue synagogue nursery school every
morning, they converse in Yiddish. Mr. Schwartzman is a New
York lawyer who specializes in international film and television
matters. He met his wife, Kyoko, shortly after she came to this
country from Japan. When Kyoko Schwartzman picks up Harry
at midday, he says goodbye to the class in English and starts
up with his mother in Japanese. When the parents converse in
English, Harry listens from a distance. Meanwhile, by hearing
each other speak to Harry his parents find themselves gaining
a substantial knowledge of one another's languages.

His parents never sit down and formally school Harry in a
language. Frederick says, "We don't push the child; we don't
use pressure tactics. He's a very normal child." It is astonishing
all the same that until the age of three, Harry only spoke English
with his friends in Central Park playgrounds and with occasional guests at home, yet within three months of starting nursery school he prattled in English as well as his peers. There has
been no diminution of skill in either home language since he
started first grade, and Harry has learned Yiddish pre-reading
in an organized Yiddish playgroup, as well as many Japanese
characters informally with his Japanese books and in games
with his mother.

Harry knows about the kimono and has his own chopsticks
and Japanese pencil box. He asks for a Japanese rice ball for
lunch. His bathroom words and his expletives for pain are all
in Japanese. But at school he says "Ouch" and if his younger
brother feels sick he tells Dada, *"Daniel tut weh."*

Kyoko and Frederick stress the value of beginning bi- or
multilingualism early. They began speaking Japanese and Yiddish to Harry (and to Daniel) at birth. Says Frederick, "You feel
silly speaking to a three-month-old infant in two different languages. Part of the process is parents conditioning themselves."
The father keeps a Yiddish dictionary handy and refers to it
often. "We don't want him to grow up speaking Nipponglais
or Yiddish that has 50 percent English in it."

The Language of Love

All the preceding ethnic families have disciplined themselves to do what comes naturally. In some families, where the parents are from two different cultures, both naturalism and artifice are at play. In my observation, the language-learning pattern of one language in the home in a bicultural marriage (that is, *two* people, *one* language) is quite frequent and among the most sturdy arrangements of all. In this pattern, the monolingually raised American who develops a great interest in another culture and marries into it, converses in this second, learned language at home, helping to reinforce the effort of the native-speaking spouse.

We all know about learning a foreign language for love. I remember starting Italian with a bilingual paperback of Dante's *Inferno*, cadged from a college beau. The beautiful young man's extempore Italian recitations echoing in my heart, I scrambled *allegro* through the tenses. Although intercultural marriages may experience great strains, I have met couples whose commitment—and romance—are enhanced by an affectionate reciprocity: He (for example) gives her love and friendship in her native language, and she gives him cause to improve his fluency constantly in his own home, just by *talking*. They tend to be remarkable couples.

John Wertime was the blondest blond I ever saw in Iran. One of four sons of a cultural attaché at various American embassies, John had been the one who developed a curiosity about the Middle East that led to graduate Iranian studies at Princeton. His last act before ending his research in Iran was to fall in love with a raven-haired beauty, Suzan. Together they planned to open a carpet and antiquities store in the United States, and to live intercontinentally, in both their native lands. The business came about (the Wertimes have opened their store on Washington's tony Dupont Circle) but not (due to Iran's political climate) the geographic flexibility. Nevertheless, their son, Sam (pronounced "Sahm" after a legendary Persian ruler), is growing up hearing his parents converse in Persian at home, and in English publicly. And they do this not because Suzan speaks a faulty English—you would take her for a native-born American—but because, first, Persian is the language in which the Wertimes met and fell in love, and second, they want to share Persian language and culture with their tow-headed, striking son. "Given my own interest in Iran," John says, "and Suzan's strong identification with and love for her country, we felt it imperative that Sam know Persian like a native."

Once established, the pattern has never faltered. In the family circle, Sam will sometimes create sentences that exhibit elements of both language. In an example from age four, "Mommy, *pawk* my *roon*" (wipe my fanny), the grammar is English but the key words are Persian. An independent youngster, Sam, at age six, sometimes says, "I don't want *baghal konam*," or, I don't want to be hugged; *baghal konam* means "let me hug you." A sentence like this, psychologists of language agree, is a normal homogenization of the languages being learned.

It has been difficult for John and Suzan to give Sam cultural experiences in Persian, except through a few Iranian friends and their children, who are mostly several years Sam's senior. Although Sam understands Persian as well as he does English, English is the language of his school and neighborhood play. John says, "He seems willing to use Persian, but it is till a struggle—one in which we are determined to prevail. We feel that we cannot let up or give up and use English with him or forget about encouraging him to speak Persian. As a matter of fact, whenever we prod him a bit he usually gives us a pleasant surprise."

French/English. Sandra-Lisa Schwartz, an architect, was born in Brussels in 1957 of a Belgian mother and an American father. Her mother and father were studying pharmacy and medicine at the University of Brussels when they met. When Sandra was three, the family moved to the United States for her father's internship, and has lived here since. Not only did Sandra learn to speak French before English but, as her mother wanted to bring some other cultural context with her, they continued to speak French at home. On her arrival in the United States, she did not speak any English at all, which proved temporarily problematic to the paternal grandparents, who spoke no

French. Says this bilingual: "My parents recount early problems involved in going away and leaving me with my grandparents for the weekend. It was a *job* to communicate with me! Cultural differences often centered on food. My grandparents merrily recount the problems involved in getting me to eat foods not prepared by my mother—like vegetables not sautéed in butter. I insisted on *pain et confiture* for breakfast, and didn't know why anyone would want to eat cereal and (oh God!) cold milk."

Sandra admits to having suffered from this different upbringing at times, but ultimately attributes to it social abilities, not disabilities. "At school people made fun of my accent, which I subsequently lost, and they realized I was being brought up differently, ate different lunches, and did not dress as they did. My earliest impressions were that the girls were intolerant of my differences—they did not know how to cope with me— where boys were more adventurous. So for many years, my friends in my class were boys. My returning to Belgium in the summertime to visit my other set of grandparents served to reemphasize the 'foreignness' of my family vis-à-vis my peers. I always missed the first day of school, because I was still abroad. It always seemed as if everyone had been divvied up into their groups by the time I got back. Of course my parents devoted much time to compensating for the problem. My mother took me to the park, and to Old Macdonald's Farm in Norwalk, Connecticut, where there were rides and animals. I remember family times together above all, when I was in the early grades." Sandra adds, "My mother tried to make our home a French hearth, of which the language spoken was only the most obvious ingredient."

When Sandra was eight, her parents met another couple, both foreign, she Israeli and he Dutch, who became their fast friends. Sandra felt close to their daughter because of shared differences; the two became "like sisters to each other." Of this pivotal friendship Sandra says, "We helped each other out of those feelings of bewilderment that came from dealing with some of the American children. We were able to discuss our experiences, and gauge our reactions together. We understood that we weren't crazy; we just didn't see or understand things as they did."

Were there conflicts with her father about not speaking English at home? "I never challenged my upbringing. The use by both my parents of French seemed really very harmonious. Very early on I felt that it was not my fault if others were not sufficiently open-minded to accept me as I was. I felt privileged to be a part of two cultures, and was quickly the wiser for exposure to them. I seldom felt miffed at exclusion from a clique. When you live in two cultures you think: Why condemn others for the crime of snobbishness for which you are yourself being criticized? From the beginning, when they established French as the language of our Connecticut house, my family has seen and done things differently from those around us. At times this may have been frustrating but, as I suspected as a teenager, I have *no* regrets."

Speaking French as "first nature," Sandra has found it easy to continue on her own. She was taught by her mother to read in French at an early age, as well. From age eight on she wrote creatively almost exclusively in French—essays about her life and feelings, stories and poetry. In high school, poetry was a particularly vital outlet. "It was wonderful," she recalls, "should my mind wander in class, to write a poem. Most of the time no one would be able to read it if I got caught." She wrote bipartite poems, half in English, half in French, and when she learned Spanish, trilogues.

In Sandra's profession, architecture, being trilingual has favored her with opportunities, experiences and a broader point of view. She has been able to read professional books in her three languages. She can meet and talk with French architects abroad and in America at openings, drawing exhibitions and the like. She enlarges on how French is applicable to her job: "Architecture is a profession comprised of fairly cultured people (more so in Europe than here) and within that context one is expected to be able to do certain things, and to have read certain things. Particularly in the light of the amount of international exchange both in the profession of architecture and the world in general, another language simply puts you at advantage over someone who is monolingual—there is no escaping this fact, in my opinion."

Swedish/English. James and Mare-Anne Jarvela, an education consultant and a technical editor for a computer magazine in New Hampshire, are raising their son Jacob in Swedish, which is actually a second language for them both. Mare-Anne was raised speaking Estonian at home in Sweden (her parents fled Estonia after the Russian invasion in 1944) and learned Swedish outside the home, in school and at play. James was raised in a partly bilingual home (English/Finnish) in the United States. In 1974, James studied Finnish in Finland, continuing his undergraduate language studies begun at the University of Minnesota. Mare-Anne was in this same class of international students. At the end of the course, the American youth followed the pretty Estonian home to Sweden, enrolling in a nine-month Swedish-for-foreigners course at the University of Lund.

Since their marriage in 1976, Mare-Anne and James have spoken only Swedish at home in the United States. When Jacob came along in 1980, it was only natural for them to continue with their baby. The Jarvelas speak *only* Swedish at home. By age three, Jacob was already dealing with a bilingual situation: Swedish at home, English at daycare and with Jacob's other family members. When "Sesame Street" is on television, his parents may ask him in Swedish about what is taking place and he answers in Swedish. Says James, "It's just a continuation of our daily verbal exchange. We might ask him about the horses in the field across the street. If we ask the question or discuss the topic in Swedish, Jacob answers in the same language."

When Jacob was two, his grandfather from Sweden visited the family for two weeks. It took Jacob a couple of days to realize that his grandfather understood Swedish—up until then only his parents had spoken Swedish with him. Jacob kept speaking English to his grandfather, while Grandpa responded or asked questions in Swedish. "It seemed that Jacob thought we were the only people in the world who could speak Swedish," says James Jarvela. "But after this initial period of the visit, Jacob began speaking Swedish, and if his grandfather (whose knowledge of English is limited) wanted to know a word in English, he'd ask Jacob, and his grandson would tell him. Jacob's grandfather speaks Swedish with a heavy Estonian accent, which Jacob was beginning to pick up when he left!"

James Jarvela speaks of what it means to him to communicate with his son in a language acquired in adult life: "In the summers we will go to Sweden whenever we can—we have been twice already—and my father-in-law will visit again, but for the most part our language world will for a long while be limited to a population of three. Yet we have a terrific sense of learning and growth. Not only does my son's Swedish get better and better, but so does mine. Sometimes we read a word or expression in a folk tale and are able to use it again within hours." for continuing Swedish education, James has books, magazines and conversation with his wife. "It is not so much that Mare-Anne teaches me new words as that with her I have the best possible forum for practice." In this dynamic atmosphere, not only does the boy learn Swedish from his American father and Estonian mother, but James Jarvela, through his son, learns little stories, expressions and customs which the mother passes on. Everybody's Swedish gets better—in Munsonville, New Hampshire!

Chinese/English. Christina Lobb, born in 1979, is being raised in a Chinese-speaking home by a non-Chinese and a native Taiwanese—in another situation bearing witness to the power of linguistic imagination, and of love. Fred Lobb enrolled in a Chinese-language course at Fairfax High School in Los Angeles in 1969. He later majored in Chinese at the University of Southern California. In 1976, he went to Taiwan for the first time. "I intended to brush up on my Chinese there," he says. "I discovered that the Mandarin I had studied at USC was much different from the Chinese actually spoken in Taiwan. I had to learn new words and, as is usually the case when learning another language, lots of slang. Since then, I've made two more trips to Taiwan. I have spent more than two years there altogether. At this point I am able to read and write several thousand characters. I can read newspapers and books. I think my pronunciation could be improved, especially my use of the tones. My wife says my Chinese is 'as crude as a butcher's'— a Chinese butcher, that is."

Lori Lobb is a native Taiwanese, whose great-great-grandparents came from the mainland to Taiwan over 150 years ago.

She knows both Taiwanese and Mandarin.

When Christina was born, her parents wanted her to grow up speaking both English and Mandarin. Fred was to speak to her in English and Lori was to use Chinese. "It didn't quite work out that way," says her father. "I was used to speaking with my wife in Chinese. As a consequence, Chinese was the language Christina heard from us both at home. The Chinese people we've come into contact with are delighted that our daughter can speak such clear Mandarin. Members of the local Chinese community, which is sizable, have been very positive in accepting a child of mixed background."

Now that Christina is in kindergarten, and comes home with English news to share, Fred is speaking more English with her. She asks daddy to tell her stories in Chinese, a Taiwanese folk tale, for example, or in English, such as *Winnie-the-Pooh*. The family watches Chinese videocassettes and reads Chinese books aloud together. On the other hand, Christina's favorite television shows are in English. Her Chinese vocabulary, the Lobbs feel, is growing, not regressing. Fred admits, though, that he has a problem keeping his own proficiency in Chinese. He says, "The only thing that would raise my Chinese back to its former best level would be an extended stay in Taiwan. Financially, that wouldn't be feasible. I have resigned myself to reading as many classical Chinese works as I have time for— the only option open—and I find that my reading has suffered the least. When I speak in Chinese at home, my vocabulary is often concerned with mundane topics such as maintaining the family budget and where to eat. It is fine to be comfortable in these areas, but I am waiting for Christina to be older to have talks on a broader plane. The very fact of her growing up should help my Chinese quite a lot."

The Language of Desire

In the afterword to this book, the linguist Dr. Wallace E. Lambert gives an "A for effort" to families who, like mine, are raising their children bilingually when there is no native-speaking relative in the house. A few brief cases demonstrate that you don't have to be in a cosmopolitan area (with, for instance, a bilingual school) to do this. It is interesting, too, to trace what happens to a successfully bilingual family as the children grow up.

French/English. On the day Geneviève was born, Nancy Gail Reed began speaking French with her; her father used English. Nancy, a French major in college, describes the impetus for putting her academic study to personal use: "I was one of those early 1970s European wanderers, another kid wearing jeans and a backpack. If there was anything I learned from all that seemingly pointless wandering around and 'rapping' in youth hostels with kids from other countries, it was that most European teenagers spoke at least one language other than their own. I decided that, if I ever had children, I would give them this gift of language." When the family lived in Boston, there were visits for Nancy and her small daughter with French friends, and French books available from Harvard Square bookstores. But they moved to New Mexico when Geneviève was three and a half; what would become of her French?

The home program is progressing fine. "Interestingly enough," Nancy Reed says, "though I haven't always been able to convince my Eastern friends of New Mexico's culture, I find there is less opposition (or verbalized doubt) to my speaking French to our daughter here than there was in Boston. New Mexico is officially trilingual (English, Spanish and Navajo) and the Hispanic mothers always seem to look in our direction with a knowing smile."

German/English. Mark Gessner, born in 1980 in rural Vermont to American parents who were themselves raised speaking only English, hears a different language from each parent—English from his mother, German from his father. What decided Bob Gessner to make this commitment to bilingual childrearing? "My reasons are three," Bob explains. "To teach Mark, to help Mary Ann learn more German, and so that I do not forget the language I battled with and won."

A schoolteacher by profession, Bob Gessner worked for six years in Germany as a flight attendant for Lufthansa Airlines. He struggled to learn the German language at Notre Dame University, then in Austria and Germany, specifically to get the job. "My time in Germany was a happy time for me; I got married, and made some money. I was sorry to leave, but we felt we had to start a life in the States. When we came back in 1979, Mary Ann became pregnant, and we started to build our house in the woods. Because Mary Ann has found a job she likes and works full time, I have stayed home to build and care for Mark. Speaking German with my son was a sentimental thing. It made me feel good in my backwoods isolation and was a covenant with our good German and Austrian friends." Mary Ann said "Why not?" and encouraged her husband to try. Bob made the decision and one day, while Mark was an infant, simply began.

At this point Mark replies mostly in English to his father, yet prefers to hear German from him. "He doesn't permit me to speak English to him," says Bob, "which turns out to be the best reinforcement there is. Our relationship is so established in the one language it would be artificial to switch now." The grandparents on both sides are supportive of what the Gessners are attempting. "Although none of them speaks German, they all enjoy the learning that is going on. They like to try out a German word or two with Mark," Bob says. "It doesn't feel artificial to any of us anymore. The one time I do use English with Mark is in exclamatory command form: '*Stop it!*' or, in exasperation, '*Leave the dog alone!*' But this is a rare thing."

Mark practices German when playing alone, just as he used to practice German words and sing in German in his crib. Old Lufthansa friends, German speakers, visit the Gessners in the Vermont countryside. Their arrival serves as an opportunity for Mark to "see that German is a real language spoken by someone other than his father," says Mary Ann. "He will occasionally respond in German, but what pleases us is that his comprehension is so high." As for the future, Bob does not know if he will continue to speak only German with Mark. "It is unlikely that I would switch," he says, "yet if I couldn't explain myself anymore as father to son I would have to." Bob teaches

German to a businessman in St. Johnsbury, reads current German magazines and writes German letters. It gets both harder and easier, he believes. "At first I was translating booklings like *The Little Duck* to Mark. Now it's longer stories like *The Mouse Tales* or *Curious George*. And I've begun to read Grimms' *Fairy Tales* in German. Last evening Mark listened to the whole of *Die Bremer Stadtmusikanten*. I was really surprised. And delighted. As the books become harder, my German gets a better workout. The effort is becoming more interesting all the time."

Spanish/English. Bilingual American children's second-language skills are here to stay, even in families having no ethnic connection, as long as the parents persevere. Kerr Thompson, a professor at Louisiana State University in Shreveport, and his wife, Susan, had the singleminded determination necessary to succeed.

Three months after their first child, Louise, now 13, was born, the Thompsons moved to Panama, where Kerr was assigned to a military unit in the Canal Zone. They decided to speak Spanish exclusively in their home, because they wanted Louise to be bilingual. Consequently Louise heard English only when they had English-speaking visitors, and naturally began speaking Spanish as "her" language.

There were, the Thompsons explain, minor difficulties. "First," Professor Thompson says, "even though Susan and I were fluent in Spanish, we felt a bit odd—phony—speaking Spanish to each other. We felt, however, that Louise needed to hear us speak the same language consistently. So we kept at it, and in a short time this problem passed. Second, when Louise herself began to speak, we had to learn—with the help of a Panamanian maid who worked for us a couple of days a week—to understand Spanish baby talk. Finally, we found that we needed to build a repertory of children's poems, nursery rhymes and songs if we wanted to provide Louise with the usual children's cultural activities without having to resort to English. This need, incidentally, has been a blessing. It forced Susan and me to extend our knowledge of Hispanic culture into a domain not generally covered by people learning Spanish as a second language. We have both discovered since then that our appreciation of a mature literary work has occasionally been enhanced by our awareness of a children's song, for example, which the author of the work we were reading was evoking."

The Thompsons returned to the United States when Louise was 21 months old and continued to use Spanish in their home. Of course, Louise soon learned that other children spoke English and rapidly switched to speaking English in most situations. "We did not discourage this," continues the professor, "nor did we try to insist that she speak Spanish with us. We were acquainted with a number of parents, Cuban refugees for the most part, who had tried to force their children to speak Spanish and who had encountered hostility and resistance." The Thompsons decided to risk the loss of active Spanish rather than foment rebellion. Nevertheless, some years later, when Louise and her brother, Currie (born in 1974, and with whom the parents also used Spanish), began to suggest that Susan and Kerr also switch to English, they refused—"We explained that, since we were allowing them to use the language they wished, they should show us the same courtesy."

Thirteen-year-old Louise and ten-year-Currie have a largely passive knowledge of Spanish that they can summon up to speak fluently. Says their father, "They understand the language well; they rarely utter a sentence in it themselves, yet if placed in a situation whee they are forced to speak Spanish, they do." The Thompsons' experiences in the summer of 1978, which they spent in Spain, are illustrative. Susan and Kerr assumed that their children would sail into Spanish immediately, where at first they hugged the shore. When after a few days, the children proved still reluctant to speak Spanish, the parents resorted to bribery: "It was ice cream after lunch each day if they had spoken a minimum amount—which increased daily— of Spanish. We also tried to help by asking Louise and Currie multiple-choice questions—'Is that a dog or a cat?,' and 'Is the dog drinking from the fountain or swimming in the fountain?" It worked. Soon the children were using Spanish comfortably. As Professor Thompson relates, "At first they spoke haltingly and made a number of grammatical errors (noun-adjective agreement, for example; but not, as I recall, subject-verb agreement). After a couple of weeks, however, they overcame their reticence and began to participate on their own in lengthy and fluent conversations with the people—particularly the children—we encountered during the rest of the summer."

At the summer's end, Louise and Currie returned to using mostly English at home in Shreveport. "I find they use Spanish when they want something and are trying to cultivate our favor!" their father observes. The Thompson parents are now focusing on helping Louise and Currie develop their written skills. In the summer of 1981 they worked on Spanish reading, using a series of books designed for a bilingual program. The family has also purchased a computer, and Louise and Currie work occasionally on homemade computer-assisted Spanish drills and games.

Even if Louise and Currie favor English over Spanish, when they need Spanish they have it. Furthermore, and very importantly, they speak Spanish without an accent, and readily spot (and are amused by) a foreign accent in others. Professor Thompson elaborates: "I recall Louise commenting at three or four that the Spanish word for 'no' (pronounced with a diphthong /nou/) is 'no' (pronounced with a pure vowel /no/). Susan and I found her comment funny, of course, but we were pleased that she was distinguishing the two sounds properly. Apparently she and Currie have both always regarded the sound systems of each language as independent of each other rather than as variants of the same sounds." Many parents live abroad when their children are small and there are many Americans who learn a language through laborious study, and *could* pass it to the children. Louise and Currie are among the fortunate few who have been given all the necessary foundation to develop their active skills with the passage of time. Says Professor Thompson, quietly beamish, "We'll do all we can to help them do so."

German/English. Although they grew up in the typical, all-American suburb of Evanston, Illinois in the 1960s, Karin, Christine and Linda Phelps were raised speaking only German until just before they entered public school. Their mother, Ruth Phelps, was born and raised in Pittsburgh by parents originally from Frankfurt and Vienna. Mrs. Phelps' own upbringing was bilingual. Her family had a German au pair girl, her maternal grandmother lived with them until her death and never spoke English in the house, and many guests spoke German. Ruth's letters to her paternal grandparents in Germany were corrected by her father, who also assigned her translations, English to German and back again, and corrected them. The children read Schiller's plays aloud, taking roles, while their musician father dressed and readied himself for his evening engagements. At 15 Ruth was taken to Germany, touring and visiting relatives who had children her age. No chance to learn was missed in this old-fashioned, highly educated bilingual family!

Leland Phelps (Christine, Karin, and Linda's father) was, in contrast, bilingual by choice and chance. Raised in Flint and Detroit, Michigan in, to quote one daughter, "your typical all-American apple-pie-and-motherhood" family, as a youngster he was not bilingual. Nevertheless, Leland set out, at age 26, to learn German and become a German professor. He met his wife at the Middlebury Language School. The Phelps girls were all born while Professor Phelps taught at Northwestern University. Later the family moved to Durham, North Carolina where he chaired the German Department until 1984. All three daughters speak, read and write German fluently.

"We were definitely raised in the old Teutonic tradition," says Karin, "eschewing consumerism, making rather than buying things like birthday gifts and clothes, respecting our elders and not being allowed to mature as quickly as many of our peers. Our parents' decisions on such matters were not questioned, unlike in many American homes." Rebellion was handled, Karin recalls, "creatively." The girls were given plenty of books, and games were devised to keep them speaking German at the supper table. Karin explains, "We never had much money, 25 cents a week allowance *if* we did all our chores, so it was a great incentive to have an additional income at supper. Everyone got ten pennies at the outset of the meal. If someone spoke more than three English words in a row, she forfeited a penny."

The parents were not rigid in their demands. For example, rather than insist that their children report on their school experiences in German, they did not protest when the girls burst in from their American school day with English tales to relate. "It seemed too important to let them release pent-up excitement without translating," says Mrs. Phelps.

Perhaps the most effective way of handling resistance to using the foreign language, the daughters agree, was taking trips. The Phelps girls were taken to Germany for three months at four, seven and eight. Since babysitters had often been German-speaking foreign graduate students from the university, the girls stayed in these students' homes without their parents during part of the stay. "We were especially pleased," says Mrs. Phelps, "when our four-year-old Linda, watching some street repairman in Stuttgart, turned to us and exclaimed excitedly, '*Mama, die können* auch *Deutsch sprechen!* ' [Mommy, they can speak German *too.*] To which the laborers responded laconically, 'Where the devil is *she* from?'"

Later, their father took each daughter to Germany alone as she reached her teens. This time it was arranged for each to attend a special skills class, such as riding school for Linda. "When the language makes sense in the larger environment," comments Karin, "it becomes effortless."

Karin sketches elements of the informal German home instruction that endured for years. "At one time my mother, who is creative and an amateur artist, began leaving letters to us from 'Puck,' a dwarf she had met in the woods in Germany, under the front door mat. These colored-pencil illustrated letters printed in German were so dear to us that for a long time it kept us busy writing (German of course) replies to his charming comments on our life and descriptions of his life. I remember one picture of myself with black and blue eyes from falling while ice-skating! It was a marvelous method of generating interest—kids love to read about themselves, and Puck loved to describe his life in the woods, and how he made his inks and writing pens. I suppose eventually we got clever enough to wonder how Puck had gotten hold of the scrap paper from the German Department's mimeograph machine on which all those letters had been written; at any rate, it didn't last forever. I wish I had copies of those letters to inspire me with my own children as they get a little older."

"Another part of their campaign to teach us German (I'm talking about the five- to twelve-year-old period) involved weekly assignments and a class. Just as we made our beds every day, and washed the dishes, and helped clean the house, so we had to write a weekly essay in German. Sometimes, instead, we spoke original stories onto tape in German, invented on the spot. We also went once a week to the house of another German-speaking family, the Pages. There we spent an afternoon or a day mixing play with actual grammar classes, writing and reading. I doubt that it was our favorite activity of the week. However, I remember having fun with much of it—there were clever games, for instance. One was Questions and Answers. Slips of paper in one heap each had a question on it while those in another heap contained answers. A player would pick a question, read it aloud to his neighbor, and the neighbor would then pick an answer from the answer pile and read it out loud. The often occasioned hilarious combinations, and, of course, an hour would pass with only German spoken. Mrs. Page also led us in eurhythmic exercises, in German."

With the spirit of play animating lessons, the girls were lured into using German. When Mrs. Phelps taught them piano she even went so far as to assume a fictive role. She pretended to be Fräulein Pumpernickel, who could speak no English, came in the front door in a silly hat, was always very patient and asked her pupils many questions about their activities in the family. The children played along with the charade. When Fräulein Pumpernickel left by the front door, mother came in by the back door and requested a report on the lesson, which, says Mrs. Phelps, was given "very seriously and most often in German." By the time the eldest daughter was a teenager, the *gnädiges Fräulein* had vanished.

The three daughters were completely convinced of their advantage in learning German when they took college entrance examinations and scored 770, 800 and 750 out of a possible 800. There are, they point out, strains in keeping up their extra language, just as there are in keeping up any skill acquired in the course of life. "Use it or lose it—it is up to each of us to keep it going," Karin says. Christine majored in French and German at Emory University, then became a group leader for the Experiment in International Living in Germany for several summers. She now teaches fifth grade in North Carolina. Karin went to Harvard University, switching from an easy German major to biology for the greater challenge. She has kept her hand in by translating scientific German texts for colleagues, "for free. I see it as a way of keeping up the skill." She adds, "I don't worry about forgetting my German. I know that no matter how difficult German might become for me through lack of use, I can regain it quickly by simply going to Germany for a brief time."

3
The Language Live-In

The live-in helper or "au pair" is an old-fashioned arrangement that is again gaining currency. In J.M. Barrie's classic *Peter Pan*, Peter goes in search of "household" help when he finds he cannot handle the rambunctious Lost Boys. They need the rule of a gentle but firm hand. Peter Pan flies from Never Never Land to Greater London to find someone to take charge. How well Peter understands children, being one himself *per aeterna*! He chooses a young and pretty yet strong-minded girl who is an experienced older sister. Captivated by her charm, the Lost Boys cry, "Wendy lady be our mother."

Your boys and girls don't have to be lost to develop great affection for a language live-in. The advantage of having a live-in is that learning a second language is reinforced daily by emotional rapport with the helper. A live-in gives the children continuous, in-depth contact with a foreign language. You become an accessory in your child's language learning; the au pair becomes the kingpin. With a live-in foreign-language speaker, a preschool child learns to organize and grasp the world in a non-English tongue. The power of the child's language becomes a special connection with him or her. The outsider becomes an insider; the experience is literally unforgettable. If a child grows up with native speakers of another language, that language is not foreign. It remains active as long as the child continues to practice it. Should the child ever need to relearn the language, having forgot it, he or she need only open his or her ears to it.

A live-in can be either a salaried nanny/housekeeper or the less expensive au pair. The live-in is ideal support for two-income families. As with any mother's-helper situation, parents must learn to adapt to a new member of the household. Women who work are usually more than willing to share their turf with another, non-family person. The job-experienced person is ac-customed to administering and delegating, and can use these skills at home. Having a live-in requires an understanding of consultation and corporate use of space. In the office you don't engage in chit-chat every time you pass somebody's desk. Sim-ilarly, just because the live-in comes to the kitchen for toast and tea while you are preparing applesauce doesn't mean you have to sit down and talk. You can refuse to lend him or her the car for recreational outings, and still be friends. She can admit to you that one of the children has been misbehaving, and ask your advice. You must learn to give her a blueprint of general obligations and each week's special events, without overseeing her activities too closely. So, if you can afford an au pair, why not get a foreign one?

The dividends of sharing your house are great. You have to dash out late at night and pick up your spouse from the airport? Ask the live-in to leave the door to her room open, let the children know that you are going and you have, effortlessly, a babysitter. Are you always running out of eggs, bread and milk? Put the live-in in charge of replenishing these basics at the corner store. Now there is someone else at home to let in the plumber and see to the children's Halloween costumes. Her first priority is your children's language, but she can be avail-able too help in all the troublesome interstices of your home life—especially when they give her the opportunity to practice English.

Nanny

In *Speak, Memory: An Autobiography Revisited*, Vladimir Nabokov recreates with extraordinary vividness the role of foreign nan-nies from the succession of young German, English and French women tutors who came to live in his aristocratic St. Petersburg home. From Nabokov's description we can understand the language live-in situation from the child's point of view, and draw parameters for success.

Nabokov learned to read English before he could read Russian. His mother read to him bedtime stories in English—hero stories, chivalric tales, English fairy stories and Bertha Upton's verse adventures of the Golliwogs, glossy picture books that he pored over on his lap when she had finished the bedtime ritual. As a child, Nabokov then said his English prayers below a little icon of an Orthodox saint and fell asleep, to dream English dreams until the Russian morning. First the English nannies, then the French and German filled out the civilized learning environment of his home. He describes "four simple souls in my grammar" as his first English friends. He thought in English because of these nannies. They were an essential element of his multilingual upbringing.

Then, for seven years, came the Mademoiselle. She brought the ritual of *dictée*, her ideas of dinner conversation, and her "nightingale" reading voice. Mademoiselle's forte was reading aloud long novels on the veranda ('We got it all: *Les Malheurs de Sophie, Le Tour du Monde en Quatre-Vingts Jours, Le Petit Chose, Les Misérables, Le Comte de Monte Cristo,* many others. There she sat, distilling her reading voice from the still prison of her person." Nabokov says his father's library, not Mademoiselle's lore, taught him to appreciate "authentic piety." But he adds, "Nevertheless, something of her tongue's limpidity and luster has had a single bracing effect upon me; like those sparkling salts that are used to purify the blood." Growing up in several languages, Nabokov clearly harvested their literary treasures. What an interesting household it must have been!

A nanny is the classic live-in. This means you employ her as an adjunct housekeeper at full salary. Her presence makes life so simple compared with some other child-care alternatives that two-career families who have the means decide to have her. You can request from a domestic employment agency a person who speaks Spanish, German, Italian, French or Chinese and expect to find her. You can also advertise in the newspaper. She may be responsible for both house care and child care. Because she is also contributing something of herself to your child's upbringing, she will feel added interest in her work. It

will be easier for her to express both her questions and com-
plaints. Be sure when you hire her that she wants to open her
language to you. There should be *no* idea of her getting paid
for formal language lessons to you or your children. It is pre-
cisely informal immersion you want, not an adjunct to the
school language program. Consider whether you, or an older
child in the family, can give her English lessons or a conversation hour on a weekly basis as part of the bargain. It is a good
experience for a teenager to teach someone else his or her first
language.

A natural time to look for a nanny is when you are looking
for a housekeeper, as the *New York Times* reported in an article
of October 2, 1979. Marcia Fox, an assistant dean at New York
University, was discussing the question of a housekeeper with
her husband, a bankruptcy specialist in Manhattan. "We decided we would try to find a housekeeper who spoke either
French or Spanish. We thought those were the best languages
for a child to be learning in New York City. Spanish because
of New York's extraordinary Spanish population. . . . A New
York child who speaks Spanish has a tremendous advantage,
I think—she's on the inside track to another culture. And
French because I think it's a language that I feel would be marvelous when she grew up, the language that educated people
are apt to speak as their second language." By two years of
age, Lauren, who was learning Spanish full-tilt, liked to listen
to her father read *Plaza Sesamo* books to her, though he doesn't
himself speak much of the language. "She sure enjoys it," he
says. "She seems to laugh in all the right spots." She asks her
mother for a bath; but she asks the family's housekeeper, who
is her teacher, for a *baño*.

Au Pair

Besides nanny or housekeeper, a more affordable arrangement
that can bring the desired foreign language into your house is
the au pair. this is a live-in young person, usually female,
whose object in voyaging to your country and your home is to
learn English. She is called an "au pair" (French for "on a par")
because she lives in your household as if she were a member

of the family. The attraction is more than money: She wants the experience of living in America. The au pair is not a servant, but helps you on an informally contracted basis.

The phrase "au pair" dates only to the nineteenth century, and was first used between the English and the French. Balzac fictionalized this kind of exchange in *Pierrette,* in which he wrote: "Two years later, she was au pair: if she earned nothing from it, neither did her parents pay any longer for her lodging and food. That's what they call being au pair, rue Saint-Denis." In contemporary usage, in America and all of Western Europe, the phrase "au pair" is established not merely as an adjective but a noun, as in "Carmella is our au pair."

To buoy our bilingual program, my family has hosted two vivacious, adventurous French-Canadian au pairs during their school's summer holidays, and two others (one an immigrant to Montreal from Nice) during parts of the school year. An ad in a Montreal newspaper brought us the first, Chantal. She returned a year later to accompany us on a family trip. During the summer after the children turned four, one of Chantal's Québecoise friends filled the same role of French sitter and fond *amie*. Like Chantal, Geneviève brought us a smiling countenance, a habit for taking long walks and an exciting soupçon of foreignness in her cooking, sartorial style, songs and games, turns of phrase and even laughter. Anne, who was with us when the twins were five, not only won their affection but gave them beautiful French manners.

The au pairs were like cousins to Emma and Burton, while, outside the home, they profited from the chance to see America and improve their English. Because of Quebec's selfconsciousness about educating today's youth in a French with an international currency, all these young women speak a French *très soigné*. As much as possible, they emphasize standard French with us, though of course the French-Canadian accent is distinctive. (The difference is comparable to the difference between American and British English.) Since it will be much easier for our family to spend time in Quebec than in Europe, we are very pleased to have Emma and Burton exposed to French-Canadian style. If some Professor Higgins detects this souvenir in their speech at a future date, it will be a vestige of a happy contact between cultures.

How do you find an au pair? There are referral services in Europe, which you can connect with by sending your request to the cultural attaché of the embassy or consulate of his or her country. I also operate a referral service to put families in touch with young people in Quebec. Another way to find an au pair is to ask a friend who travels abroad on business (medical doctors and corporation executives are good possibilities) to ask a host in the foreign country whether he knows of a possible candidate. A person who comes via personal referral will probably be satisfactory. Be sure she comes because she wishes to, of her own accord, not to please her parents. If you have family ties with an old country, you may want to use them. Be frank about the kind of help with the housework and child-care experience you would like. It's best to find an au pair 16 or older, though families in the States suggest to me that they can accept a somewhat younger person, as young as 15, if the children to be cared for and talked with are post-toddlers.

There are certain major newspapers where you can expect a response to an ad for an au pair. If you begin the procedure a year in advance, you will have time for an exchange of letters back and forth, to be sure you find someone you will like. For our basic four languages the addresses and names of some papers are:

German: *Frankfurter Allgemeine Zeitung,* Hellerhofstrasse 2/4,
6000 Frankfurt-am-Main
Süddeutsche Zeitung, Sendlingerstrasse 80,
8000 Munich 2

French: *Le Monde,* 5 rue des Italiens, 75427 Paris
Le Figaro, 25 avenue Matignon, 75380 Paris

Italian: *Corriere della Sera,* Via Solferino, 20121 Milan

Spanish: *ABC,* Servano 61, Madrid, Spain
El Universal, Bucareli 8, Mexico City, Mexico
Novedades, Morelos 16, Mexico City, Mexico

Some au pairs actually advertise themselves for placement. Buy a copy of the *International Herald Tribune,* where the prospective au pairs often advertise. You may also wish to place your ad in this publication, which is read by English-speaking people all over Europe, the Middle East and Far East, since English is such a common second language. The classified ads are paid in dollars to the New York City office (477 Madison Avenue, New York, N.Y.) The classified section where the ad will appear is also more legible and widely read than in many bigger papers.

A good source for the language live-in is a nearby university with foreign students. You give a student a room in exchange for conversation and help around the house. Try posting large index cards around the campus, stating what you seek and offer, your phone number and a note on proximity to the school and how it can be reached by public transportation. Do not include the address. These go in key locations. Take or send one to the student employment office, the off-campus and graduate housing office, any foreign student office and the office of the academic dean.

Usually the help you ask for will include some light babysitting. Because the Morrises live in a bilingual city, Miami, they wanted their children to learn Spanish. A Venezuelan graduate student, a poet, answered their ad on a bulletin board at the University of Florida. Daphne Morris didn't at first feel he would be a good babysitter for the younger child, a year old, but in interviewing him she learned that he played the recorder. The older Morris child wanted to start an instrument, so the young man's responsibility became Spanish conversation and recorder instruction. Sharing music also helped develop a friendship between the young man and the children. Soon Randall, seven, could not only play the recorder and speak some Spanish but knew some beautiful South American folk songs. With the money not spent on sending Randall to camp, on music lessons or on babysitters (Raoul was soon trusted to tend the baby), the family made an off-season trip during the next year to Mexico.

Having a student room with you is something that might not appeal to you for a full year, but be fine for a summer or school term now and then. Another couple, New York academics, knew that they would be living in Tanzania for a year. Half a year before this trip, through the Columbia University Student Affairs Office, they found a student from Kenya to live with them for six months, so the children could learn some Swahili before the big adventure. "It meant putting the boys into one bedroom in bunk beds and we found ourselves lounging on the weekends less than usual, but it was well worth it for the almost magical transition the boys made to Tanzania. They made friends in Swahili right away. They even knew the international rule for soccer, thanks to their Columbia student's tutelage. I don't think they would ever have made local friends any other way, because the school they went to was for other foreigners."

Hiring an Au Pair. There are federal laws governing the hiring of foreign nationals. In looking for an au pair, you must keep in mind that there are two ways to employ him or her, legally. The first, and simplest, is to treat her as a visitor. The United States commonly grants six-month tourist visas to visitors. Often this can be extended for another three to six months. When the au pair applies for a visa, she applies as a tourist. She says nothing about working. As far as the Immigration Service is concerned, she is here to enjoy herself. Once she is here, you pay her according to a private, prearranged agreement. Technically, this is illegal, but in general the law is not enforced. The Immigration Service has no way of monitoring what she does while she is in the States. To work for you, she needs no papers, and no bank account. Even if you adhere strictly to the letter of the law, you can still pay her informally and consider it pocket money, compensation for her expenses or travel money with which to see America. This is as legal as it need be, and is the most commonly used system.

The reason that almost all au pairs work slightly outside the law is that the United States, unlike most European countries, makes no provision for au pairs in its immigration laws. The laws are thus unrealistic in this respect because they don't take citizens' needs into account. Richard Madison, an immigration lawyer in New York City, is author of *The Greencard Book*, a useful guide published in New York in 1981 by Visa Publication Corp. He says, "The laws in this minor but sensitive area are usually ineptly worded and rarely enforced. If you could round up all the millions of illegal aliens in the United States, the economy would collapse!" The Immigration Service stipulates that a foreigner come either as a tourist or as an employee. If the latter, he must go through a lengthy and involved procedure to apply for working papers, which are difficult to obtain. European countries, on the other hand, have long enjoyed the institution of au pairs, and regulate their legitimacy by calling them temporary workers. For this reason, European countries usually exempt au pairs from the formal requirement of working papers. Since United States law does not thus distinguish au pair work from other kinds of work, it is often necessary to work around it.

Although you can pay your au pair modest wages without having pangs of guilt about the legalities, you do have to observe the duration of the visa. When the visa runs out, the au pair should return too her native country. If she does not leave, nothing is likely to happen. But if she goes back after eighteen months instead of the six that she was allowed, she may have difficulty getting her next visa. A U.S. counsel might note that she overstayed and make it difficult for her to return to the United States. If the overstayed visa comes to the attention of the Immigration Service, she could be deported.

She may eventually be tempted to ignore the visa time limit and stay on indefinitely. Should she leave your employ, however, it may be difficult for her to find another job since she has no social security number or card.

Because the informal arrangement is the easiest route for an au pair, we have hired several French-speaking girls from Canada. An au pair from this side of the ocean has many advantages over transatlantic arrangements:

1. The au pair is cheaper! Instead of paying for a round-trip jet fare, you pay train or bus fare for her from her school or home across the border.

2. She can go home again without great expense. For example, you might find a college-age student who is taking a year off, who can come to live with you for the length of a school year. You might want to give her a round-trip ticket home as a Christmas gift if she is with you during that period. Or if a grandparent dies, she needs a wisdom tooth extracted or she decides to stay on after the summer and wants to fetch her fall clothes, she can easily go home for a short visit. (All of these things have happened to au pairs from Quebec staying with us, and they were absent only for a long weekend or a week.)

3. Your au pair need not worry about a visa. Even though she crosses the Canadian/U.S. border, or flies from Puerto Rico, for example, she does so as a tourist. Often her passport is unstamped or she has no passport at all. (A European's visa is stamped for three months, or in some cases six, unless she enrolls in a full-time program at a university or school for languages.)

4. If your children form an attachment, they can see her again much more easily if she is a Cuban-American from Miami than a Spaniard from Spain. Twice we have invited our au pair from a former year to come on a later summer trip. Her help is super, and it is fun to reestablish old ties.

5. The au pair's knowledge of American culture before coming is usually greater than a European's would be. Likewise, her expectations may be more realistic.

6. You can interview the candidate by a long-distance phone call. You can take the names of two references (which you should probably do anyway), or her parents, and call them too, instead of writing.

We have found two other advantages in having au pairs from Quebec. Canada is a bilingual nation. To get a good job, fluent English is essential. French Canadians read English well. Their spoken English ranges from fair to good. An au pair from Canada will be extremely motivated and positive about her stay with you. The English she speaks with you and your children fits in beautifully with her own life plans! Similarly, brought to the States to speak French, she does so with utmost pride.

Some newspapers where you can run an ad for North American Spanish, French, German and Italian au pairs are:

French: *Journal Français d'Amérique* (biweekly), 1051 Divisadero Street, San Francisco, CA
          France-Amérique (weekly), Trocadero Publishing, Inc., 1556 Third Avenue, P.O. Box 415, New York, NY

German: *New Yorker Staats Zeitung & Herald*, 36–30 37th Street, Long Island City, NY 11101

Italian: *Corriere Illustrato* (weekly), 1000 Lawrence Avenue West, Toronto, Canada

Spanish: *Miami Herald* (daily), One Herald Plaza, Miami, FL 33101

You will find a listing of other ethnic newspapers, by language, in the *I.M.S. Ayers Directory*, which gives a circulation figure for each.

A sample ad, requesting an au pair girl or boy for an American family living in Boston, for the summer of 1984, to care for two children aged three and four, might run thus:

French: Cherchons garçon ou fille comme "au pair" pour famille américaine à Boston. Eté 1984. 2 enfants, agés de 3 et 4 ans. Ecrire au: (address).

Italian: Cercasi ragazzo/a "alla pare" per famiglia americana, a Boston. Estate 1984. 2 bambini, 3enne e 4enne. Scrive: (address).

German: Suche "au pair" Mädchen/jungen Mann für amerikanische Familie in Boston für Sommer 1984. Zwei Kinder, 3 und 4 Jähre alt. Zuschriften an: (address).

Spanish: Se necesita niñera para cuidar niña y niño y vivir con la familia—norte-americana—quienes residen en Boston. Verano 1984. Comuniquése: (address).

The second way to employ an au pair is to hire one legally. This procedure takes between one and two years to complete. According to the immigration lawyer Richard Madison, a lot of advance planning is required as well. "[You need] the dedication to stick with each other. It may work if the doctor and the doctor's spouse go to the same inn year after year, meet the innkeeper's daughter, and plan way ahead. It is not going to work from a casual meeting on the Spanish Steps."

As part of the procedure for obtaining a Labor Certificate, you must show that there is no ready, willing and qualified American worker available to fill the position. This means advertising in the paper for a tutor, and demonstrating that no respondent was found, but consult a lawyer before placing an ad. The ad cannot be too specific. "Must speak German and be university graduate" is fine, but "Swabian speaker, experienced with houseplants, between 19 and 21" is clearly not; it sets up too many barriers to a local person. Besides offering proof that no American citizen can fill the job, the potential employer has to promise to pay wages at the going rate. Getting an au pair into America is an involved but not insuperable process, provided you have a lawyer and enough lead time.

Can you keep the au pair? If she comes as a visitor for six months and you want her to stay longer, a special request can be made to the Immigration Service to extend the visa. You and the au pair must show good reason for the extension. The safest way to present this good reason is with a lawyer's help, but you can, again, do it alone. Madison offers this advice: "To say 'I've been six months with the Smiths, and am really enjoying teaching their children Norwegian' is *not* a reason that will be honored by Immigration for an extension. If the authorities believe the purpose for the visit is completed, or that the visitor is trying to establish roots, they won't give him one hour more. 'I've not yet been to the Grand Canyon' *is* an adequate reason if the young person has traveled widely in this country during the first six months. But her sudden desire to tour will probably be discounted if she has traveled little to date."

Alternatively, if the au pair comes as a visitor for six months, and you wish her to stay longer than authorized, you can begin the process of applying for a Green Card (worker's permit). As long as she hasn't worked without authorization since arriving here, she can procure one. The government will not usually refuse a person a Green Card simply because he or she has stayed too long. The reasons for exclusion—there are thirty-three!—relate in general to moral turpitude, drug smuggling,, thievery and certain types of prison records.

Another way to skirt these legal problems is to invite a student from a foreign country to live with your family. Ordinarily, a foreign student is not permitted to work in the United States. That would violate his or her student status. On the other hand, if you find a student at a university and offer lodging in exchange for conversation, you may have the start of a relationship that endures through the person's undergraduate or graduate career. As long as the arrangement is informal, and no job is being taken away from an American, or formal salary paid, you stay within the law. You can also feel that you are promoting a foreign student's sympathy for American life. Note that the line is a fine one and the distinction important between this student lodger and a hired tutor. Mr. Madison comments: "If the person says 'I'm a tutor, pay me so much per hour or week,' and you agree, you are violating the law. The law asks: Why hire a foreign employee rather than an American?"

Find out about health and accident insurance for another person working and living in your home, but do not let your conscience prick you excessively over employing an illegal alien. If this is a reliable person whose destiny you grow to care about, you may be able to help her get a Green Card. That she has been of illegal status here before applying does *not* disqualify her from obtaining a permanent work permit.

For permanent residency for your foreign worker no lawyer is required, but you can avoid problems if you have a good one. The immigration lawyer is a specialist; the lawyer dealing with domestic law would have to use much more of his expensive time to get the same results. Richard Madison's office is witness to this efficiency. He has a student working for him who can take ten cases to the immigration office and wait in the long lines common there, instead of lining up himself ten times. The immigration lawyer knows as well the best hours to go, and shortcuts.

Finding such a lawyer is a matter of calling the local or county bar association's referral service. The lawyer should advise you on whether the case can be successful, on the precise strategies to be used, and can tell you approximate steps, time and costs in advance. The lawyer should be able to give you a fixed fee for procuring a Green Card for a particular person. "Don't pay the second installment if you don't get the next document you need," says Mr. Madison. "And only go to an immigration-experienced attorney."

You are probably going to have to hire your au pair sight unseen. To reduce the risk of an unpleasant surprise, correspond plentifully before he or she comes. If you find references obfuscatory, as I do, a letter from her parents can still be nice. You'll do better if her family is involved and positive about the arrangement than with a stray cat. You should exchange photographs. It's important to ascertain that she has enough English to get around town. You don't want her to be entirely dependent on you for all commerce with the outside world, and mute in relationship to it. Other questions to ask include the following:

1. Does she plan to go to college or take courses while staying with you? What are her goals for the visit?
2. Has she come from a home with children?
3. Has she had much to do with children in other ways?
You may want to ask whether she smokes and whether she has a valid driver's license and driving experience.

You should come to some understanding in advance, on paper, about what the procedure will be if the arrangement doesn't work out. Will you split the airfare or pay for her return flight if the arrangement disintegrates? Or is she coming to the United States anyway, to prepare for or enter a degree program?

You must decide how to pay her, what pocket money to offer. It should be enough, say, to buy herself weekly entertainment and a pair of American jeans. If she has heavy babysitting responsibilities the rate should slide upwards. However, you are responsible for her room and board, use of the telephone for local calls and other domestic amenities, and these are her most substantial compensation. The person who feels her services merit a salary should apply for a nanny position, not come to you as an au pair.

When you select an au pair, keep in mind that she will above all be your child's foreign-language friend. One success story of such a live-in comes from Agatha Christie, whose novels, you may remember, have apt sprinklings of French. The Mistress of Mystery writes in her autobiography about the rocky start her French got from book learning, and how it flourished when she had a French-speaking companion at home.

When Agatha was five, her sister came back "finished" from a Paris school. The big sister, Agatha Christie recalled, "endeavored to cope with my education by teaching me French from a manual called *Le Petit Precepteur*. She was not, I think, a good teacher and I took a fervent dislike to the book. Twice I adroitly concealed it behind other books in the bookshelf; it was a very short time, however, before it came to light again." So Agatha tried to commit the perfect little crime. In the corner of the room was a glass case containing her father's stuffed bald eagle. She "insinuated" *Le Petit Precepteur* behind the eagle into the unseen corner. When a thorough search over several days failed to turn up the book, Agatha's mother offered a prize of a delectable chocolate to the child who could find the book. Agatha fell into the mousetrap! She conducted an elaborate search round the room, finally climbed onto a chair to peer behind the eagle, and exclaimed, "Why there it is!" A scolding followed, not a chocolate (not, the author deemed a half-century later, one-hundred percent just).

When Agatha was six, her father, an American gentleman expatriate, did as so many Europeans and Americans did for several generations before World War II to economize: he rented the house and moved to the south of France. During their six months there, Agatha's mother engaged for her a series of French teachers. "I was docile as usual," the author recalled, "but apparently bone-headed as well. Mother, who liked quick results, was dissatisfied with my program." The third try was a spur-of-the-moment choice of the dressmaker's assistant fitter. Agatha's mother had noticed the girl's good humor with her sharp-tempered employer, and on the third fitting broached a conversation. Agatha's father, hearing of his wife's choice, protested that the girl wasn't even a governess. Christie continues: "My mother replied that she thought Marie was just the person they needed. 'She knows no English at all, not a word of it. Agatha will *have* to learn French. She's a really sweet-natured and good-humored girl. It's a respectable family. It's a perfect answer!' How it came about that in less than a week Marie and I were able to converse I do not know. The language used was French. A word here and a word there, and I could make myself understood. Moreover, at the end of the week we were fast friends. Going out with Marie was fun. Doing anything with Marie was fun. It was the beginning of a happy partnership."

A particular pleasure to Agatha was her nightly representation, with Marie, of various fairy stories. Agatha chose the character she wanted to be, and Marie was pressed into service to be everyone else. They went through "Sleeping Beauty," "Cinderella," "Beauty and the Beast" and so forth, performing entirely in French.

The details of your arrangement with the au pair can be settled when she comes, but you will want to work out the terms of the basic agreement beforehand. Insist gently that she bring a modicum of her own pocket money (I advise a minimum of $200) to start off. From local babysitting and other odd jobs she may be able to earn additional cash quite well once she is acclimated and known in the neighborhood, and your own children will be her best advertisement. You don't want her to borrow from you for stationery or other supplies in those first weeks, or suffer silently because she can't afford to pay her way at the pizza parlor or skating rink with a new friend.

Sample First Letter to a Prospective Au Pair

Dear Angelika,

My husband Ray and I live in the Cleveland, Ohio area with a family of three energetic boys. We would like to know if you might be interested in living with us for six months to a year, helping us with our German, and in our daily activities. Ray and I are both 33. Ray spent most of his youth in the Far East and Middle East with parents employed by oil companies. I grew up in Chicago, but my parents were born in Austria and spoke German at home. I am a native English speaker but remember quite a lot of German, which I am now passing on to our sons—John, seven; Charles, five; and Barry, two.

Our home is twenty miles from the center of Cleveland in a suburban community with parks and small lakes nearby. I used to work in an academic field, teaching the deaf, and still work with deaf children one day a week in the public school system. Ray's job involves microcomputers and their industrial application. The company where he works is also where your friends the Saltons work. Most of my spare time is spent at home with the boys or with them at their soccer club. Ray's spare time away from home is devoted to music.

He plays the clarinet and sings in a community chorus. We have one car, which I usually use or keep at home during the day, since Ray frequently bicycles to work.

We are middle-class and live simply. We do not spend our money on many material things, but rather on good food, the arts and the foreign trips that we all love. Good child care in German is our primary reason for seeking an au pair from abroad.

We can pay your roundtrip air fare to Cleveland, plus $100 a month pocket money. You will have your own room and share the children's bathroom (the house has three on the two floors). We will provide your food both at home and when we eat at restaurants. I will ask you to help with housekeeping, such as making the children's beds with them, dishwashing and laundry, and with some meal preparation. The housekeeping amounts to about one hour a day. Three additional hours each day, usually in the afternoon, should be given to practicing German with the boys. Your weekends will be free, except for either Friday or Saturday evening (the day will vary from week to week), when Ray and I go out alone, leaving the children in your charge.

There is a community college fifteen minutes away. It has many special cultural events, a coffeehouse for students and free movies at least once a week. I know the professor of German at the school, who promises to introduce you to students in his classes, if you wish.

We would like to know more about you. What are your personal interests? What experiences have you had away from home? What experience do you have with children? Please tell us something about your family. What do you expect from an au pair position, and why do you want to come to America? If you wish, have your parents tell us something about you and their feelings regarding our proposal. If you think you would like to come, please send us a phone number so we can call you soon.

Lastly, please remember that although you will have many opportunities to speak English, in our home you will be using German most of the time. We hope this will be a good feature of the stay for you—not everything will be new and strange—but it means your English will often take a "back seat."

Thank you, Angelika, for considering our offer. Please contact us soon with your reply.

Sincerely,

Kathy Janis

An alternative to a foreign au pair, a live-in native-speaking tutor from the United States, can be found through a Bilingual Education Service Center. These are discussed, and several addresses listed, in chapter seven.

When you consider hiring an au pair, you must ask yourselves whether your home is one in which she is likely to be content. Will she be happy? She must have places she can go to practice English, or a time when she can practice English with you. She will need to have contact with other young people her age. (This need not, by the way, happen quickly.) She may want to attend courses and to earn money from odd jobs outside the home. If she comes from downtown Copenhagen, is she prepared for the fact that you live 40 miles from the nearest small town? If she is from Naples, does she understand about Montana's winters? We have loved our Québecoise visitor for this remark, expressed when the first daffodils poked up their heads in April on a 45° day: "Oh, spring comes so early in New York!" Having an au pair can work out smoothly if you plan well.

Not everybody has the room for an au pair, but with a little organization it is possible for most households. It takes space; yes, but how much? Not a lot. She will need her own room and a bathroom of her own, or one shared with the children. The room need not be fancy. Our au pairs have often stayed in the room that is now Emma's bedroom: a sunny room, well-lit and adequately furnished, but with a roof that leaks from time to time, because of an aging Yankee gutter. When there is a rainstorm, the au pair has the choice of enduring this Chinese water torture or evacuating to the couch in the den for the night. Before the first au pair came, I would have done anything to correct the leak. What could be less hospitable than a leaky roof over one's head? I thought. But the au pairs have seen the trickle for the inoffensive flaw it is, because they are young and motivated to evaluate the situation in terms of its total benefits, not to look for disadvantages. Foreign live-in visitors are more concerned about being treated with respect by the children and by you than about having elegant quarters.

Even the tiniest room can be outfitted with a mini-fridge and single-burner hot plate, mounted on a square of asbestos, so that she can eat a simple meal—what person of this age eats anything else!—in private in her own room, if she chooses. If possible, provide her with a bicycle. That's absolutely all you need to do to prepare your home for an au pair.

Some problems with an au pair may be of your own creating. Here is an example *not* to follow. The wife of the vice-president of a large company, a woman of German birth, went to great effort to glamorize the room where her au pair from Switzerland was to stay. By the time Honi arrived, she was exhausted from scraping, painting and sewing curtains and a matching bed-spread. Then she refused the girl's offer to wash the dishes twice the first weekend—Honi was not likely to ask again. Worst, the woman bent over backwards linguistically, con-stantly helping Honi with her English and totally abandoning the purpose of her visit—to help her children with their Ger-man. The very first Saturday the au pair, not required to baby-sit, met friends from her flight in Manhattan, and returned at one A.M. When the woman mournfully told me this tale, I applauded the girl's independence at 19 in making friends and so quickly. But the hosting parent was offended. Didn't Honi know she would worry? And her husband had had to open the door for her at that "weird hour," when Honi returned. Tell the au pair to call you with her whereabouts if she will be in after a certain hour, so that you won't worry. Then give her a housekey. Avoid being thrust into the role of parent of a rebellious teenager. Most of the young women who will come as your au pairs have been living with their families, since young people in Europe usually live at home longer than Amer-icans do. It is a treat for them to have adult privacy and inde-pendence for the first time. Give them all the reasonable cautions you must, but let them explore their freedom too.

Let the au pair know the terms of the job in advance. To what extent will she be a family member? How much child care and housekeeping will she have? At what pay? At the first stage— that of the initial letter—what she needs is a general idea. Some things should be firmly etablished, such as money and whether smoking is allowed. But much is open to change.

You should be aware in bringing over a European au pair that there are practically "au pair rights" in Europe, so well developed is the position for a young person going to another country for cultural and educational enrichment, who chooses to live au pair. In France, for example, the rights and responsibilities of an au pair are subject to regulation by the Ministry of Labor. Her duties must not exceed five hours a day, and her work schedule must allow her sufficient time for her studies. In return for her work, an au pair receives room and board and (as of 1982) a minimum of 700 francs (about $100) per month for incidental expenses. An au pair is entitled to one day off per week, which must fall on a Sunday at least once a month. The trip to and from France is her responsibility. In addition to the usual au pair situations there is also a modified version whereby an au pair works approximately ten hours per week in exchange for a room in the home of a French family.

The American version of the position is different in two essential points. First, many prospective au pairs need all of their airfare paid. Second, the length of stay is limited to the six months' duration of the visitor's visa. Nevertheless, the European version gives us a yardstick. If you are paying for airfare, it is logical to expect that the au pair will receive a lower amount of pocket money than she might in Europe. I advise strongly giving two days off. In this way she will take part in American life more fully than if she is cloistered *chez vous* six days a week.

When she arrives, give her a "welcome wagon" kit, one that will help her make her way in the English-speaking world. It should include:

1. A map of the neighborhood marked with the basic stores you use.

2. Information on public transportation to the same cultural and social points that are important to her life back home— shopping center, church, municipal pool and so forth.

3. Information on concert series, film festivals and other special cultural events that are free or low-cost, and can be reached in her free time.

4. Instruction on using an American telephone, and emergency numbers.

5. List of American holidays and what will be closed on those days.

6. Explanation of postal rates and post office hours.

It is important to help the au pair structure her time with your children. You know how they learn language; she must learn. The au pair is not a professional and will welcome guidance, at least for a while after she arrives. She needs your direction about songs and games, whether to correct the children's grammar and how to keep her language pure (the children should perceive her as not speaking English). Capable she may be, but run through everything with her carefully. And be patient: as a foreigner, she will have to understand your information before she can act on it, whether you are speaking English or a basic form of her language.

Daily directions can be written or oral. I prefer to leave a note magnetized to the refrigerator door at the beginning of the day, and to discuss her work with her at the end. You can be specific on what to read with the children, since reading is an especially important activity. If your child was at the airport yesterday he might like to read about airplanes today. If he was painting with colors, maybe he would benefit from *Petit Tom et les couleurs* (or its Spanish, German or Italian translation). Or perhaps it will be a story you began to read aloud at breakfast. This permits you and the au pair to take turns reading a story to the children that might take more than one or two sittings, like Hans Christian Andersen's "Little Mermaid" (available easily in all the above languages), without either you or she growing hoarse. Second, you can jot down the day's activity, something, perhaps, that will take the group out-of-doors; or easel painting; or a project involving hammer and nails on a rainy day. Third— and this is my hobbyhorse—show her how to work with the children. However recalcitrant they are about cleaning up, children like to polish wood, scour sinks and do other jobs that use tools and show results. They learn language with the au pair when sharing jobs, because their mood is methodical and concentrated, and the verbs are action verbs and the nouns wholly concrete.

She will appreciate ideas, an informal curriculum. Tell her that when she is with the children for several hours spanning a mealtime, the program will be outdoor play or a walk, reading and writing, listening to songs and singing. You can say, "In our climate we consider a light rain or 30° Fahrenheit day good weather. Please take the children into the fresh air every day"; or, "The children like to curl up with you and listen to a story while dinner's cooking." Sometimes note the page in a crafts book and leave out all the fixings. In short, help the au pair with ideas and projects for the children. If they become used to the rhythm, they too will take the lead. By age four a child likes to play a story book record and follow along in the book. If the au pair can memorize and tell him when to turn the page, her job for an hour is as good as done.

I set the children tasks, like learning 12 parts of a car in French. (I'm bound to learn a new word myself!) The reward is a fat felt-tipped pen, or a kiss. I urge them, before their afternoon with Geneviève, to ask her to tell them how maple sugaring is done in Canada. It is not hard to come up with this sort of inspiration on a daily basis when a foreigner is living with you and spending time with the children regularly.

Put her in situations where she can do delightful things with the children, and can dispense treats. This is easy after the children are about three years old. Arrange an ice-cream treat on her day. If there is a performance of children's theater or an appropriate movie, the children may enjoy translating fine points to their au pair.

Our children enjoy seeing a lifestyle so contrasting to ours. The au pair polishes her nails, or meditates in a half-lotus position. She posts magazine pictures on her wall, she eats pizza ambling down the street instead of in a restaurant. And for her the telephone is not a prosaic interruption but may be the emotional focus of a day—*will* François call her from Montreal? All this is new to the children.

Confusions are intercultural, too, as well as moments of understanding. Working them out is good experience for the whole family. Children gain insights into the social contract. One au pair they may fall in love with, with another the rapport is more one of mutual respect: both can be successful. Tolerance often comes in the wake of a clashing of swords. Here are some of the gustatory misunderstandings a family may encounter.

1. Which meals are main, which minor; this is a salient cultural difference. Your au pair may call lunch dinner and expect it to be the day's main meal.

2. Though she may be an experienced cook, she may not know how to make a kiddie sandwich.

3. These days, Americans are growing more concerned about the freshness of our food and are more often cooking from scratch, which draws us closer to the eating habits of Europeans. But our habits of keeping meat in the freezer, considering four-day-old bread fresh, nibbling vitamins at breakfast like candy, and zapping dinner in the microwave may confuse an au pair. But you will be pleased that your foreign au pair has probably been brought up with less taste for junk foods than Americans have. Seeing her eat a baked potato and green salad for lunch, may encourage your vegetable-shunning six year old to assay them too.

If, on some rare occasion, you should go into her room, look at the clippings she has selected to stick on her walls, the souvenirs on her bureau. Notice what she wears in a day. Her tastes and style will reflect her nationality. See this as enhancing her value, because it does! She shares the trappings of her culture with the children—food, games, a drawing style, a way of wearing a scarf—as well as language. (And what is language without culture?) The benefits do not come at once. Don't expect her to walk in like a costume doll and enrich your cultural lives. She is cautious, and she has come to observe your culture. Gradually, gratifyingly, the coloration of her background shines through.

Alyssa Leshem, an Israeli ex-ambassador's wife, describes the French girl who took care of her first son in Zaire. "We found her in Israel and invited her to come to Zaire. She had been with Father Abee in India and described the *volupté* of living on the ground and lying next to lepers. The girl was exuberant and wonderful, caring about the world and our children. She read *Paris Match* and *Le Monde* snippets to Matti, who was two. "De Gaulle" was one of his earliest words. I attribute lots of his interest in the world not to travel merely but to this young girl and their fast friendship."

Chantal had many relatives stop by during the nine months she lived with us. They are farmers and carpenters from a village in the Quebec countryside. In the summer they had one thought—the beach—and our children once picnicked with Chantal and her parents. Your children will be curious about the au pair's family, will love to meet them and will remember all their names. They will understand that, because the au pair's family loves her too, she cannot stay forever. (That she is going home to somebody makes it all right to let her go, in the children's eyes).

This is a complex relationship. She is a member of the household, but only temporarily. She should be extended a measure of privacy from your lives, as well as privacy regarding her own. To insure our own privacy we ask the au pair to stay off the first floor from eight to ten P.M., when my husband and I have dinner and curl up on the couch. Our batteries for sociability recharge in that period of time. Our intimacy as a couple has its night bloom. You also owe it to her to keep your wallet out of sight, close your bedroom door and not streak to the bathroom in the buff, if she travels that same route. You ought not to have an altercation with your spouse within her earshot or, in most cases, discipline your children when she is present.

The appeal of the arrangement between the au pair and you is that both parties will learn the other's language. This is its *raison d'être*. However, she will learn English essentially outside her job—either from you or, better, from activities outside the home. The children must perceive and relate to her as a foreign speaker, a parcel from another culture. Thus, she will feel a tension in her situation. She comes to learn English; you bring her to America to hear her native tongue. In general, au pairs find it a pleasure to speak their language with the children. It's up to you and the children to broaden their English experience outside the home. Make it clear that *on parle français* or *si parla italiano* in the house. Be sure the au pair carries this out. That means no English-language radio, television or records when she is "on the job." The best way to dissuade her from using the television as a babysitter is to shut your television up in her room. Then it is a tool for her to learn English in her free time, but off limits to the children during the hours when they are in her charge.

To compensate her for using her native language in your-home, you should find opportunities for her to practice English elsewhere. In this she will need assistance, although once the roads are pointed out she will traverse them largely by herself. If you let her flounder, she may feel she is making no progress. You can approach this objective in several ways.

1. Enroll her in an English as a Foreign Language program or school. Get in touch with a college she can reach by public transport. If you need her days, this can be weeknights. If you need her nights, this will be days. A drawback is that you will probably have to pay for her schooling.

2. Enroll her in a high-school night-school course, or at the YMCA. There are many English courses to be found in various places. The level need not be exactly hers but it should not be wildly different. If she has studied English for six years in secondary school, she will not appreciate being in a class with twenty Japanese housewives who are struggling with the sound system of a Western language for the first time.

3. Arrange a tutoring exchange for her by putting an ad on a bulletin board or in a newspaper. This will work if she speaks a language many people want to learn—Spanish, German, Italian or French. If her language is one less commonly studied on our shores, there may be a university nearby where it is offered.

4. Give her entree into community clubs and organizations. Does the au pair have sports skills? A sports club might suit her. It is relatively easy for an au pair who arrives from abroad with her tennis racket to find friends. That her partners may be housewives and retirees won't deter her from having a good time and learning a lot of English. Even a bar or ice-cream parlor is serviceable, because there will be evenings when she would simply like to get out of the house. It is not important that she be exactly the same age as the people with whom she socializes. Our sophisticated early-20s au pair went off with a Lutheran high-school fellowship for glorious Saturdays at the shore.

Check into the young singles meeting places in your area if she is over 21. The best thing that can happen for her English is dating. I have found that the most efficient way to help an au pair is to introduce her to as many dateable young men as possible. An au pair with an active social life learns English and stays contented. I encourage an au pair to invite male friends home for lemonade and pretzels. Sometimes it is appropriate to help her evaluate dating material. She may find it hard to size up an American male. We allow our au pair an overnight visitor—male or female—one or two nights a month.

5. Help her earn extra money by working during her off time (if she wishes). If the au pair is staying several months, you can put an ad in the local shopper or town newspaper the very first day, saying she is free to babysit and do odd jobs at given times. The ad might read: "Young foreign woman living with Springtown family available for part-time babysitting, cleaning, yard work and the like. Transportation please. Call Carlotta mornings." By indicating the time of day you won't have to take Carlotta's calls. Suggest the going rate to her, rehearse with her the vocabulary she needs to negotiate a job and tell her that if employers want a reference they may speak to you. One of our au pairs hit the jackpot. She received 70 calls, which she pared down to a half-dozen people who telephoned her occasionally, at the times she suggested, for babysitting and secretarial help.

Geneviève wanted to earn some extra money and educate the natives (us), so she organized a French cooking class for us and two other couples for whom she babysat. It took place Sundays at noon and was conducted in French and international sign language. We all shared the price of ingredients and each had a prepared main dish or dessert for the evening meal. The women abandoned the class—cooking just wasn't recreation for them—but the men continued and had a lark. Before the classes ended, the husbands had learned to make *oeufs en neige*, tarts and several winy, creamy dishes that made them slightly inebriated. Geneviève also demonstrated foods appealing to children, such as stuffed eggs with pimento and green-pepper faces, and carrots cut on the bias and steamed and sautéed. Her parting gifts to Emma and Burton were egg cups.

It will greatly amplify the au pair's efficiency if you spend time using the foreign language with her and the children. This may mean simply passing time together. If you are a non-native in the language, it will also mean checking vocabulary with her. This happens in several ways. For example, there is probably an apt, colorful phrase for "It's raining hard" in both languages, such as, "It's raining cats and dogs." One of you uses it in passing or questions it, and a brief language discussion ensues. Or, she does not understand a phrase in a rock song heard on the radio or in a newspaper headline, and you decode it. You can then ask her to explain it in her language. If she is not highly conscious of her own vocabulary, so that the word does not come immediately, be patient; it will. Often, when a native speaker of a language is separated from the context of the language, vocabulary slips away, hides in the mind's recesses. Then again, words do not always have exact equivalents from one language to another.

You can sit down for an impromptu language lesson too. I think of these as naming sessions. At the bank, in the photography store, at the amusement park there is a vocabulary that you would like to conquer. If the au pair is with you, she can name everything in sight, the way the children do for the extraterrestrial in *E.T.* It can be tiring for her, of course, so you mustn't overdo it.

The entry of the parent into the language-learning scene can have a magical effect on children's language learning. In John Updike's story "Avec le Bébé-Sitter," Mr. and Mrs. Kenneth Harris uproot their family of three young children and take them to the south of France in the middle of November. In chilly Cannes, the Harrises set up housekeeping, and three weeks later acquire a "badly needed babysitter . . . a short, healthy widow of about forty." But the relationship with Marie sticks like a wheel in the mud. The children act bristly and frightened of Marie. "Hermetically sealed inside her language, she must have seemed to the children as grotesque as a fish mouthing behind glass. They clustered defiantly around their parents, routing Janet out of her nap, pursuing Kenneth into the field where he had gone to sketch, leaving Marie alone in the kitchen whose floor she repeatedly mopped in an embarrassed effort to make herself useful. And whenever their parents left together, the children, led by the oldest, wailed shamelessly while poor Marie tried to rally them with energetic 'ooh's' and 'ah's.' "

One afternoon, when his wife is at the Musée d'Antibes, and as usual the children are fleeing from the French sitter, Mr. Harris is riled enough to try to solve the impasse. "I think we should have a French lesson," he announces firmly, guiding the children to the living room. He sets Marie the task of naming everything in sight. It goes fine until two-year-old Vera toddles out to the kitchen and returns with a stale cupcake. Marie calls it *gâteau*, but Vera insists on "coogie." The lesson concludes in tears. A good idea, but it had a bug in it: Language learning traffics in lively emotions and does not develop from a mere rational accretion of words.

In the Updike story, after the children file out, Mr. Harris confronts the subject of home. In his infinitesimal French, supported by pictures on his sketch pad, he confesses, *"J'aime une autre femme"* ("I love another woman"). Suddenly the impasse is broken. Informality enters the scene. From that afternoon on, child care and language learning go swimmingly. Jolly volubility replaces grammatical set pieces. The children, "feeling the new rapprochement [between the sitter and both parents] under Marie's care developed a somewhat independent French."

To be informal you must make an honest gesture of communication that unlocks your self-expression and makes the children trust the au pair too. It is like throwing on a light switch, connecting the circuits. If pushed out alone onto the gangplank of friendship and told to jump in, the children clutch. but if the water looks good, they dive in. Treat the au pair with respect and warmth, and watch the children's foreign-language skills zoom, as they catch the ball and run with it. In a trusting environment, children relate to the new person in her language unreservedly.

Thus, when you set up the arrangement, remember that the au pair is an extension of you. During the time she is in charge, she should have as free a rein a possible. She will also do your householding when you are giving the children your attention. So don't fall into the role of anxious employer, or let your hostess instincts get the better of you, or you will end up with a *fainéant* (do-nothing) au pair. Take caution from the depiction of Samantha Upward and her au pair in Jilly Cooper's study of English society, *Class*. Samantha gets foreign au pairs to help Zacharias with his French. Gideon, her husband, hopes for Brigitte Bardots, but "Samantha has so much middle-class guilt about employing anyone, and spends so much time scurrying round doing all the work, that the various Claudines and Marie Joses soon become au pear shape."

The au pair can't always merely sit with books and your children and exude the desired foreignness. Sometimes she and they should be mother's helpers. This is how the extension of language use occurs. She shouldn't have to do drudgery—that is not why you hired her—but she can be expected to do some housework associated with child care. If she has sufficient time off to be her own person, she will not object to pitching in to do certain tasks for set hours during the day or week. This is known as light housekeeping, yes? What is *heavy* housekeeping? Since the American household banished washboards, there is no rational distinction. "Heavy" is, I guess, the housework we hate. This may well be different for you than for your au pair; find out.

Put her in charge of certain daily and weekly tasks. For example, marshalling the children to put away the toys. Indoor or outdoor errands—which are her forte? One au pair is a good driver and will take the children hither and thither to friends and appointments, another will mend and make the floor shine. It's wonderful to arrive for a changing of the guards and, instead of spending the first half-hour cleaning up the kitchen and restoring order to the living room, to be able to sit down for a few minutes of intimate interchange. Anyone can find a housekeeper, babysitter or tutor, but an *au pair*—she is a very special addition to your life.

It is very advantageous if both parents deal with the au pair. Both spouses, therefore, should be involved from the beginning. One may coordinate the foreign-language side of things, plus designate and check up on housekeeping tasks. The other may be the moneybags—handling pocket money, household expenses and a Christmas bonus. Often the au pair deals with one of you in English, the other in her native language, which has merits on her side and yours. The point is, really, that she has to cope with both of you. This keeps her on her toes. Second, you and your spouse must abide by the same ground rules with her and expect the same of her.

At Sunday breakfast you hash over anything that has come up on her side or yours. Could Michelle rake some leaves while watching the children next week? Could you or your spouse arrive home early on Friday because an American friend has invited her to an early movie? Is there adequate heat on the third floor? Most contact with the au pair is in-flight and one-to-one. A breakfast meeting is a chance for a round-table discussion.

Treat the relationship with the au pair as a friendly, flexible contract. Speak plainly and allow her to do the same. Otherwise both parties are walking on eggshells. For intance, Helga, an American banker's wife, brought over Danielle, an au pair from Belgium, whose constant chatter was so irksome to Helga that she joined a riding stable over an hour away from home, and rode out her frustrations five days a week. Tina, an art historian who invited a young Greek girl into her home to teach her children, after meeting her while on an archaeological dig, felt equally displaced, in this case by the friends of the gregarious lass, Sylvie, who made Tina's house the rendezvous for the (polite, her employer admitted) gang. Tina self-sacrificingly put up with it, and kept the au pair until the prearranged six months were up. But Sylvie was left in the dark as to why the relationship with the children's mother cooled, and Tina's daughter's "amazing" Greek faded fast. If you value the service your au pair performs, set the ground rules clearly and have open communication regularly during her stay.

A final hazard must be mentioned, and that is the sexy footnote to this otherwise chaste chapter. A number of women avowed to me that they had nothing good to say about the au pair because she and the spouse became infatuated. Either there was evidence of sexual betrayal or the winds of attraction were blowing when the girl was sent home. This seems to be an upstairs/downstairs phenomenon—stealing kisses from the European au pair instead of the chambermaid. It is not a conventional problem; nevertheless, since marital fidelity is at a premium, guard it with reasonable caution. Don't go away for three months leaving your Teutonic beauty in charge of your children, husband and the rose bushes, or *she* may be plucked. Instead of making the au pair an exotic stranger your husband never speaks to, but only has fetching glimpses (and dreams) of, bring her into his conscious life, giving him a friendly role to play as her employer. Hanky-panky between Papa and the au pair is, sadly, real or imagined by many wives who make a clinical comparison between themselves and the figure of that nubile creature in halter top and jeans.

Seeing the young woman again. It can be terribly important to maintain contact with the au pair when she has become a significant person in your children's lives. One family, concerned that their children not come to see good friends as replaceable, worked out a system whereby the children live abroad for a few weeks with each of their favorite au pairs on their summer trips with Mom (Swedish-born) to Stockholm. We fell into a terrific pattern by accident. We needed a babysitter while going on a trip to write a travel article, and invited the previous year's au pair to come along. It was a great success. Now, as much as we are able, we intend to braid the au pair from the past year into next summer's holiday—into our children's lives in the present. The renewed friendship is wonderful for Emma and Burton. The children have the opportunity to express everything that they had saved up with their new verbal powers, improved since the au pair was last with them.

Having the au pair back or visiting her abroad is not always feasible, of course. Anybody, though, can stay in touch by letters, birthday tokens or a visit when—even years later—you are in her country. Alyssa Leshem, the Israeli living in the United States, still exchanges birthday cards with the young women who lived with her family in that cherished period when her sons, now in their 20s, were small fry. Alfredo and Harriet, whose four children have all grown up in this country speaking good Italian, have been clever in bringing every au pair from Bologna. Their two trips to Italy in the last ten years have each been smiling reunions when they arrived in that city.

4
Program

Every bilingual family situation is different, especially in terms of personalities. However, there are five guidelines that are central to the success of any bilingual upbringing:

1. Start young.

2. Teach by immersion rather than instruction.

3. Be consistent and disciplined in your use of the second language.

4. Take full advantage of play as a mode of learning.

5. Teach reading and writing as well as oral fluency.

6. Provide the child with a social sphere including, at least intermittently (summertime, for example), peers who also speak or are learning the language.

7. Keep up with your kids.

Starting Young

The optimal age for starting language learning is day one. What baby hears, baby imitates. Before baby surmises that one language works for everybody (false!) show him or her that different languages work with different people. "The only language people ever speak perfectly," observes Maria Montessori in *The Absorbent Mind*, "is the one they learn in babyhood, when no one can teach them anything." Williams Girards, a Johns Hopkins psychologist, has said, "Babies and young children are literally language-learning machines. This is the thing they do best. Any reasonably intelligent child under three years of age can manage two languages." There is neurological evidence that only a young child establishes a center in the brain for the second language system—learning to think in that language automatically, rather than to translate mentally from some other system. The formative period diminishes but does not seal off until about age 12, when the initially uncommitted part of the brain, which the child could have used for an additional language, has been taken over for other functions. When you change your baby's diapers, sing and talk to him in the second language you have chosen, and your baby will soon be cooing in Spanish, Chinese or Dutch.

The best tactic is interaction. Engage the baby in pointed conversation. Most of it will be play. Does the language you will be using have separate words for different degrees of hair curliness? Find out what they are, along with words like "bangs" and "sideburns" and use them at once with your baby, with dolls, members of the family and magazine models as your visual examples.

Toddlers' favorite subjects are fulfilling play commands ("Bring me something round . . . something purple"), all the colors and sizes, and the names of well-known animals. Mr. and Mrs. Zarhovic-Bookman, two university professors, an anglophone and a bilingual whose native language is Serbo-Croatian, have a daughter who is actively bilingual, conversing with her mother in Serbo-Croatian. Says Milicia Zarhovic-Bookman, "Since Karla was several months old, I made an effort to talk to her a lot [in Serbo-Croatian]. The younger she was, the more boring and tiring was the task. When she started going to day care, I would pick her up and, for lack of anything better, I would describe the streets that we passed to get home. Then, at home, for at least three hours, she would listen to Serbo-Croatian in the following manner: (1) Either I would tell stories, read books (in Serbo-Croatian acquired when I was in Yugoslavia) or play, but always I talked and described what we were doing. Then, when I cooked dinner, I described out loud what I did (it made cooking even more tiring!). (2) Sometimes we visited Yugoslav friends, so Karla heard us talking. (At this point she was usually on my knees or hovering). (3) When my parents visited there was less pressure on me since she heard us conversing and they played with her, also talking all the time."

A traditionally observant Jew, Zev Stern is attempting to raise his son Nehemiah Akiva as a Hebrew-speaker; the boy's mother addresses him in English. Zev was present at his birth and began cooing to him in Hebrew from that day on. When Nehemiah was seven months old, Mr. Stern described his use of Hebrew with the child: "When Nehemiah is awake during my morning prayers, blessings over food, and such, he listens intently, much to my delight. On the Sabbath I sing the traditional songs to him. Since Hebrew is a language for common as well as religious use, I also 'talk' to him about everything from the weather to my long-distance running. He is beginning to babble, and when he says 'Da-da' I correct him with 'abba,' which he said once during a two A.M. wake-up episode. My wife, who does not speak Hebrew, talks to Nehemiah in English."

The child presented with a second language (whether this is inside or outside the home) dives in fearlessly—a strong reason for starting young. Take, for example, Wilfred Alde, the child of German immigrants who came to this country in their early 20s. Instead of falling into the habit of speaking English at home, Mr. and Mrs. Alde spoke German to each other and to Wilfred, destining English to be his second tongue. Recalls Ingeborg, "It would have been much easier to speak that horrible mixture of two languages that many immigrants use among their friends who understand both, but when my son was small I worked very hard to get along in pure, unadulterated German. Several of our German-American friends had children at about the same time we did, and since Wilfred's social life revolved around them he never heard English spoken except occasionally on television. The day came when he went out to play with a neighbor's boy. They were both three years old at the time, and I expected all kinds of questions: why did his new friend talk funny, why couldn't he understand him, or something else in that vein. Nothing! They never had any trouble communicating with each other. It still seems incredible to me!"

Immersion

The reason most Americans do not learn foreign languages well is that we learn them in the classroom. Almost everything is wrong with this environment. Though language is primarily oral, classroom instruction concentrates on reading the printed text. Where fluency is largely unconscious, the classroom is highly self-conscious. Where language expertise comes mostly from use and feedback, a school gives the individual student only minutes a week in which actually touse the grammar and vocabulary that he spends so much silent time learning. And even if there are simulated dialogues, it takes an uncomfortable mental squint to relate suddenly in another language with peers perceived wholly in the native one. The conventional academic route may get children into college, and may teach them many skills they need in life, but is inadequate for learning extra languages fluently. To master a language one must grow with it intellectually, take the time to absorb and to express.

To learn a language effectively you must believe you need it to make yourself understood. You must become excited and caught up in something not bound to judgments and evaluations. Usually, the conditions are wrong in school. For the most part, schools assume that foreign languages can be learned exclusive of context, that progress can be made despite hearing everybody else's mistakes, and that the real action goes on between the child and the textbook. Don't become discouraged; get smart. By approaching language learning with versatility, your child can become bilingual easily.

The program, basically, is to immerse a child as actively as possible. This process can be as simple and directed as that of giving a baby a bath. You draw a bath to the right depth and temperature. You can do it in a plastic dishpan or a fancy basinet, or you can hop into the tub and have your bath with the baby. For toddlers, you may toss in toys and bubble bath, to make it fun. Bath time is a challenge for the five or six year old who wants to do it alone, but still needs you in the act. Likewise, language immersion requires a program with safeguards and opportunities. Your job is to be sure the quality of the second language suffices, and that there is sufficient quantity and variety. Language play corresponds to the water play of the bath, as a means to an end. Talking with other than loved ones and eventually reading and writing the language, the child needs you first as an impresario, then as an adjunct. You immersed the baby, the older child immerses himself.

In Molière's *Le Bourgeois Gentilhomme*, Monsieur Jourdain, the *arriviste*, receives a buffoon's lesson in the philosophy of language. Dazzled at the Grammarian's distinction between consonants and vowels, Monsieur Jourdain rushes to try out his Fs, FAs, Rs and RAs. Further verities are yet to come. All that is not poetry is prose, the philosophy master tells his pupil. "My word!" says Jourdain. "For forty years I've been talking prose completely unawares, and I'm the world's most obliged man to you for letting me know." Molière serves up a double joke: first on the overgrown student who, grasping language's toenail, thinks he has touched its heart; second, on the academician, for misrepresenting the study of a language's formal elements as essential to its use.

American children no more need grammar lessons in the second language than you needed to take English lessons when you were a child. The secret is simply to have an active and correct use of language in the home. At five, my children mixed up the imperfect and past perfect of the French verb *devoir* (to must, have to, ought). In fact, from the time they began to use this rather difficult verb they merged *Il a du* and *Il devait* into, instead, the nonexistent *Il du-vait*. I heard the error a lot because, as you will discover or have discovered, children often trot out the grammar they sense a need to get straight. I batted back reformulations of their sentences with the correct use of *devoir*, and by five and a half, they had the two tenses down pat.

Do not correct the child's grammar in the second language with admonitions, any more than you would in a first. You don't want to clip your child's wings with reprimands about errors, or explicit grammar lessons. Niceties spoken and written come later, when the bilingual child reads, and vocabulary learning slows down. Treat the second language as you would your native tongue.

Don't translate, even when your child would understand better in English—even when you are discussing an emotional issue, such as punishment. Jean Cabral is raising three boys to speak English and Spanish in the Dominican Republic. Jean's husband, an industrial engineer, is Dominican and she is a former elementary school teacher from the American South. The company transferred them abroad, first to Portugal for six years, subsequently to the Dominican Republic. The elder two sons (in their early teens) were bilingual in English and Portuguese first. Now, like the youngest, they are bilingual in English and Spanish. Jean spoke no foreign languages until the first transfer, and although she learned both Portuguese and Spanish from "intense social contact" she speaks only English to the children. "From the time all three boys came home from the hospital, I have spoken to them in English. I chattered in English all day long: 'Here is your milk,' 'Come to Mommy,' 'Let's change your diaper.' I commented about what I was doing for them, what was going on around them, everything. When they were older, I read them nursery stories at every meal, every day. I took them to children's movies in English. But most important, I talked to them in English all the time and *never* translated for them. When you translate, the child hears only the translation. When, intead, you explicate by discussing the word with a child in the language, the child explores a concept mentally." This is an essential rule of the immersion method.

Before learning to apply the rules of language with consistency, all children overgeneralize them. Children constantly revise and refine their internal grammar, as my chldren did with *devoir*. First they cope with clear-cut questions, then sort out subrules in increasing detail. According to linguists, the process of refinement continues until at least the age of ten. It probably takes considerably longer for most children to be able to compose the full array of complex, adult sentences. By the time children are six or seven, however, the changes in their grammar are so subtle that they may go unremarked. Children often circumvent points of grammar they have not yet dealt with, relying on simpler patterns. Do not expect your child to speak like a well-schooled adult!

Bilingually raised children will attack any subject. For this reason their grammar is often irregular. They are unafraid to push their language to its limit of expression. They will fill in words they don't know when writing a composition. This is good, and to be encouraged. If they "hear" a word in the inner mind, whether or not they know how to spell it, they want to write it in a sentence. The academic student is rewarded above all for a neat figure-eight, but the home-tutored child skates an icecapade. Formal grammar is relatively useless to the young child still learning to function in the language.

Veena Oldenburg, an Indian political scientist married to an American and living in the United States, describes immersion in her multilingual home: "Languages flew around my house, and the children learned to cope." Servants, depending on whether they were Muslims or Hindus, spoke Urdu or Hindi, her grandmother spoke Punjabi, and so did the driver who drove her to school. Behind the walls of her school, by decree only English was spoken. Veena spoke three languages fluently by age five. "I had to talk to all these people. I had no choice. You can survive and then later you can choose among the languages and dialects, a directed choice."

Instead of offering grammar lessons, consciously embroider on your children's speech. For example, to the statement "The fox found the nest," you can say "That sly old fox found the nest, didn't he?" A study at the University of Pennsylvania, by the psychologist Keith Nelson and several colleagues, has shown that one way adults help children learn languages is to elaborate slightly on what the child has said. In one study, the researchers sometimes played verbal tag with the children, aged two to four and a half, over two months time. For example, they answered a statement with a question, as in the fox-and-nest exchange. Children exposed to such responses spoke longer phrases and sentences, used more auxiliary verbs, and were generally more advanced linguistically than a group of children to whom the adults gave replies that were either new sentences or verbatim echoes. A simple embroidery can be done when a child uses a weak vocabulary word where you can supply a strong one. In Italian, your child might say, "Do you have something to erase with?" You reply, "Here, take this *gomma* (eraser)."

Overlap language learning with daily activities. "I would I had bestowed that time in the tongues, that I have in fencing, dancing and bear-baiting," says Sir Andrew to Sir Toby in Shakespeare's *Twelfth Night*. If your family is to be bilingual, make sure that at least some of your activities, without being lessons, are heavily weighted to verbal exchange and listening to language. The recessive language must be drawn out. My French dictionaries are as close as the cookbook shelf and telephone stand, but other than an occasional dash to reference sources like these, I never have to set aside time for French. Children learn the second language by being surrounded by it all day long before they enter an English school and at home thereafter. Be sure they use it to accomplish the everyday tasks of living with you. A four year old should know how to talk about dusting the corners free of cobwebs, carving a pumpkin and washing the car. A five year old should hear the words associated with visits of the mailman, electrician, meterman and so forth, and body parts in some detail beyond what a toddler knows. If you are hearing the language less about the house this season than last, ask yourself whether the children need to hear you talking about some of the concrete operations you and they do: You can bike or play Parcheesi in Italian!

As the child's language awakens, you need to draw out less. For two weeks, of evenings, my husband and I were standing on the twins' highchairs painting the dining room mauve. The children wiped up drops, and found us equipment. Burton said, "Dad, I want you to listen *Pierre et le loup* so you can learn French." In the same vein, Burton pointed out all the painting tools to his father in French ("*Ça c'est un pinceau; ça c'est un seau*"). After Chris had echoed '*pinceau*," "*échelle*" and "*seau*," and we had listened to another French story record, *but not before*, I switched on New York's "best" rock station.

Try to give the children some practical return on their efforts as soon and as often as possible. Whether it is something as simple as being able to read a street sign in, say, New Orleans, or a storefront sign in a Hispanic neighborhood, let them see that their learning has benefited them in some obvious and useful way. Stefan Demetriadis, seven, used his knowledge of Greek to understand dinosaurs better. His parents pointed out to him that the scientific terms were actually Greek words describing the dinosars, and then began translating dinosaur names for him. Then he began trying to do this for himself, matching the names with the characteristics of the dinosaurs, as described by their names. Next they did the same for medicine, biology and other scientific terms.

Take children to events where the language is spoken in a natural environment, to social, cultural, patriotic, religious or political activities. Here they can hear the second language in its natural habitat and gain a better understanding of the verbal and nonverbal elements. Go where the language is used in ethnic neighborhoods as well, to the restaurants, department and grocery stores, movies and cultural clubs. If possible, attend an ethnic wedding.

Music and song are marvelous ways to get into the culture too. "Hear it, sing it, dance it!" says a Greek-American mother, giving her formula for keeping up a language at home. Singing is of inestimable value in giving a child language patterns before, perhaps, the child is even using them in speech. Also, by repeating a song, the child imagines himself a native speaker. When practicing a song at other times, when it springs from their hearts, children play with it, substituting nonsense lyrics that frequently are consonant with the grammatical pattern. Even if you wanted to be good as gold in church or synagogue when you were a child, you probably found yourself substituting other words for the second, third and fourth stanzas of hymns. It is exactly this kind of exercise that language laboratories mandate. Isn't singing—memorizing as many songs as possible and watching the children sing them back—infinitely nicer? Singing as a technique for language-learning is further discussed in chapter eleven.

Often, children ask to be read the same story over and over. In that case you can change several words, to make the reading more complicated. Often this means varying from your simplified version to reading word for word. Ask them what the new words meant, and explain to them. Leave the story book out or return to past chapters the next day. Ask them again, to see if they remember the new vocabulary. If a word strikes their fancy, think immediately of a way you can use it later. Build vocabulary so subtly that the children don't feel you are being pedantic!

Make sure that the children learn about the cultural background so that they understand the importance of that language, its place in modern life and how it relates to the American experience. There are excellent books on ethnic groups in America, such as the series from Lerner and Dial. (See chapter seven for titles and publishers' addresses.) See also the last chapter in most of the books in the Heritage series by Dillon Press, and Dillon's Swedish/Danish/German *Ways* books for older children and adults. Gladys Meyer, a retired professor, was the daughter of a German pastor and an American mother who learned German from his mostly German-speaking congregation. She tells how, before World War I, her mother supplemented the children's respect and affection for their German heritage, often with English. "My mother read the autobiography of Carl Schurz aloud to us in English. She gave me the legends of the *Niebelungen* in English, which I read at seven or eight. The first opera she took me to, at age eleven, was *Parsifal*. It was unforgettably exciting seeing the German opera in an American audience."

Make a conscious effort to extend your own vocabulary. Jean Mitchell's father was a writer, so he could take his work with him, as well as his family, when he traveled. Three out of the first six years of her life were spent in the south of France, in the course of three separate trips. When they returned to the United States, in the depths of the Depression, her father felt he had made an investment in his daugher and he didn't want her to forget the French she had learned. They spoke no English for the next 25 years. "Interestingly enough, my mother, who had a good accent, did not join in the bilingual goings-on. My father's accent was atrocious (in the sense that it was his), but he read a great deal in French and was constantly imparting new words to me. My vocabulary to this day is unusually large for someone who isn't French."

When you impart a new word, bring it to life. Take a hint from the classroom teaching style of John A. Rassias, professor of Romance languages and literature at Dartmouth College. Whether he teaches beginners French, Spanish or Greek, he is an actor on stage. He exudes emotion and uses gestures to make unfamiliar words comprehensible. Give the children commands and stage directions. When my children were learning French as babies, I didn't need to reinforce their learning with theatrics. But now that they are studying German as a "foreign" language, I tell them to hear the meaning in each word. *Müde* sounds tired and *Ich weine* (I cry) can't be said without a sob in the throat. We collapse on the bed as we talk in German about being tired, and verbs like "to cry" and "to shout" were the first learned and used in German because I taught them to Emma and Burton by the dramatic approach Professor Rassias advocates.

When the children ask you what a new word means, either from a book or conversation or because you have used it in speech on purpose, practice with it without delay. The stimulus might be a nature book saying, "The Asian elephant is smaller than the African and tames more easily." "What does 'tame' mean?" the young child asks. "Taming is what the little prince did to the fox" or, "The lion who jumped through the hoop at the circus was tamed by the lion tamer," the parent replies. Then the child comes up with other sentences using "tame":

Snow White tamed the dwarf.
Bambi tamed the big stag.
Snow White and Rose Red tamed the bear.
Pinocchio tamed Geppetto.

These are the actual sentences my twins, at five, composed for the word "tame." They are a little off-center but are close to the actual definition of the word. This is a vocabulary-building technique familiar in the later grades and junior high in written school work. It is most effective, I think, used orally on the spot, when the children are stimulated to learn an isolated word.

Make sayings and adages a part of your speech. Our English speech has become impoverished in traditional short sayings, but now you can learn some in the second language. Your bookseller will help you with a book of popular sayings in the language, such as:

French: *Proverbes à la douzaine.* Told by Anne-Marie Dalmais, illustrated by Benvenuti. Paris: Flammarion, 1976.

German: Lippl, Alois Johannes. *Eine Sprichwort im Mund wiegt 100 Pfund: Weisheit d. gemeinen Männer in Spruchen und Reimen.* Munich: Süddeutscher Verlag, 1972.

Italian: *Italian Idioms with Proverbs.* Compiled by Vicenzo Luciani. New York: Vanni, 1981.

Spanish: *El Libro de los 500 Refranes.* Compiled by Carmen Bravo-Villasante, illustrated by Carmen Andrada. Minon Vallodolidi, n.d. Distributed by Bilingual Publications.

From the Information Center on Children's Cultures (331 East 38th Street, New York, NY 10016) you can get the titles of books of sayings in many languages. The Center will send titles, and even, at the cost of photocopying, a few pages of books that would otherwise be difficult to acquire. Because the specialty of this center is languages spoken by children in the Third World, your bookseller or a cultural institution—the Goethe House, Alliance Française or Istituto Italiano, for example—are better sources than the Center for such books in German, French or Italian. Addresses for these institutions appear in chapter seven.

Florence Evans wrote to me in her eighties. Her parents came from Sweden to Massachusetts. She spoke English to older brothers and sisters, Swedish to her mother. Sunday school and church were in Swedish. From Sunday school and from her mother she learned a wealth of sayings. "I still remember a good deal of Swedish," she said, "though there is no longer an opportunity to speak it." Americans who grew up in an ethnic heritage before World War II were brought up on sayings like those that hang on the wall of Mrs. Evans' breakfast area, printed on ceramic plates. These are the favorite Swedish expressions of her mother:

Morning time has gold in its mouth.
Morgonstund har guld i mund.

Talking is silver, but silence is gold.
Tala är silver, men tiga är guld.

Away is good but home is best.
Borta är bra, men hemma är bäst.

When asked, without a moment's hesitation, Mrs. Evans told me some of her own favorites, translating from the Swedish:

Comes the day comes a way.
Kommer dag, kommer råd.

When it rains gruel the poor have no spoons.
När det regnar välling har den fattige ingen sked.

Never criticize half-done work.
Aldrig skåda halv-gjort arbete.

An inch on the end of the nose makes a good deal of difference.
En tum på näsan gör mycket.

If you've said A you might as well say B.
Om du säger Å, sa må du säga B.

Florence and her siblings were brought into line at the table with: "Let the food silence the mouth!" Florence adds, "Having known a second language made it easy for me to learn Spanish and a bit of German in school. I have forgotten most of the Spanish and German, but I remember the Swedish that I learned in early childhood extremely well."

The success of your bilingual childrearing depends on your child's ability to experience feelings in both languages. To this end, discover poetry, the language of the heart, with your child, reading aloud and reciting it. Nadia Rakoff and her husband are American born, of Russian families. They have three children, now all teenage, and all have spoken only Russian in the home. Nadia used to learn rhymes by heart from children's books to recite to the children as babies, or sometimes she tucked letter blocks into a bag when strolling out. "When the children were two," she says, "books were the most important tool. Especially important from even before that were books with lively pictures and rhymes that were catchy and fun. When taking walks with my babies in their carriage, I used to recite these rhymes to them, so that now they feel they know

them too, without actually ever having memorized them."
When you read a bedtime story, include a poem as the grace
note. If you enjoy the poetry and find it echoes something else
in your life, your child will begin to recall poetry too, carrying
the benefit of the rhythms and cadences over into all his language self-expression.

Prayers also are written in poetic language, and in many
families they are language as well as religious instruction.
Emma and Burton have learned a number of prayers in the
French Baha'i prayer book for children. They find the prayers
fascinating because the mystical language is perfumed with the
scent of faraway. When they say the prayers they naturally
chant, almost sing, them.

Cook in the language. It takes precise listening and speaking
to give and take directions. The child tastes words with the
food. When you cook with the child, memory and words reinforce each other. Says Edward Bailey, a graphic designer and
illustrator living in Vermont: "I remember as a teenager being
in Germany, and wandering into a *Konditorei* in Düsseldorf. I
randomly pointed at something that looked delicious, and
when I bit into it outside the pastry shop, I knew that taste! It
was *Lebkuchen,* what we call German gingerbread. And I knew
that I had eaten it many Christmases before in Porto Alegre in
Brazil at my grandmother's house. We are of German and Ty-
rolean origin on my mother's side. That household spoke German. Ummmm!" If language were taught entirely as a cooking
and eating class in school, as a series of rehearsals for a play or
as a series of preparations for and celebrations of appropriate
holidays, children might absorb and recall it better. Why? Because cooking concentrates, narrows and attracts our mental
attention and our senses as well. Cooking words are the last
words a person forgets when his or her ethnic language fades.

Our children make up crazy recipes or try to devise edible
ones. Crazy Salad, for example, uses the kitchen words that a
child learns early from spending time in the kitchen. It also uses
the imperative mood. Each person either writes down or de-
vises and commits to memory five to ten steps for making a
crazy salad for a particular occasion. The format is like a recipe
book, hence the string of imperatives. Throw in a rule like,

"Every new direction must involve a new verb," to add piquancy to the game. We carried the game into real life when the children told me recipes, in French, for omelets filled with an abundance of vegetables taken straight out of the bags from the supermarket and sautéed.

Consistency

If the mood of language acquisition is playful, the structure of learning must be clear and strict. We learn language because it is a primary means of communication. A child is motivated to learn two or more languages because he encounters people and situations where the second language is essential.

There are three basic types of bilingual structures: (1) inside the home one language, outside another, (2) one parent, one language, (3) daily interaction with a nonparent native speaker of the second language, as with an au pair or grandparent.

Exposure to the second language must be consistent and regular daily, throughout childhood and into the mid-teens. (From this point on, use can be more desultory without loss of fluency.) I think of the flirtatious exchange between pretty Miss Everdene and the sergeant on "the verge of the hay-mead" in *Far from the Madding Crowd.*

"Seeing she made no reply [to his conversational gambit] the sergeant said, 'Do you read French?'

'No, I began, but when I got to verbs, father died,' she said simply."

The language spoken in the home should be used consistently rather than fitfully. A language should be learned in its entirety. Hardy's Miss Everdene was unlucky in more than love in stopping French short of the verbs.

Either all adults in the household speak the second language to the child, or one principal person does. One adult speaker is enough, provided that adult addresses the child exclusively in the target tongue. If you are the only speaker of the language, you must speak it with some confidence and you must persevere. You are going to speak it entirely to your child from the moment you decide to rear him bilingually. While perfect fluency or a graduate degree in the language is not necessary, you should be beyond the stage of translating in your mind. conversance with "kitchen" Spanish or a solid foundation in college Spanish will suffice. Mary Gail Reed, a speaker of French as a second language who is passing it on to her daughter as a mother tongue, explains: "You don't have to be too hard on yourself. You may not be able to carry on a philosophical discussion about Camus with your college professor, but you can carry on a conversation about airplanes or birds with an eager child."

You may be eloquent on the Bauhaus movement or Symbolist poetry but a wash-out on animal sounds, kitchen utensils and nursery rhymes; or perhaps reading in the language is uphill work but you are at ease in a homely chat with your great-aunt. In either case, you face the same challenge, developing new muscles in the language. Most important is your commitment; you must *be* the second language for your child.

Set up a consistent pattern of usage with the child as early as possible. He must understand when and where to expect English to be spoken, when his other language. The pattern might be: The second language at home, English at the daycare center; or, the second language with Daddy, English with Mommy. If a parent switches to English whenever he or she is tired, angry or "just doesn't feel like it," the child may be confused and unhappy. Chances are he will finally switch to English completely, since at least that is one language to which he is exposed consistently. Dolly, a character in Tolstoy's *Anna Karenina*, spoke to her children in English and told them to answer her in French. As Tolstoy suggests, this is no way to teach a language and, indeed, no way to bring up children.

Many parents who immigrate to the United States abandon their native language and become English monolinguals in the home, to help their children move ahead in school. How benighted! They often wait until the child is of school age to begin using the original language, and then may do so imperfectly. The result? The children are cut off intellectually from the language of their heritage, and their parents have made a futile sacrifice. It is important to remember that your offspring are getting excellent exposure to English from the environment at large. The Mexican-American author and critic Richard Rodriguez describes how school authorities came to his house when he was a child and convinced his parents to cease using Spanish in the home. Henceforth, for Richard's supposed benefit, they spoke with him only in English. Rodriguez' regret is expressed in the title of his fascinating autobiography, *Hunger of Memory*. In effect his parents abandoned him to the majority culture by following the dictates of the school. Their decision left the bright youngster with a sense of loss for the Spanish discarded at home. One Saturday morning, he entered the kitchen when his parents were talking to each other in Spanish. He did not realize it was Spanish until, the moment they saw him, they switched to English. "Those *gringo* sounds they uttered startled me. Pushed me away. In that moment of trivial understanding and profound insight, I felt my throat twisted by unsounded grief. I turned quickly and left the room. But I had no place to escape to with Spanish. (The spell was broken.) My brother and sisters were speaking English in another part of the house . . . . I would have been happier about my public success had I not sometimes recalled what it had been like earlier, when my family had conveyed its intimacy through a set of conveniently private sounds." Being consistent means continuing with the second language even after your child enters school.

How does consistency work? Kitty Drick, whose parents were a case of reverse immigration, returning to Czechoslovakia after her birth, offers an example of how parallel languages should work in the family. "My parents," she recalls, "decided to make me thoroughly bilingual and leave nothing to chance. Papa spoke only German with and to me from the time I was born, while Mama and everyone else could speak Czech to me. This created no problem, so that between the ages of two and three I did not even mix the two languages." L.C. Audette, a lawyer born in Ottawa, Ontario, describes how the languages were entwined in his household in French Canada. Both parents were of Scottish and French heritage, and fluently bilingual. "Great care was taken in the house to ensure that all the children spoke both French and English. There was an implicit law that we simply spoke English to my mother and French to my father. So basic was this atmosphere that, turning from one to the other, I would instinctively and unconsciously switch from one language to the other, even in mid-sentence."

In his mid-teens it began to strike him as odd that his parents, "a good, very happy, old-fashioned marriage," should sit alone evenings chatting away, one in French and the other in English. By then, because of very real effort in the early years of the marriage, this unusual form of communication had become totally natural to them. They were oblivious to the fact that they were speaking different tongues. Explains Mr. Audette, "To all of us, this atmosphere was a godsend. I, for instance, never learned the 'other' language; there was not an 'other' language; there were only the two in which I had been brought up." A former prime minister of Canada, Louis S. St. Laurent, phrased a similar situation in his own life amusingly: "I merely thought that all children spoke to their father in one way and to their mother in another." As a result of the neatly equilibrated home language situation, all the Audette family was completely bilingual. Adds the lawyer, "Such a complete balance between the two languages had one unforeseen minor problem which I shared with my brothers. The person with whom we were conversing controlled our linguistic thought processes. With a person known to me as anglophone I think in English and 'translate' if I am compelled to speak French. With a person known to me as francophone, I think in French and 'translate' if compelled to speak English."

If this system is used, each parent must be a steadfast speaker of one language with the children, not a bilingual converser. The children must learn to be the interpreters, switching from one language to the other; their minds are the bridge, not you. Barbara Bamberger and her husband immigrated to Israel after their marriage. Unlike many people who came to Israel from Western countries in the 1930s, 1940s and 1950s, they are part of a generation who want to maintain their English-world heritage too. Says Barbara, "I always speak English to my kids unless there is a guest or friend of theirs over who doesn't understand. If they don't understand a word, or something that's more of an idea, such as the day of the week, I don't translate. I explain it in English or I try to put it into a frame that they can more or less grasp by themselves, such as: 'Sunday is the day after Saturday. On Saturday we don't work.' It is easy to fall into the trap of answering your child in whatever language he or she speaks to you. Sometimes it takes a conscious effort not to do that, for consistency's sake. We find it important also not to translate simultaneously because the children will hear the sentence in whatever language is easier for them."

When J.P. Cosnard des Closets and his American wife returned from France to Connecticut with two-year-old Sean, they had a summit conference on the big question: "What language are we going to use with our children, where and when?" They decided they would speak French in the house and English outside, "when we walked, as it were, into America." But they noticed very early in the game that the rule was not working, even for themselves. For instance, when friends, the parents' or Sean's, came to the house, they all switched to English. It was done, as the father describes it, "out of the most elementary sense of courtesy." Eventually the child himself decided the big question. As Mr. Cosnard explains, "In our family it happened that Sean, seemingly indifferent to our 'decision,' began—and never stopped—speaking only French to me and only English to his mother. He knew that, from his point of view, it was natural to speak French to his French father, English to his American mother."

Thus, you must decide, from the beginning, that you will be consistent at all costs. From that decision, you will find that you fall into good habits uncompromisingly. Krystyna Poray Goddu was brought up in the United States of Polish-born parents, speaking Polish and English. At 28 she is still fluent in Polish, as are her younger brother and sister. They were not allowed to speak English at home unless someone was present who spoke no Polish. "It was a rule we abused, of course," notes Krystyna with a twinkle of mischief. "Nevertheless, it *was* a rule." The parents were on constant watch, however, because they didn't want the children to lose the language. They and the grandparents "never failed" to criticize the combining of two languages in one sentence, and joked with the children about their mistakes and mispronunciations, "certain of which have become part of our family vocabulary." Once, she recalls, the children were caught for the "millionth time" fighting among themselves in English. *"Po Polsku!"* (In Polish!) screamed their mother, to which the children retaliated by saying they didn't know any bad words in Polish. So she taught them a few mild curses, the equivalents of "Jesus Mary," and "damn." The children had great fun thenceforth, using the swear words and hearing their parents use them. Most importantly, the mother had made her point that Polish was for *all* occasions at home. Be prepared for your children's lapses, for contingencies and unexpected situations; but be resolute.

Another parent, Dr. Waltrud Buser, who has raised four children, all American-born, bilingually in German and English, crystallizes consistency's cardinal rule: "The parent speaking the foreign [second] language has to converse in it with the children *at all times* [except when English speakers are present who might feel excluded and consider this rude]. You cannot make this a sometime affair."

Consistency requires discipline . . . when you least expect it. For example, at some point your comfortably bilingual children will wish to respond in English even though they understand the second language. Don't condone this. A pattern of English response to the second language is not nearly as effective as encouraging the children to respond *in* the second language. If the child hears the language but doesn't speak it, he will not gain a thorough understanding and fluency. Even when children report a conversation that went on in school in English, they will, if bilingual, translate a good portion of what they have to say into the second language, as indirect speech. "Davy says that his cat had kittens," the child says in Spanish, reserving English for choice direct quotes of what Davy may have said. English, of course, also crops up in the vocabulary of every language; for example, in German: *Sein Bruder gab ihn ein wind-up car* (His brother gave him a wind-up car). Says Wanda Moscicki, "Whenever I talked to my parents in English, they said they didn't understand what I was saying. I used to get angry at them because I knew they *did* understand. After all, they understood when other people spoke English to them. But now I am very grateful that they did that."

Be firm. An example of firmness comes from Viviane and Michael Gould, who speak only French at home. Their older boy had limited contact with English until he attended pre-school at two years of age. A definite problem, reports Michael, developed when he was three: "Peer pressure was such that he demanded that we speak only English at home. We firmly refused. He made a fuss, but gradually he accepted French at home." Opines Dr. Gould, "Parents have to be firm for it to be a success. For the last four years or more, my son has been proud to speak two languages."

Some parents devise a multiplicity of ways to encourage the child to respond in other languages, some devilishly clever. Konrad Bieber and his wife were young when they emigrated to France from Germany, and they became trilingual. In the United States, they decided to raise Tom with French as a sec-ond language. Recounts Professor Bieber, "It may seem out-right demagogic, but since we had no real psychological guidance, we had to operate according to what seemed to us expedient. When Tom, age seven or eight, started answering in English to French spoken by his parents and other adults, we felt it would be counterproductive to appear punitive. How-ever, I started initiating a policy that seemed to pay off. All stern orders were given in English—'Empty the garbage pail,' 'Make up your bed,' and so on. All permissions—'You may go over to Billy's house,' 'After dinner we'll go to the Dairy Queen for dessert'—were given in French. Unfair? Perhaps. But it did work in the long run. More active use of language was en-couraged. Also, up to the time Tom was eight, I used to be deaf to requests voiced in a language other than French—outside of immediate after-school hours. The result was that at age seven, Tom said to his pal Johnny, 'My poor father, he doesn't un-derstand English,' even though, of course, I used that language at times in his presence."

Consistency is easier to maintain than it sounds, because your children are your speaking partners, not adversaries. An example of the structured way children operate comes from Marion Fraser, an American raising her daughters as Portu-guese/English bilinguals in Brazil. Both girls chose a particular language for each of their Portuguese grandparents, who like to use English with them from time to time. They spoke English to the Brazilian grandfather, who is fluent in it, and Portuguese with the grandmother, and treated the two as if there were no communication between them. "When they were with both grandparents, they would tell a story to the grandfather in English and then turn too their grandmother and tell her the whole thing in Portuguese—although I'm sure they were well aware that both grandparents were bilingual."

The Aldes of Illinois, German by background and parents of Wilfred, whose first language was German (until three, the only English he heard was on television), devised a "pay for speaking English" system when Wilfred was in grade school. Mrs. Ingeborg Alde passes on the system: "For every English word or sentence used at home by any of us, a coin had to be dropped into a piggy bank. This kept my son on his toes because he was naturally eager to score over his parents. Mother, of course, had to pay most often!" Another bilingual family sits down to dinner with five nickels at each place setting. Speak English and one of your nickels goes back into the family pot.

If you start when your children are young, you can predict the uphill as well as the easy sections of the road. You begin by exerting yourself to speak the "different" language to a gurgling baby who doesn't even speak one language yet. Then life gets easier until the child makes an anglophone friend, and is stimulated in English by a good preschool or first grade. Soon you find him second-language friends, take him places where the language can be heard, and read or discuss gripping books with him. Now it's smooth going again. The next test comes at the cusp of adolescence (unless you are the exceptional bilingual family who manage a truly dual social world). If a teenager wants to dissociate from the home language, the solution is to weave new friendships and activities into the children's surroundings, not to switch to English. Ride out rebellions against the language, as you must other rebellions. Be firm about speaking the language you have established with your child. Children eventually see the rewards of speaking the extra language. Some families say they avoid insisting, others say frankly that they do insist. If the language is present in force, children come round either way. Their foundation will be all the firmer, however, if the parents persist in maintaining a bilingual home. Both Rudolf and Waltrud Buser are from Germany. All their four children, the oldest one past 20, were born her and have been brought up bilingually. According to Mrs. Buser, there was rebellion often: " 'Why do we have to speak German?' the children would ask. The language was enforced by house rules and the constant admonition, given about a million times a day: 'Sprich Deutsch!' [Speak German!]." Mrs. Buser tells this anecdote: "As a teenager, our son dreamed that a burglar invaded our house, threatened me, his mother, with a revolver, and demanded money and valuables. My answer to the burglar was 'Speak German!' As the children grew older, they realized the benefits of a second language. Now the three older ones say it has been of value to them that we were so adamant."

Expect that your children, sometimes, will be embarrassed about being different in the eyes of their friends. Try to foster the sense that this difference is, rather, a uniqueness.

Don't be troubled that your child mixes the languages. Later, as he intellectualizes language, he will eventually sort the strands out. Roger Lewis is an American with a French wife. Although they were fairly careful to speak their own languages to their daughter, Nathalie, at 14 months her vocabulary was eclectic. When Nathalie began to name things, *chien-chien* signified dog, and *nez*, nose, but she always said "book," not "*livre*" and "crackers," never the French equivalent. Professor Lewis wrote to *Parents* Magazine that he was worried by the mixture, and received in an unpublished response from Dr. Virginia Pomeranz both approbation and the observation, based on her more than 25 years of practicing pediatrics in New York, that children growing up in a bilingual household invariably do as Nathalie does. She wrote "They use, in any particular situation, whatever is the easier word for them (Nathalie obviously prefers '*chien*' to 'dog' and '*nez*' to 'nose,' but 'book' to '*livre*'). But that *is* a choice, and it doesn't reflect a youngster's understanding. Right now your daughter doubtless understands both languages. And by the age of three years, she will be speaking both and—assuming you are speaking correct English and our wife correct French—she'll be speaking them both correctly. There isn't any conflict; she's learning from you both."

Make dinner conversation a forum for practice. Joseph Kennedy's family dinner table was a stage for training statesmen. Your dinner table can train multilinguals. Kennedy questioned his children and they answered with the liveliest possible intelligence, with solid argument or a *bon mot*. Each member of the family was expected to bring interesting, witty conversational tidbits to dinner. A well-known psychiatrist who specializes in adolescents, of Viennese background, told me that dinner conversation was the foundation of her method of German home education. Why don't her bilingual children rush from the dinner table to basketball practice or to phone their friends? Why does the family linger instead of cutting dinner short to watch television? First, the rules on watching television are strict. Second, joining the dinner table is a privilege offered the children when they reach about eight. This may not suit the relaxed lifestyle or closeness of your family, but if you do find it appropriate, it can be a useful attitude to adopt. It is natural that the second language be queen at the family dinner table. Gladys Meyer, age 75, tells how in her childhood home both English and German were always spoken, but with German reserved, on the whole, for family religious life and the dinner table. "My parents really saw education as the road to the celestial city, and as the youngest child I was exposed to much beyond my years."

Nehemiah Stern, a baby whose father and mother speak to him in Hebrew and English respectively, has a Hebrew alphabet chart above his crib. Next to each letter is a picture of an object that begins with the letter. Of course, Nehemiah does not yet recognize the alphabet, but he is accustomed to the decor of his room. Traditionally, the alphabet is learned at about nine years of age in Jewish homes, and mothers bake sweet cookies with a Hebrew consonant and vowel printed on each. The child is presented with a cookie and gets to eat it if he or she can read the syllable. The idea is for the sound of the Torah to be sweet on the child's lips.

Play

Learning an additional language through spontaneous communicative interaction—play—makes the child a good learner in other areas. When confronted with new information, bilingual children know how to get down to business, eliminating chaff and guarding the kernel of what is useful. Play does *not* mean play-acting; when children learn languages they are themselves. To quote John Locke, "Particularly in learning of languages, there is least occasion for posing of children." Make most games you play with your children word games, and play them at odd moments, when they are the most diverting. Here are some examples.

Vocabulary Drill. Lay out three or four lotto cards, name the pictures, and have the child name them. The child closes his eyes. Take one card away and the child must guess which is gone. Do the same with other sorts of pictures cut from magazines.

Bring Me Back a Word! In this eminently simple and perdurable game, everybody brings one amazing word to the dinner table, starting with A-words on Monday through G-words on Sunday, if you stick with the game for seven nights. Everybody tries to remember all the words to the end of the week. As with all memory games, children play as well as adults. This is fun for a family where one parent does not speak the language well; anybody who can read a dictionary can take part.

Categories. An adult names an object and the child names its category (furniture, food, animals and so forth). This can also be done with lotto or flash cards.

Bilingual Photograph Album. Make a book about a child, using unwanted photos. Use an old-fashioned black-paged album. Seal photographs under clear contact paper. Either write or type captions on slips of paper and place them next to the photos, or write the captions on each page with a white ink pen. Judy Cohen, whose husband is Dominican and whose son Alex is bilingual, made a bilingual album for Alex about the family before she went into the hospital to have their second child. It is best to make the captions bilingual because a child will want to share the book with friends.

Fill-in Stories. Tell stories in the foreign language, allowing the child to fill in content words from his existing or new vocabulary. For example: "Once upon a time there was a little _____, and she loved to _____. . . ."

Merry Metaphors. Inventing phrases, metaphors and names is an activity that can be done anytime, and with any age child. I go for a walk with the children. We see a bush. I say (in French) that the bush looks like a "plush flower." Burton says it looks like a "marriage of flowers." Emma tries to top us, and we continue on our walk.

Odd Families. This is another game of the same ilk. After reading the book series about the guileless, amoeboid family the Barbarpapas, we began to call ourselves *la famille Fleur: Jardin Fleur, Bouquet Blanc, Sarcler Grain, Arrose l'Azalée* (the Flower family: Flower Garden, White Bouquet, Hoe Seed and Water the Azalea). Then someone else started a family called *Fatigué: Lapin Fatigué, Paupières Fatiguées, Poisson Fatigué* and *Fleur Flétri* (Tired Bunny, Tired Eyelids, Tired Fish and Wilted Flower). You might want to start with a family called the Happys. When you and your children play, one person might become Happy Jumper, another Mostly Happy or Happy Smile. Write the names on name tags; design a "family" T-shirt. This game may be over in a quarter-hour or develop into a continuing motif. In either case, it is an anytime game in language education.

Trying out a new word can be a game in itself. Allow children to "malaprop" words when they are moving their mouths around them for the first time. At one point, Emma fixed on the word *donc* (thus, so). For the weekend, she was the epitome of the French logician. She would say, "I'm wearing a dress, *donc je ne salis pas ma robe* (so I don't soil my dress)." I did not correct her misusage. When the twins honed their use of *on* (the pronoun "one"), the third person indefinite was in ascendancy in their speech, so that the "we" form was practically eclipsed. "Is it okay if we go outside" became "*Ça va si on va en dehors?* (May one go out?)" Once practiced, *on* became properly assimilated into their speech.

Talk about word roots upon occasion. Cultivate, in this way, a child's natural interest in how a word is "born" or assembled. Once, when I was in college, my English professor brought his little daughter along to dinner at my dormitory. A bouquet of pansies brightened the table, and he explained lightly to the child the word root of these and other of Shakespeare's flowers (pansy: from the French *pensée*, thought). A parent's lesson, conveyed so naturally, enhances a child's capacity to learn vocabulary by scrutinizing familiar roots. French has some wonderful flower names: *coquelicot*, which is onomatopoetic, *pissenlit* (piss-abed, named for its diuretic property), and *paquerette* (little Easter flower), to name just three. In German there are not only *Vergissmeinnicht* ("forget-me-not") and *Stiefmütterchen* (little stepmother, the English pansy) in the easy etymologies, but many more less obvious, such as *Edelweiss* (noble-white). In Italian, your child can guess how *viola del pensiero, bella di notte, girasole* and *passiflora* (also known as *fiore della passione*) were named.

Differences. This is a somewhat taxing nonsense game my children and I derived from a song on their French alphabet record for the letter D. What is the difference, asks the song, between a *D-ragon* and a *D-romedary*? In French, each player asks what is the difference between two things. A hotel and a house? A hill and a mountain? An elephant and a turtle? One of the players tries to give a precise difference. "One is low and one is high" is not sufficient to distinguish the hill from the mountain, because someone else can respond, "So is a chair." "One is easy to walk up, and one hard" is accepted by the players more readily. Like all the word games we play, this one can become a bit silly and yet be a success. Thus, to some questions the asker knows the answer or senses a correspondence, while some—like the question in the D song—are stunningly improbable.

Invent poems with your children. The essence is that the rules be easy. Children of five can handle a rhyme scheme like *abab* or *abba*. Older children like to collect rhyming words first and then compose a poem around them. Poems can be created in a group; each person adds a line or couplet, and everyone's imagination has equal play. That one child's sentence construction outdistances another's is immaterial to the game. That the metaphors or constructions are plausible nonsense *is* important.

No More Applesauce. In this game, the first player makes a statement of quantity using a noun, such as: "No more applesauce." "A lot of applesauce" says the next person, substituting a different modifier. "Still more . . ." continues the next, and round and round the game goes. When our inventiveness is exhausted, we either drop the game or latch onto a new noun, as long or as evocative as possible.

You and I. Usually we think of word games as complicated, but sometimes they are very simple. Here is one that is just right for practicing and extending vocabulary, and is creative besides. The players engage in a badminton match of metaphor, with results that are frequently highly nuanced. Each player in turn says, "I am *x* and you are *y.*" The only rule is that *x* and *y* are nouns that relate to each other in some respect. They must rhyme, or match poetically, or simply be so surprising that they make everybody laugh. Here is a partial "contest" recorded when Emma and Burton were four and a half (and in a honeyed mood):

> "Moi je suis la bouche et toi tu es les lèvres."
> "Moi je suis le t-elle-ephone et toi tu es la t-il-ephone."
> "Toi tu es l'oiseau et moi je suis la plume."
> "Moi j'étais l'oiseau et toi tu étais l'aile."
> "Moi je suis le gaufre et toi tu es le miel."
> "Toi tu es l'auto et moi je suis la phare."

(Me, I'm the mouth and you, you're the lips./ Me, I'm the girl-telephone (*elle* = she) and you, you're the boy-telephone (*il* = he)./ You, you're the bird and me, I'm the feather./ Me, I was the bird and you, you were the wing./ Me, I'm the waffle and you, you're the honey./ You, you're the car and me, I'm the headlight.)

Parcheesi is excellent for counting and quick, repetitious talk: "You goofed," "Red is bumped," "Home safe." A child of five can play quite well, sometimes developing strategy even if still unsure of the words for numbers after ten. A game with a younger child may take 40 minutes. Keep the board out and pieces set up, and play in two installments.

Reading and Writing

The child who gains a taste for reading in the target language knows more and identifies more of its vocabulary and grammar. Reading in the language from an early age is insurance against loss of fluency. Many children grow in their command of a language but are incapable of writing or reading more than a few basic sentences. "My parents did not want me to grow up hating the language," says one Chinese- American. "They never insisted I write Chinese, although we spoke Chinese among ourselves at home. As a result, my Chinese is only a social asset, not a business or commercial one. It is embarrassing to me not to be able to read a word in Chinese. My native language is foreign to me when written." It is not wise for parents to wait until the child is in high school to encourage him to read books in the language. When a bilingual student studies his extra language in an English-language school, it is curiously *not* a breeze. The student may make fun of the teacher's pronunciation, become so bored he can't learn anything or be rattled at being graded. To be graded as less than perfect in a language learned orally in the home compares with being told you write mediocre English when you speak it fluently. Study of the written language begun too late can turn the student against it altogether.

Why did David Chavchavadze of Washington, D.C., an émigré from Russia in the 1930s, keep his Russian while many others lost it? What accounts for this relative rarity—growth of fluency in the retained language—in the immigrant story? He says, "I was already a fluent speaker when I first remember myself at age three." His Russian nurse came to the family in London when David was one. Before that, he had a British nanny and appeared, his parents said, ready to speak English, when the process was suddenly reversed. David recalls, "Of course my Russian nurse—Nyanyushka was what I called her—worked on my Russian by correcting it. But what I remembered most was her reading aloud to me from the classics. By age 11 she had read both *War and Peace* and *Anna Karenina* to me and she would even read American or English books, like *Tom Sawyer* and *Alice in Wonderland*, translating into Russian as she read."

After Nyanyushka left, when David, at age 14 to 18, was away at boarding school, he made his own efforts to sustain his knowledge. He plugged away at school, reading Russian literature, and all at once, through reading, felt his Russian greatly improve. "We were assigned *War and Peace* and, age 16, I forced myself to read it in the original. After a week of utter torture (the assignment was to read 100 pages per night), something snapped in my mind and I have been able to read Russian almost as rapidly as English ever since." Thanks to early exposure to literature with Nyanyushka, Russian literature became for David a lifelong discipline and habit of mind. Russian literacy nourished David's Russian language fluency through periods in life when he used it less.

A family need not be highly educated to be literate in a home language. Lillian Cracchiolo of Mineola, New York, was one of six children all born in Brooklyn whose parents had arrived from Italy in 1910 and who spoke only a dialect of Italian in the house. The six all read Italian. "We didn't own a book of our own but frequented the library at every opportunity. We brought home Italian books for my mother and books for ourselves which we read from cover to cover. In my opinion, it served us better than the classroom for spelling and grammar."

Becoming literate in a language is the best way for the language to grow from childishness to maturity, through contact with the flower of the culture. A recent study of reading abilities of students from homes where English is not the dominant language shows that the degree to which this is an advantage or disadvantage correlates closely with socioeconomic factors. Not surprisingly, families having a more educated background in their ethnic language raise children who perform better in English reading and literature. Theodore Andersson, a key educator in the bilingual schooling movement, has given much attention to the issue of "biliteracy" for children whose native language is not English. His conviction is that children whose parents speak a second language in the home can and should be taught to read the second language as early as at three years, so that they are literate in it when they enter kindergarten, and are first exposed to English.

Because the school language will be key for all further learning once literacy is reached, the child's home language slides to second place, if a child doesn't begin to read before kindergarten. The oral language is perceived as less useful, a "kitchen" tongue needed only for conversation with loved ones. Professor Chester C. Christian, Jr. of Texas A & M University, an "anglo" who has reared his daughter to speak Spanish, extols the benefits of early and continued literacy in the home language, and hopes that it will increase in America. "Such literacy could provide a form of creative cultural pluralism that would offer both individual and social alternatives not now readily available to most citizens of the United States . . . . And, more than any other possible result of bilingual education, the development of skills to be used permanently in reading and writing two languages potentially could magnify the personal and social benefits of learning in more than one language—from enhancement of the self-concept through improvements in intercultural and even international relations." The failure to develop bilingual literacy, Christian asserts, implies a discriminatory view of minority culture and language.

The ease of the task varies with the language. To learn Japanese is a slow accretion of mastery of characters. The process does not in any tangible way help in learning English. Contrarily, many languages, such as Spanish, Ukrainian and Armenian, have a letter-to-sound correspondence more logical than that of English, and so are ideal for the fledgling reader. If the alphabet of the recessive language is different, as in Russian, it is especially important that the alphabet or writing system be prominent in the home before the child goes to school. While some children learn to read on their own, others need support over a long period. This is as variable in two languages as in one. Do not worry about your teaching or reading technique—reading methodology is a science largely for the use of one teacher coping with a classroom of pupils. Do concern yourself with compensating for the fact that your child will be reading English road signs, car models and billboards all in the Latin alphabet, and in English. One clever mother from India tore out pages from a Bengali nutrition comic book and pasted them onto the back of cereal boxes when her children, little cereal-fiends, entered the first grade. An ambitious father from Jordan was fired up by the idea of teaching his baby to read himself, and carried out the program—in Arabic. "Our first child really could read one and two syllable words by age three," he says. "My second took it all in but did not read until six. But the prereading was just as valuable for her. Like her brother, once she could read, her language boat had two oars, which she continued to row ahead. Would she have mastered Arabic script if it had been presented simultaneously with English? We doubt it."

Not only is the ability to read important, but identification with the habit is crucial. To prepare the child for a higher, elite bilingual literacy is an essential objective. The child's identification with the language must help him develop a literate identity. The family is the principal agent. Preschoolers whose parents spend much time reading tend to see themselves potentially as readers themselves. If an influential person at home becomes excited about books with the child, the child sees himself as a reader. This is as true in German, Polish or Portuguese as it is in English.

This is not to say that you should rush hysterically to teach your preschooler to read. Through storytelling, singing and rhyming you have already laid an effective foundation for literacy. A four year old who knows literature by heart interrupts his bedtime story to say you skipped over something. This child is prereading! Parents, no matter what their degree of literacy, can use letters, words and books to associate literacy with their home language. Then, at the kindergarten stage, the children can be taught to read the home language slightly in advance of the school curriculum. Through the early grades, sit down after school with your child for a short second-language reading and writing session. Or, if it suits you better and you can afford it, rely on a tutor who loves books and writing to do this in your stead.

To the older child it can be a challenge to take national achievement tests in the language. Stress that this is an extra ability and encourage the child by responding with pride if an eighth grader passes the German examination for a sixth grade level. It devastates a child to be below grade level at school, but children schooled well at home in a second language are inclined to be more philosophical, thinking in terms of progress and not labels.

The Lucentini children, like their parents, are being brought up bilingually. They are 12 and 14 and the second language is Italian. The parents have had them take the examinations at the Scuola d'Italia in New York City along with the children who attend that school. Paola Lucentini comments, "Italian children have to pass state examinations at the end of fifth and eighth grades, covering the preceding years *in toto*, in order to continue. The Italian government sends a *commission* over in order to examine the children who are here. Eric and Jack took the fifth-grade test together in 1981. My husband prepared them for months and it was so hard because *all* the material was new. All that ancient Roman and Italian history, endless memorizing of names, emperors, events, kings. Literature, poetry and math were all different and they had trouble understanding some of the problems. Also there were tons of grammar, the kind that's barely touched on here in school, so it was really from scratch. This every night for months—anyhow they passed. Then, last June, Eric took the eighth-grade test and squeaked through. So far they've submitted themselves to all this extra studying with more or less good grace and cooperation, helped by the promise of a beautiful present whether they pass or not. Last year Jack got a present even though he wasn't taking the exams, just for sitting there and listening to Eric's lessons." The Lucentinis believe their sons will have a real choice between Italian and American universities and eventually the option of employment that relates to Italy if they wish, because of their preparation.

The Fischer family's program also involved additional homework. Asked whether her daughter rebelled, Mrs. Fischer observes, "Rebellion? No, that would be too harsh a word. She did sometimes object to writing a German page and reading from a German book each day. I insisted anyway. I had to compensate however: Letters in German to relatives or friends were accepted as her 'German page' and the book pages were always from her two favorite books, Pearl Buck's *The Dragonfish* and Edith Zellwecker's *He Had a Daughter Named Peter*. Eventually she knew one of them almost by heart. She liked to write little stories and plays too, in serial fashion, a page or so a day. At one time she wrote a mystery for me, because she knew I liked mysteries. (The dog did it!) This of course was several pages long and covered several days of homework."

Study with Mom or Dad does not interfere with the affectionate relationship. Done in the detached spirit of learning, it becomes a memory to laugh about and cherish. Mrs. Fischer tells how the language homework evolved: "Progressively, as she made more friends and wanted to go out to play, she started procrastinating. I never gave up. Although we had a few fights, I felt and still feel that this was vital to maintain her written German. The home training went on until she graduated from high school. During her last year of high school she took an advanced placement German literature exam to get credit for college. Our sessions were sometimes harder than pulling teeth. On the other hand, she became interested in many of the stories and plays and we had enjoyable evenings too—especially as long as these evenings did not interfere with her social life!"

Keep the sessions short—20 minutes per day or a half-hour three times per week. If you can, find a pleasant tutor to work with your children of ten or older, instead of yourself. Sitting down around the table with children to work on a bit of composition or reading is a long, beautiful tradition. Instead of helping your child only with the school homework he hates (why else would you get asked?) you cover together fresh material and attend to knotty problems on the spot. If for some reason all this sits poorly with your child, consider, as an alternative, a group afterschool program.

In our family, the breakfast table seemed an ideal time to go over a few flashcards. I made big, bilingual flashcards out of poster board (the babies can read using simple, short, large words), with French on one side and English on the other. It is my husband, surprisingly, who uses them French side up. He finds that the twins enjoy reading French with him because they feel they are all three learning together, which is true. With written French, he doesn't have to worry about passing errors on to them, as he would in speech. By six, the children and he were dictating back and forth. *"Proust est au lit"* I hear him call out as I shuffle downstairs in the morning, and the pencils scratch in concentration. This reading taught by a man who has only a slight inclination to speak French with us gives the children special pleasure. What explains his enthusiasm? We adults will endure the discipline involved in raising bilingual children because of the stimulation we feel, and, frequently, the benefit we receive of learning with them.

Your child can keep an "open" diary in the second language. This is a diary you can read, but not a classroom assignment read by strangers; it is more intimate, and allows for some candor. Give him a blank book and ask him to write three or four paragraphs a day; with practice, these may grow to great length. We kept diaries in Paris recording what the children did on their afternoons off (half-days) from school. *Mon Mercredi* recounts the adventures of a year of Wednesdays, each with a page of writing and a page of drawing in a 100-page spiral. A Hungarian-American, Kati P. Csatary, describes how her father assigned her to keep a diary in Hungarian ("on seemingly inane topics") from the time she was eight. "Day after day I would write almost exactly the same thing: Today it rained, we walked to the store, my mother was baking something delicious, etc. My brother soon followed in my footsteps; it was a chore over which we often agonized. Today those diaries are very amusing. We are glad our parents required this of us. The main objective was to teach us correct Hungarian spelling and to develop our vocabulary and usage. Our mother (*edesanya*) made sure we wrote daily, and we would leave notes for our father (*edesapa*) to explain the meanings of new, unfamiliar words we read in books and newspapers. Often, I would discuss these words with my father at three in the morning when he came home from a ten-hour workday . . . . At age 12, I realized that my grammar and spelling were more accurate than that of a 16-year-old boy from a remote Hungarian village, with whom I was corresponding. We also surpassed relatives who had lived in this country for many years and had the awful but 'quaint' habit of mixing in English words and expressions, of running words together and misspelling them. So, today our language skills compare favorably with those of recent arrivals from Hungary.

Your child may enjoy writing to a pen pal or overseas relative. The spirit of a language is revealed most beautifully in letter-writing. It is exceedingly hard to write a letter as a native would. The best we can hope for is to express ourselves without horrendous gaffes. General rules for adult or child are to keep the letter short, simplify sentence construction and embellish polite formulas. American letter-writing style tends to be less formal than that of other countries. In Italy, Germany, Latin America, Spain and France one starts out a letter with greetings and pleasantries and then moves on to the news of a broken leg or new braces. Friendly letters from abroad are a pleasure to read, and can give us a taste of current, idiomatic usage. Thus, you may enjoy a foreign-language correspondence as much as your children do. To achieve a properly polite tone, it helps when writing in a foreign language for the children to imagine they are writing to a count or countess. Naturally, if your children are corresponding with other children, they need not be so concerned with stock courtesies.

Since letter-writing is subtle and close to the soul of a language, you will benefit from reading about this complex and revealing subject. A few guides are listed in chapter six.

Tell your children over and over all the positive aspects of being bilingual: career development, travel, friends, being a little different, how happy it will make grandma—whatever facet most appeals to them. For example, if you back bilingual childrearing with the promise of fairly regular trips to the country where the language is native, you will give your child a sterling reason to progress. A young bilingual architect, Sandra-Lisa Schwartz, grew up in America, speaking French with her Belgian mother and English with her Americn father. "I'm not sure anyone can expect a child to be motivated without a goal in sight," she says. "In my case, learning to keep my French was a necessity, as I was to return each year to Belgium. The goal was also in sight, and was one that I believed in. In Belgium I reaped the fruits of my labors. It was a real test: a challenge to be met and a victory to be enjoyed."

Keeping Up With Your Kids

If your own knowledge of the children's "extra" language is incomplete, and you are not content to stay at your present level, the following procedures will help:

Read light fiction. I subscribed to Harlequin romances in French from Canada, for the au pair to read. Now I keep one on my bedside table, along with a more serious book (in English). I mark new words and turn down the corners of marked pages. After the confection is finished, I consult my dictionary. Harlequin Enterprises Limited (225 Duncan Mill Road, Don Mills, Ontario, Canada M3B 3K9) can send addresses of overseas offices in Brazil, Finland, Greece, Germany, Italy, Japan, Mexico, the Netherlands and Sweden, to subscribers. Mysteries are another exemplary popular genre because you are watchful as you read for clues usually expressed in arcane, specialized and often useful vocabulary. Might there be a connection between the ink-stained pipe shank in the hand of suspect X and the screw-threads of the shattered lacquer fountain pen found by the victim's body? I had better look up "shank" and "screw-threads" if I want to make sense of the plot.

Keep dictionaries all over the house. Scatter them the way a smoker does ashtrays. Essential places are within arm's reach of the dinner table and where you talk on the telephone, to glance at in idle moments. Asked by French people how I learned French, I like to answer, "From the dictionary." Other parents of bilingual children who speak primarily English will know just what I mean. Once you know a basic grammar and have a good accent, the way to swing from the low rungs to the high bars is by increasing your word power, *word by word.* It is said that it takes seeing and hearing a word ten times to learn it, but when you have children waiting like thirsty plants for new words, your memory for them improves. Keep a dictionary in the glove compartment of the car as well. I find I need new words all the time when I travel.

Keep a list of words and phrases that your big dictionary has failed to define. "Rag bag," "From little acorns grow big oaks," and "bean curds—will *'le tofu'* do?" form the to-be-checked list on my kitchen bulletin board at present.

Turn on a shortwave station. Instead of your usual AM or FM, while you are doing housework, listen to the Top 40s or classical music in German!

Experiment with the cuisine of your "second" country. When you want to try out a new dish, or look up the roasting time for a duckling, consult a second-language cookbook. It will probably mean using metric measures, which should present no problem now that cookware stores are stocking metric measuring utensils.

See movies in your second language. Try never to pass up foreign films (new or revived) in your area. This can be extremely useful—especially if you can avoid looking at the subtitles!

5
Oral Materials

The premise of this book is that language is oral first and read and written second. Learning a second tongue should imitate and intensify the casual oral modes in which a mother tongue is learned. Modern communications technologies make available a wide range of audiovisual materials that can help the prereader learn a second language, and a young reader expand it. Among these are recordings, radio and television programs, cassette tapes and other products, some of which are outlined below.

Children's Songs

Songs teach rhythm, cadence and vocabulary. Young children can learn a song that has new words and syntax well beyond their own level of speech development. Traditional songs have beautiful traditional words and phrases that the child can learn in no better way. In English, for example, every child knows the word "bough" from "Rockaby Baby"—a word now otherwise consigned to usage in Christmas verse. Children can practice songs alone in their beds or while playing blocks or taking a walk. A melody makes a language lesson palatable. When a child is first immersed in a language outside the home, in preschool, the first language he learns is usually song.

In many languages, children's songs are the rich folk counterpart of Mother Goose in English. In French, for family songs we like the Folkways recording *Chantons en Français* (two discs with a booklet of words in French and English), and *Sing Children Sing: Songs of France*. The *Sing Children Sing* series also includes *Songs of Mexico, Songs of Italy,* and *Songs of Austria* and is issued by Caedmon/United States Committee for UNICEF. Many contemporary French children's recordings are jazzy, melodious and—very important—not unappealing to an adult. Our happiest musical discovery has been the six-disc, wildly fanciful *Chant les Mots* (RCA, A. Colin Burrelier). Cassette/story sets (predominantly lyric) by Cassettine (Vif-Argent, 56 bis rue du Louvre, 75023 Paris) come packaged in a pretty, laced-together cassette. Long reviews of a few records are carried in Loisirs-Jeunes' bimonthly publication *Jeunesse Loisir*. Many of these recordings can be found in the United States. Loisirs-Jeunes (36, rue de Ponthieu, 75008 Paris) will provide you with a short list of new recordings upon request. See the catalogue of the National Textbook Company (8259 Niles Center Road, Skokie, IL 60077) for song recordings in four languages. Recordings remain with the children as they grow, and so are a sensible investment. Good songs sung at the age of four will not seem babyish at eight. Holiday songs for everybody are readily available at import record shops and from import booksellers. Many recordings of Italian Christmas Songs, such as *Buon Natale da Nino Rosso,* are available from Rizzoli (712 Fifth Avenue, New York, NY 10019; branches in Los Angeles, Chicago, Washington, and Atlanta).

The Children's Center, United States Committee for UNICEF (311 East 38th Street, New York, NY 10016) is a rich source for lists of children's holiday and game songs in recordings, as well as of songbooks, especially in those languages not widely spoken in America, and in Spanish. In addition, Folkways Ethnic Series offers *Children's Songs from Spain, Latin American Children's Games Songs, Italian Folk Songs, Dutch Folk Songs, German Children's Songs, Children's Folk Songs of Germany, Israeli Songs for Children, Jewish Children's Songs and Games, Yiddish Folk Songs for Children* and *Russian Songs to Teach Russian*. All Folkways records come with a booklet that gives the words to the songs in the original language as well as in an English translation, plus an explanation of the ethnic significance of each song or dance on the record. For dance music, performance instructions are also included. All the large Spanish materials distributors emphasize Folkways in their catalogue; look for other, imported items as well.

If you are not fluent in the second language, it is essential that the recordings have word sheets or booklets. The game songs, holiday carols and folk songs on these recordings are sometimes in a "light" dialect. Songs written especially for children may also use some informal "nursery" talk. Even when you understand the songs, the lyrics are nice to keep in the glove compartment for singing in the car.

Recording/Book Story Sets

These are a melange of stories from the corpus of international children's stories. *Blanche-Neige* ("Snow White") seemed far too hard for Emma, but when the Disney album cover appealed to her I let her play it. All one January, at the age of three, it was her favorite record. In this much-loved story she sometimes wanted Daddy to play the part of the prince and sometimes Burton (more amenable, but no kisses please, *"trop mouillé"*— too wet). Because of the visual support of the album's cover and illustrated script, *Blanche-Neige's* popularity zoomed. The first weekend Emma didn't turn the record over, but played the first side again and again. Between playings, she wandered to the coat pegs and collected winter accessories to do some dressing up.

Our first fairy tales were a group of book/record sets of juvenile classics, *Collection Peluche,* from Casterman: *Les Trois petits cochons* and Perrault's *Le Petit chaperon rouge.* Children can understand and listen to *Le Petit prince* or even *Cyrano de Bergerac* performed by the Comédie-Française long before they can read them. The spoken word conjures up pictures, and pictures anchor the language in a comprehensive world. Few children would read and enter into Kipling's prose, but via recordings in many languages (in French, the series is *Contes histoires comme ça*) the Just-so Stories can burn into a child's mind. My children talked like Gérard Phillipe and Gina Lollabrigida in *Fanfan la tulipe,* for weeks of swordplay and gallantry after seeing the film in France. I chose to take them to see that film, knowing that there was a cassette we could buy afterward. The children mentally rescreen the movies *Tintin et la temple du soleil, Lady and the Tramp, and Rox and Rouki,* seen abroad, as they listen to the cassette tapes.

If these materials strike you as mere frills compared with, for example, a dictionary, a recording of familiar children's songs or an alphabet primer, reconsider. For contemporary children ages four and older, dramatizations of stories on records or cassettes are among the most important materials available. You don't have time to read aloud to children all the second-language works you would like them to know, you may be the only person in the family able to read aloud in the non-English language. But you can flip stories onto the cassette recorder at opportune moments, and keep new ones coming as the children grow. Children sometimes like to listen with you in the same room. They can stop the tape and ask you a difficult word or speech they really want to understand. Listening to the recording, you and your child share a smile or a sigh where, when reading aloud, it's a cuddle.

What story recordings can you expect to find? A series of recordings is available from Bilingual Publications (1966 Broadway, New York, NY 10023), based on children's classics, with musical accompaniment and sound effects. It includes *Little Red Riding Hood, Ali Baba, Aladdin, Puss in Boots, Pinocchio, Snow White* and *The Pied Piper of Hamelin.* The famous Latino folktale *Perez y Marina* is available, read by storyteller Pure Belpre, from CSM (14 Warren Street, New York, NY 10007), and the publisher Frederick Warne, Inc. (2 Park Avenue, New York, NY 10016) sells the book in a Spanish version. A selection of familiar stories (two per tape) in Italian, such as *Puss in Boots, Ali Baba, Aladdin* and *The Country Mouse and City Mouse* are available on cassette from S.F. Vanni, 30 West 12th Street, New York, NY 10011. As for German, dramatic readings of familiar stories, poems, Grimms' tales, Rip Van Winkle and even German recipes are distributed by Wible Language Institute (24 South 8th Street, P.O. 870, Allentown, PA 18105). Wible also lists dozens of cassettes in Spanish for the legends of Saint Nicholas, fairy tales like "Thumbelina" and "Goldilocks," and literary classics like *Heidi* and *Robinson Crusoe* (these last two have three tapes each).

A good au pair has a capacity to read aloud longer books. While a read-aloud with *Maman* was still one Babar book, my au pair Geneviève polished off a paperback children's biography of Louis Barille, which the children found enthralling, in two days! "I'll miss my Anne," sighed Emma a week before Anne, our au pair from the Côte d'Azur, departed for home. Before she left, I handed Anne several blank cassettes and asked, the next time she sat down and read to Emma and Burton, would she flip on the *magnetophone*? The result: handsome tapes that match some of the children's French books. Children at an age when print still shuts them out love a "talking book."

Language-Learning Recordings

Many commercial services provide audio-visual materials specifically designed to teach language. You may use on yourself to brush up on the language you are speaking with your bilingual child. Or perhaps another person or your spouse is the principal speaker of that language, and you want simply to understand what they are saying. It is also possible to give a child a start on an entirely new language using one of these recorded courses, provided the child is extremely motivated— by a future trip to Granny's house in Denmark, a move abroad, or even a desire to skip first-year high-school Spanish and get to a more interesting level of study. The virtues of some specific courses are described here.

Linguaphone. (World Languages Courses, Inc., 313 Nolana Avenue, McAllen, TX 78501.) 28-day free trial offered. 34 languages are available, including German, French, Spanish and Italian, and as well Arabic, Russian, Japanese, Modern Greek, Hindi and both Mandarin and Cantonese. It is the only audio system that offers three types of spoken Arabic: Egyptian, Algerian and Modern Standard. You listen to and repeat conversation on the tape, and the book provides grammar lessons and a vocabulary.

Living Language. (Crown Publishers, Inc., Department 814, 34 Englehard Avenue, Avenel, NJ 07001.) This is a 40-lesson course of four records or two cassettes, with a manual and dictionary that can be especially useful to someone who used to know a language and who wishes brush up on it while his child is learning it. The ten foreign languages offered include two versions of Portuguese, Continental and South American; in addition, English as a Second Language courses have been prepared for Chinese speakers, French speakers, and so forth.

Berlitz. (Berlitz Publications, 866 Third Avenue, New York, NY 10022.) Berlitz sells a Comprehensive Course is French, Spanish, German or Italian. With diligence it is possible to learn a language from scratch using the Berlitz taped conversation course. Children's Berlitz records are also available. These systems are expensive but can often be borrowed through your public library.

National Audiovisual Center. (General Services Administration, Washington, D.C. 20409.) Offers courses in 40 languages, including French, German, Italian, Spanish, Cantonese, Greek and Swedish. The number of instructional tapes in each course varies. For example, Cambodian has 146 tapes, French has 111 tapes, but Hausa (a major language in the Sahara and a trade language in much of West Africa) has only 15. The courses are broken into sections and you can buy one set of tapes at a time. The NAC tapes have far more material at each level of skill than do the shorter Berlitz courses.

The adult Berlitz course can be used by a child between six and twelve, even if children find themselves mimicking some unchildlike dialogue. By contrast, the NAC programs are more useful for family study than for a child's self-study.

Conversaphone. (Ronkonkoma, NY 11779.) Comes in 40 languages with one to four tapes for each. This is a children's language course based, like the adult courses, on listening and repeating. The lessons, however, are briefer and the subject matter is to scale. Four consecutive lessons chronicle a trip to the zoo, another introduces names of the features of the head and the parts of hands and feet. The dialogues are easy to memorize, and the courses admirable but short.

The Learnables. (International Linguistics Corporation, 401 West 89th Street, Kansas City, MO 64114-0697.) Available in French, Spanish, German and Mandarin Chinese, are audio-visual courses that teach comprehension of 3,000 basic words and grammatical constructions. In this method, you look at a series of pictures while the tape repeats the appropriate name or short sentence. Each sentence is correlated with a picture in which the meaning of the sentence is indicated. The entire series consists of 8,000 pictures and sentences presented in eight books and 41 40-minute to one-hour tape cassettes. Four levels of tapes exist for each language. By the time they reach the last book in the beginner series, learners can respond to complex sentences, comprehend interesting stories and use the conditional. *The Learnables* can be used with young children if an adult points to each correct picture as the tape describes it or else watches the child point to the picture, to be sure he is staying with the lesson and not getting lost. I came across *The Learnables* in the *Growing Without Schooling* newsletter, in a report by Ann Bodine, a professor in New Jersey who home-schools her children. Before their twelfth birthdays, the Bodine children had learned the equivalent of several years of academic French, which neither parent spoke, by using these materials.

Book/Recording Learning Aids

International Linguistics Corporation, producers of *The Learnables*, has sets of pictures that adhere to a background but can be removed (like flannel-board pieces), depicting a kitchen, airport, beach and supermarket. These are excellent aids to vocabulary building for a child. If you want to use textbooks with your children, give their ear a chance: Use systems of textbooks with an audio component. I recommend the following:

Hablan Los Niños by Dorothy Bishop. Spanish. (National Textbook Company 8259 Niles Center Road, Skokie, IL 60077.) You can buy three years' worth of the tapes and books of this school-textbook program. Filmstrips are also available.

Deutsch für Dich. German. (Continental Books, 11-03 46th Avenue, Long Island City, NY 11101.) This is a series whose main goal is to teach eight-to-twelve-year-olds the conversational aspects of the German language. This is done by presenting typical, everyday situations relevant to this age group. Each volume consists of 14 chapters with a main dialogue, pictorial presentation and various exercises. With cassettes.

Komm Bitte! by Hermann Schuh. German. (Also from Continental Books.) A clear, amusing beginner's course, emphasizing 250 of the most important words and grammatical structures, designed to teach comprehension, speaking, reading and writing in that order, through workbooks and tapes.

Du und Ich. (Langenscheidt Publications, 46-35 54th Road, Maspeth, NY 11378.) A thorough program comprised of a teacher's manual, songbook and recordings, for the parent or teacher who already speaks some German. Originally designed for kindergarteners learning German by immersion in South America, the course is appropriate for all elementary grades.

The Pappenheimers by Tamara D. Stehr. (Langenscheidt.) Described as an Animation and Vocabulary Guide. It was written to accompany "The Pappenheimers," a television series of German language and culture. The first section uses colorful cartoons to retell 26 animated segments from the show; English translations are provided. The names of these segments—Pirates in a Bottle, The Wasp in the Torte, and The Crazy Soccer Ball—give you an idea of what fun they are. All vocabulary used is found in the second section, a comprehensive glossary.

Italian Conversation by Adele A. Gorjanc. (Boston: Branden, 1976.) Italian. This is a very attractive self-teaching book, geared for travelers but more comprehensive by far than the usual traveler's phrasebook. It deals with everyday situations, has lots of proverbs and anecdotal vocabulary (as when the client complains of split ends at the barber's). There are no tapes for this course, but I include it because it so clearly stimulates oral practice.

Open Door to French. This package, by Margarita Madrigal and Colette Dulac (who runs the Madame Dulac language schools), is Regents' conversational course in French for beginners. A set of four long-playing records of all dialogues, conversation and vocabulary is available to accompany this book. It explains which words are similar in English and French and discusses how to form French words, and thus is well-suited to the school-age learner. There are no dreary exercises; rather, short, snappy lessons introduce vocabulary gently.

Movies

Nothing immerses a child in language like a film. Whether your child understands 50 percent of the film, or 80 percent, seeing it is a vastly more important experience than a T.V. show. Even the four or five year old with a short attention span can enjoy a feature movie by making two trips out to the lobby for soda and popcorn. Don't be too fussy about that films you take them to. Anything that you would let them see in English is acceptable. After children see a number of movies, they gain the same expectation adults have that the movie will begin to resolve its story after the first hour, and last two hours, and they will watch patiently. Tell the children some of the story beforehand. Ferret out films shown noncommercially. For example, Italian-American clubs screen features from Italy and soccer films, and high schools show features occasionally in languages that correspond to those taught. Let the foreign-language department chairman of your local high school know about your little speaker, and room will, in general, be made for him or her to attend.

Large public library systems have film libraries and will allow you and your children to see foreign travelogues and documentaries and even foreign art-film features in a public viewing room. If you or a friend have a video recorder, television foreign movies in your language can be recorded for many reviewings. Check all art theaters that show films in German, French, Italian and occasionally Spanish. There are, in many cities, Spanish-language movie houses and other cinemas with an Italian, Spanish or other language night.

Cable Television

Cable television programming exists in many languages, such as French, Danish, Spanish, Polish and Chinese, carried on cable systems in various parts of the country. Most foreign-language channels are carried on a time-share basis, which means the foreign language source shares the channel with other productions in a given day or week. The comedies, sports events, films and other performances can enhance your child's exposure to native speakers and the popular culture of the target language. In the several hours of programming shown each week, stations tend to cull the best material from a season of television back in the home country, with news and talk shows produced locally. The Portuguese Channel (Channel 20) in New Bedford, Massachusetts has shows nine hours a day, seven days a week. They send television crews to Portugal and the Azores every year to cover special events!

Local stations can also arrange to have on loan copies of certain desirable or favorite television programs that are shown in an area elsewhere in the country to a larger population of speakers of the language. For instance, the "novelas," television serials so popular in Brazil, can be viewed on the New Bedford Portuguese Channel and rented or purchased through the station.

Should you as a subscriber desire certain foreign language programming, you can work through local-interest organizations, showing the cable television companies a demonstrated desire on the part of a group of subscribers for specific programs. "As a service business, we would do everything possible to satisfy you," says Robert W. Cacace, general manager of Cablevision of Westchester (New York). According to Mr. Cacace, "The newer, state-of-the-art cable systems being constructed in big cities across the country will provide from among 80 to 200 channels. Additionally, cable systems are now either being constructed or contemplated in most of the Western

European countries. As the systems are put into place, there will be a need for more programming. The scenario often described in our business is one where most languages would be represented by at least one programming service."

Betty Graham of Glendora, California watches Spanish on KMEX, Channel 34. "They show about ten or twelve hours per day. Some of their programs are excellent. I would particularly recommend two of them: "Mexico, Magia y Encuentro" and "300 Milliones." "Mexico, Magia y Encuentro" is aired on Sunday afternoons. To me this program is the epitome of what Mexico is all about. It shows all areas of Mexico, the food, the traditions of each particular region of the country, the music, the religious beliefs, the problems of their people, and their hopes. It is extremely well done, wonderfully presented and very interesting."

"300 Milliones" is made in Spain and transmitted via satellite to all Spanish-speaking countries and to those, like the United States, that have a high percentage of Spanish-speaking residents. It represents all Spanish-speaking people, and the title is derived from the fact that there are about 300 million in the world today. The quality of the program is outstanding, and it, like "Mexico, Magia y Encuentro," has a cultural orientation, presenting poetry, music, art, traditions and beliefs of Spanish-speakers worldwide.

Short-Wave Radio

Short-wave radio can bring many languages into your home, in addition to what may be available locally on AM or FM. Most countries broadcast in short wave. Although they direct a preponderance of English-language broadcasting to our shores, considerable programming is conducted in most European languages. There is a wide choice of Spanish from South America at any hour of the day. Arabic comes in clear from Mecca during certain hours. Deutsche Welle broadcasts German throughout the day. Russian and Chinese are available over long periods. We listen to French from South America, and over Radio Canada International. Popular songs are played along with perhaps more news commentary on South America than is of interest to us. Thus, short-wave is very useful for practice in the less popular and widely spoken tongues.

Short-wave programs are not geared to children. However, there is some music and, for the older children, everything from soccer to political analysis. News programs are very useful for the adult who needs to build vocabulary to describe space exploration, nuclear-arms negotiations or the events of the French Revolution (usually discussed around Bastille Day).

We use a nine-band portable world receiver. The model is so small you can prop it up on the bed next to you, or take it at night out onto the beach, where reception is good. The transistor can also go on a trip abroad if you wish to listen to news from home. Our radio is rated "amateur." Other makes and models, called "professional," have features that improve the usefulness of the short-wave. They may have the ability to clean up the static in a program that crackles at you, and they have a computerized tuning device that allows you to switch in to a number without manually tuning to a band. Another feature is the computerized timer that can be added to many models. Most people listen to short-wave at night, when the English programming is broadcast. You can look up a program you want to hear in the guide and record it, without even listening while the program is being taped.

Two guides will help you use short-wave, Sony's *World Band Radio* and the *World Radio/TV Handbook*. Sony's guide lists programs separately by time of day, station, topic, country and frequency. Using the station/country guide you can find out when and on what frequency German programs, for instance, are available. The *World Radio/TV Handbook*, published annually by a firm in Copenhagen and distributed by Grand Central Radio (155 East 45th Street, New York, NY 10017), is fatter and has more details, but is basically similar. Contact a consulate or cultural organization for further assistance in finding your language. Usually a brochure summarizing programs will be sent; Deutsche Welle (HA Öffentlichkeitsarbeit, Postfach 10 04 44, West Germany) sends an illustrated monthly guide.

Games

I recommend board games for two reasons: When children can play a board game, they become partners with others. Secondly, they can share a foreign game with English-speaking peers in ways they can't usually share their non-English language. Old-favorite games from certain countries can be great fun for the child of six and up. See the paperback book *Board and Table Games from Many Civilizations* by R. C. Bell (revised one-volume edition). Its distributor, World Wide Games (Box 450, Delaware, OH 43015), makes many fine wooden board games that originated in the Orient, and Table Croquet, Pouff, and L'Âne Rouge from France, Italian (or French) hoops, Dutch shuffleboard, and Mexican Balero. There are also educational language-learning games, such as kits of cards games like "FOU" (FSL Publications, P.O. 184-A, Douglastown, New Brunswick, EOC 1HO Canada), which teach the fine points of intermediate French grammar. You may also wish to purchase traditional childrens' games, such as the French Jeu de l'Oye, during a trip to the foreign country. Or you can order a multiple-game board from the foreign country, along with a handbook of accompanying directions. Just as you and your children read the directions in the second language, it is natural for the play to be in the same language. Ordering directly from a game or toy store abroad is exciting. Here are some large stores that can help you:

German: Kunst und Spiel, Munich 40, Leopoldstrasse 48, West Germany

French: Le Bon Marché, 22 rue de Sèvres, 75007 Paris, France

Italian: Baby's Store, viale XXI Aprile 60, Rome, Italy

Spanish: Garbancito, General Moscardo, 3y5 Madrid 20, Spain

Monopoly in Spanish, French, German and Italian is available from the National Textbook Company (8259 Niles Center Road, Skokie, IL 60077). Players use pesetas to buy properties named for locations in Spanish, francs to buy in France, marks in German, lire in Italian. Scrabble is excellent for vocabulary building and spelling practice; you can purchase Scrabble in the above four languages plus Russian and Hebrew—for the most reasonable price around—also from National Textbook. Remember Clue, the game you liked as a child in the preelectronic-game age? Its name and all the sleuthing fully translated, Clue has maintained its popularity in France, Germany, Italy and Spain today.

Take a trip through the subways of Paris with a board game designed for two to four players and appealing to an age range from eight to adult: Paris Metro. It can be ordered directly from Infinity Games, Inc., 6801 East Thomas Road, Scottsdale, Arizona 85251.

6
Book Materials

There is no frigate like a book
To take us lands away. . . .
—Emily Dickinson

For you, Emily Dickinson's famous words take on special meaning. Books are the frigates that carry your children every day to the faery chateaux of the Loire, the Black Forest of Bavaria or into the pampas of Argentina. The child reading Erich Kastner in the original becomes intimate with German city life, Astrid Lingren makes Sweden a permanent spiritual home and French fairy tales of the Bourgogne or Provence communicate national character better than any sociology lecture. Books are portable yet an inexhaustible source of language and culture.

Compare an alphabet book from Czechoslovakia with one from Italy and you will see different toys, different domestic environments, different faces; there will be a different feel to the paper and another sense of color and pattern. If you follow a bilingual home program, your child may never need to resort to a grammar or conventional language-learning book, but he will have many foreign book friends. Your bilingual child will, at an early stage, become not only bicultural but bi-bibliographical.

One way to ensure that your child's second language doesn't wane in the English-speaking world is to create a home setting that is rich in literature. Bilingualism makes it essential that you become a real book-loving family. Books provide support as stand-ins for the cultural aspects that are absent. Books help wean your children from the "It's Daddy's language" point of view in the most positive way. This is the beginning of love of literature and of realizing parallels between literature and life. Children relate to books as very concentrated doses of the world.

A seasoned mother once expressed to me that a succession of beautiful moments made all the trials of raising children worthwhile. This is certainly true when it comes to materials for your bilingual child. Getting English-language materials is as easy as dropping by the public library, local bookstore or garage sale. Acquiring foreign-language materials often takes dogged effort and ingenuity. Of all the areas of bilingual child rearing, getting the *stuff* is the most arduous. But if the orchard is hard to find, the fruits are delicious and abundant. Books in your child's second language produce positively beatific moments—often.

At three and a half, my daughter played Snow White with a French child she had never met before. When they named the little girl's stuffed animals after the Seven Dwarfs, they shared the same French vocabulary for Sneezy, Dopey, Doc and the others. The names were new to me; my daughter had picked them up from her French recorded version of "Snow White and the Seven Dwarfs." Similarly, I experienced *Peter Pan* afresh when Tinkerbell became *Clochette* and the Indian Princess *la Tigre Princesse*. My husband and I smile to ourselves when the children talk about hamburgers with a touch of a New York accent and then ask for their book *Le Jour quand il a plu des hamburgers*, pronouncing the last word with the French inflection, "am-boo-GEHR." They'll hunt up a French poem in their favorite poetry book that had been lost in the toy chest for months to point out falling leaves, or a certain rhyme or a child in a poem they know, named Frederick. By reading French, my children have broadened their sense of themselves as Americans: Josephine Bonaparte, Emma's heroine, was born in Martinique; the legendary Québecois runner *Cheval du Nord* (Horse of the North) is an inspiration to both children from the book of the same name; they hold as heroes the French who left

Nova Scotia and settled in the Louisiana bayoux.

People who become fluent in a second language through scholastic study often credit the love of books or of one book as the springboard of their enthusiasm. Here is how Paris-born New York City lawyer Raymond d'Escadron describes his pivotal movement towards English fluency: "I came to an English boarding school at age 13. The boys took pity on me and gave me *Dr. No* to read. I'd read lots of simplified and textbook editions of English books, but I stayed up nights to read *Dr. No*. I read it and I read it and Ian Fleming's English (really quite good English) became mine."

From fairy tales, hero stories, funny books, contemporary realistic stories, poetry—all the literature you would want your child to encounter in any language—language learning can benefit greatly. As with song and oral literary forms, children can enjoy a book that is somewhat beyond their ken and come away with passive, or recessive knowledge of important new words. They can polish their grammar and learn new expressions by reading a book that is easy. Listen to a college professor and author of children's books, Peter S. Neumeyer, on the influence of German books in his bilingual upbringing on his adult intellectual life: "Books were extremely important in my German upbringing. I read all the time. I read anything—though that 'anything' tended to be pretty good, albeit eclectic. My father still had the German equivalent of *Boys Life,* which I devoured; a life of Frederick the Great, equivalents of *St. Nicholas Magazine;* Kafka—my father read him aloud; Rilke, early and often. As a child, I wrote German only out of necessity—'Thanks for the birthday socks'—but I read voraciously. I'm told (and it must be as a consequence), even though my German is somewhat shaky now, that what I speak is classy. And that makes sense, for I'd never read anything else!"

Professor Neumeyer's upbringing was literary beyond the norm, but the primacy of books in his childhood typifies American families whose children are successfully bilingual. Books work their way into the child's command of the second language with stunning results, provided reading is a major second-language option in your home.

Below are kinds of books you should stock or borrow, and a few examples.

Story Book Classics

Picture books without words range from the exquisitely hushed world of John S. Goodhall's *Naughty Nancy* to the standard compilations of pictures of objects with which children are perfectly familiar by the time they abandon the crib. You can use picture books without words to build language. Think in terms of making simple sentence captions. The wordless picture book is like a film and your words are its subtitles. Pop-up books are less available from libraries than other wordless books, and must be bought; they generate much good talk and play. Some pop-ups even offer delightful local color of the country of their origin; for example, De Paola's *Giorgio's Village* and the current reproductions of the books by the German Meggendorfer, the grandfather of pop-ups.

Roger Lewis, a professor of English literature at George Mason University, reads aloud to Nathalie, age four. "A few evenings ago, Nathalie and I were 'reading' Peter Spier's *Rain*. This book is all pictures, no text at all. Nathalie has always liked it because it can be read to her in either English or French. Moreover, as no language defines the situation, it can as easily be read as a girl-centered story as any other way." All parents of young bilingual children also cheat and read aloud English-language books in the other language. Nathalie blithely asks for the French version of a book that they have in English. Children who are aware that a book can be read in either language join the parent from time to time in adapting the English book to the non-English. One evening as Nathalie was listening to her father read Maurice Sendak's *Where the Wild Things Are*, something interesting occurred. "I was doing my best with a rather freehand, spontaneous *Où se trouvent les choses sauvages* and she was following along, but I got stuck with the line 'till Max said, 'Be still!' I fumbled with '*Soyez tranquilles*' and other wrong synonyms for 'still' till *she* came out with '*Ne bougez pas!*' That's exactly right, and showed, I thought, that she was at home in the concept in French, whereas I was tangled up in a word-for-word translation—an elementary schoolboy error."

Many translations are available. Some are international editions, books that are produced in several or many languages. Try to acquire internationally known books like the Barbapapa collection, Sendak's *Nutshell Library*, or Tomi Ungerer's *The Three Robbers* (each of which is available in Spanish, Italian, French and German).

Golden Books are often found in translation, as are books created by the Disney studios featuring familiar Disney comic book characters. At three, Emma and Burton memorized their favorites among the lower-grade books, such as Walt Disney's *Oncle Donald et ses neveux*, whence Burton became Oncle Donald for Halloween. (See chapter seven, "Finding Materials," for the names and addresses of publishers of Disney books abroad).

The story of that very special bunny, Beatrix Potter's *The Tale of Peter Rabbit*, is a book that has been translated many, many times. In French, the translation is so jewellike that it has itself become a classic. Astonishingly, although the twins had heard the cautionary tale dozens of times in French, and knew from it phrases like *thé à camomille* and *se faufiler sous la barrière*, when their father read them, at four years, *Peter Rabbit* in English, they insisted it was a "new story." Another English nursery tale whose Gallic version approaches art is *Le Hibou et la poussiquette*, Edward Lear's *Owl and the Pussy-Cat*, translated by Francis Steegmuller. The couple dance, of course, *au clair de la lune."*

Reading classic children's books makes a child part of the international community: Japanese children may think Pinocchio is Japanese, but they can talk about him with children from Norway or Bolivia. Fill your collection with international classics, vintage and recent. Especially if you are a non-native, this is less formidable than plunging into unfamiliar foreign literature. Also, you will know what you are getting when you order a book sight unseen.

Literary classics are the stuff of culture. The German who doesn't know Heinrich Hoffman's *König Nussknacker* and *Struwwelpeter* isn't German. The French gain their sense of drollness from *Puss in Boots* (and their inclination for bloodcurdling crime movies from *Bluebeard*). Nearly every Italian child has wept through that great story of compassion, *Cuore*, by De Amicis, and gained a moral sense of the relation of work and play from *Pinocchio*. Each culture has folk characters and classic stories like these so intrinsic to it that they must be considered essential for the bilingual child. These are stories that will be read aloud and the reread, over and over.

First read these classic books aloud; later, the children will read them themselves. Simplified versions are fine. Book importers tend to be felicitously traditional in this regard. They stock the higher level of classics, such as *Swiss Family Robinson*, *A Tale of Two Cities* and *Around the World in Eighty Days*. Don't worry if they seem too advanced for your child—the treat of being read aloud to places almost no demands on his skills. Stuck once, waiting in a very slow line with only a volume of the adventures of the gentleman-burglar Arsène Lupin—meant for older readers—to hand, I read half a chapter aloud to Emma and Burton. Closing the book, I said something like, "Whew! That was tough going." Emma retorted, "What do you mean? That was terrific!" If you suspect you are forgetting about some classics, get a critical work on international children's literature from the library, and make a list of the essential titles that you would like to have your child read. Your task is simplified by the fact that whereas a multiplicity of presses small and large bring out original books, translations of well-known children's books tend to be done by a few major firms in each language, such as, in Italian, Arnoldo Mondadori; in French, Hachette, Gallimard, Flammarion and Larousse; in Spanish, Biuguera and Alianza; and in German, P. Suhrkamp and Droemr-Knaur.

Nursery Rhymes, Fairy Tales and Short Folk Forms

Nursery rhymes play a very important role in growing up. They are the encapsulations and clarifications in brief story form of the child's basic concerns and motives. Reciting them, a child and parent act out intense emotions in a relaxed mood. While your spouse or babysitter reads the English-language Mother Goose with your child, you can read translations and equivalents. It is an extraordinary experience to read Mother Goose in Spanish, French or German, while some of their counterparts are just as spicy and entertaining. Even in translation the jingles rhyme, and though it may be that the stories are rendered less vivid, you and the children will enjoy reciting in German what you know in English—it makes a two-part harmony in the mind. If the nursery-rhyme book's pictures are not exceptional, you can recite the rhymes with the child while he or she plays in the tub ("Rub-a-dub-dub"). Keep this first poetry book in the glove compartment of the car for extending your child's and your repertoire. Older children extend the horizon of their literary tastes far beyond the likes of Mother Goose, but continue to recall them with love. Some American editions in foreign languages are:

Cooney, Barbara and de Kay, Ormonde. *Mother Goose in French.* New York: Crowell, 1964.

Pomerantz, Charlotte. *The Tamarindo Puppy and Other Poems.* In Spanish. New York: Morrow, 1980.

Tortillitas para Mama and Other Nursery Rhymes. A selection of traditional Latin American rhymes in Spanish and English. New York: Holt, Rinehart and Winston, 1981.

Alexander, Frances. *Mother Goose on the Rio Grande.* Skokie: National Textbook: 1977.

Fairy-tale anthologies are often big, gorgeous volumes. One illustration per story is a must if your child is to make ample use of the book from the listening age to the reading. The following qualify as deluxe:

French: *Il Etait une fois . . . Vieux contes français.* Illustrated by Adrienne Ségur. Paris: Flammarion, 1951.

German: *Märchen.* Illustrated by Marlene Reide. Annette Betz, 1975.
Deutsche Heldensagen. Gerhard Aick, ed. Heidelberg-Schlierbach: Ueberreuter, n.d. Available from Continental Books.

Italian: Froud, Brian, and Lee, David. *Fate.* Milan: Rizzoli, 1981.
Grimm. *Fiabe.* Translated by M. Castagnoli. Turin: Einaudi, 1970. *Enciclopedia della favola: Fiabe di tutto il*

mondo. Rome: Riunti, 1981.

Spanish: *Mejores cuentos juveniles.* French and European Publications. In two volumes. Barcelona: Labor, 1966.

Playlets of fairy tales in script form, ready to be performed, will appeal to the theatrically inclined child of seven to twelve. Every major language has full-length versions prepared for children's theater productions, and brief one-acters are frequently available too; for instance, *Teatrino de Cappuccetto Rosso,* seven fairy tales for performing, from S. F. Vanni (30 West 12th Street, New York, NY 10011). Be ready to condense the stories or simplify them for the younger set. In French, for example, you can change the historic (past definite) tense into the easier past indefinite (*le passé composé*), or the present for the very young listener. For the older child who branches out into reading fairy tales on his own, look for the collections of folk and fairy tales assembled by region, which European publishers often have in children's versions, with minimal dialect.

Due to their good sense, clear values and brevity, fables and proverbs are easily retained by the child. A book of fables is central to the child's foreign-language book collection. "Just like 'The Country Maid and the Milk Pail,'" your child will say, when somebody "counts his chickens before they are hatched." Or, when a runaway cat is enticed back with tuna, "Gentleness succeeds where force fails." We found La Fontaine's best-known fables an entry point into literary expression, and magnificent for reading aloud. These and other renderings of the stock of European fables come in lovely editions in many languages. We like both the selection from Casterman, illustrated by Simone Baudoin, which dresses animals up drolly like Renaissance burghers, and the classic nineteenth-century Boutet de Monvel edition, with its double-page row of pictures for every fable. Remember that children can understand languages and sophisticated ideas more easily when heard aloud at age three than when read at seven. My daughter loved *Pot au lait* because of the girl in the dirndl skirt, and asked me to read it when she only understood a fraction. By age five, she could put the story to use intellectually. Proverbs too are worth their weight in gold. *Proverbes à la douzaine,* told by Anne-Marie Dalmais, and resplendent with bright illustrations by Benvenuto, and pub-lished by Flammarion, has stories in French illustrating familiar proverbs, which are given in Spanish, Italian and German as well.

Poetry

If you are a lover of language, you probably cannot live without poetry. Yet it is an acquired taste. Poetry speaks to us in lan-guage that is most pristine and liquid. Commerce in poetry makes a child aware of language's power. It counteracts the blandness and misusages of media-talk. Moreover, while you may have trouble finding equivalents of true-to-life fiction or the best American picture-books in some other languages, es-pecially those with smaller native populations in the United States, poetry is, outside America more than here, recognized as children's birthright. Having said this, I must add that the only successful way for a young child to experience poetry is orally. A child needs to hear the warmth and wit of a voice, to hear poetry *performed*. Poetry anthologies that can be enjoyed by children from babyhood through years nine to twelve include:

French: Jean, Georges. *Les Voies de l'imaginaire enfantin*, for very young readers;
99 Poèmes, 9 contes et 9 comptines. Centurion Jeunesse; and the nearly yearly collections by Jacques Charpen-traux for Editions Ouvrières (12, avenue Soeur Ros-alie, 15621 Paris Cedex 13).

German: Bogner, Ute. *Die schönsten Kinderreime*. Munich: Del-phin, 1983. Available from Kerekes Bros. (117 East 87th Street, New York, NY 10028).

Italian: *Pin Pidin: Poeti d'oggi per i bambini*. Edited by Antonio Porta and Giovanni Raboni. Milan: Feltrinelli, 1979; and, for teens, Drago's *Poesia per ragazzi in Italia*. Flor-ence: Giunti-Marzocco, 1971.

Spanish: *Antologia de la literatura infantil Española*. Collected by Carmen Bravo-Villansanta Arena. A seminal work of children's literature that includes folklore and poems. Madrid: Escuela Española, 1979.

Dictionaries

Children from two to seven like picture dictionaries, no matter how small the pictures or undistinguished the editions. This is a genre you will find in every language. Flipping to any page, a child finds an object, action or event represented that is apropos of his or her life at the moment. In my opinion, these are more useful than the simpler abecedarium (alphabet book) which is also such a ubiquitous children's-book category. By the time a child who reads a lot with his parents is able to read the words listed under each letter, usually at about six, he has probably advanced well beyond the A-B-C approach alphabet books use. To help your child establish letter-sound correspondence, you can use a picture dictionary and have him guess the words whose initial letter is represented.

Picture dictionaries are likely to be excellently illustrated and designed, and often are well bound and printed as well. The large, colorful cardboard *First Dictionary* by Richard Scarry exists in many languages, such as the Italian *Primo dizionario* from Mondadori (1981) and German *Mein allerschönstes Wörterbuch* (Munich: Delphin, n.d.). Other outstanding beginner's dictionaries include: *Mein Erster Brockhaus* (Weisbaden: F. A. Brockhaus, 1982), René Guillot's French *Images en mots* (Paris: Larousse, 1970) and *Mon Larousse en images* (Paris: Larousse, 1956), *Diccionario bilingüe ilustrado* (Spanish; published by Voluntad in Bogota, Columbia, 1978 and distributed in the United States by Bilingual Publications) and *Il Mio primo dizionario illustrato* (Italian; Mondadori). *The Cat in the Hat Dictionary* (Random House), available in all four major languages, has the virtue of lively sentences illustrating every word.

Even at this stage it is better for your child to have an Italian/Italian dictionary than an Italian/English one. The point is that *finestra* means *"una apertura fatta nel muro per dar aria o luce,"* not "window." An additional, bilingual dictionary is handy when you must find the word for "poison ivy," but it is the foreign language dictionary—picture version now and adult version later—that will help to broaden the child's understanding of the language.

As soon as your child reads, buy a second or intermediate-level dictionary, one level above the picture dictionary. A simple dictionary with about 4,000 entries, simple text and copious color illustrations is best. Several good second-level dictionaries are:

French: *Mon Premier Larousse en couleurs*. Paris: Larousse, 1953.

German: *Kinder Duden: mein erster Duden.*

Italian: *Dizionario della lingua italiana*. Milan: Rizzoli, 1977.

Spanish: *Mi Premier Larousse en colores*. Buenos Aires: Larousse, 1967.
 Diccionario bilingüe ilustrado (the second and third volumes of the set that includes the easy dictionary mentioned above); *Mi primer sopena*, a 1000-word dictionary with 700 illustrations, more advanced than the Larousse, published by Ramon Sopena, 1967 and *Diccionario*, a general Spanish/Spanish dictionary whose very readable print makes it excellent for young people, published by Trillas in Mexico and distributed by Bilingual Publications.

Technical Books for Children

These answer such questions as "What makes a car go?" and "Where does a rainbow begin?" Children of five to ten, when they want to know the answers, will ask you. Since technical information is the hardest kind to come up with in a language not natively yours, or one in disuse, the non-native speaker will especially appreciate these books. You may have doubt that these books will really thoroughly cover the questions your child poses. But it is to your advantage that technical books raise as many questions as they answer. These are books about how the world works. Scan them when you buy them so you know when to consult them and when not. Call these "question-and-answer" books when you order them from a bookstore, and specify the age-level or level of difficulty you desire.

Encyclopedias

The dictionary carries one as far as the French word for fox terrier, but what if your child asks why it wags its tail, or where fox terriers come from? At age seven or eight children can begin to use a children's encyclopedia, like the magnificent French Hachette or the German Junior Brockhaus. The American-born parent raising a bilingual child or even the native-born speaker needs an encyclopedia. It gives children the vocabulary for knowledge *in* the target language. If your child's essay topic at the local American school is the hydraulic lift, or dolphins, an encyclopedia in the home can be a boon. The set will not gather dust! An encyclopedia isn't an item to buy now and salt away; it should be used from the moment it enters the house.

We began with *Le Livre des mots* (Paris: Deux Coqs d'Or, 1981), a French edition of *Richard Scarry's Best Word Book Ever,* which has been translated into various other languages too. It is a preschooler's browsing encyclopedia. At five, our children were consulting the basic beginning French encyclopedia of knowledge by the author and illustrator Alain Grée, the *Collection Cadet-rama.* The series, about 20 volumes, includes an atlas, and volumes on the sea, the automobile, space and energy. The Grée albums are available in nine other European languages, and Hebrew and Arabic too. Similarly organized is the valuable *Meine erste Bücherei* (Brönner Kinderbüche, 1972); 30 titles in German. In Italian, the *Il Mio libro* series from the publisher Anthropos has slim volumes on nature, prehistory, geography and so forth, while Mondadori's *Guide* cover topics like Mushrooms, Dogs, Wild Flowers, Minerals, Dinosaurs and Birds.

By the time the children were six, even though they were not ready for a *World Book*-level encyclopedia, *I* was, to answer their increasingly sophisticated questions. During a visit to the American Museum of Natural History, Burton wanted to know about shamans (we were in the Asian section). I promised that before the next trip to the museum I would buy a general encyclopedia that would have, in French, the answers to such questions. We love the *Nouvelle Encyclopédie,* published by Hachette, which is conceived in accordance with the research needs of a child. Its 20 128-page volumes document animals' instincts and habits, dinosaurs, the Far West, pirates, the conquest of the sky, prehistory, cinema, "mysterious tribes and peoples" (and that includes Siberian shamans) and technology.

I suggest starting with an encyclopedia of this sort, listed for ages 12 and up, though Hachette does publish another, in French, organized in a similar fashion, but easier. You can write for their brochure (Editions Hachette, 79 Boulevard St. Germain, Paris 75006, France).

Several good German encyclopedias are available:

Meyers' *Grosses Kinder-Lexicon* (4000 entries; Diographisches Institut, 1982); *Das Moderne Kinder-Lexikon in farbe* (Munich: Bertelsmann, 1979); *Die Welt von A-Z.* (Two volumes, 300 entries with 300 color illustrations; Munich: Jugend und Volk, 1978); In Italian, *Arcobaleno: Enciclopedia per tutti i ragazzi.* (In ten volumes; Novara: Istituto geografico de Agostini, 1978); In Spanish, *Enciclopedia Basica Sopena* (from Spain; five volumes; Sopena, n.d.).

Comic Books

Don't forget Bat Man and Wonder Woman, the Hulk and other superheroes; get the kids reading. Because you want to hook your children on the written word in the target language, present them with a varied diet. These are only one kind of comic book you'll find in this broad and valuable category. American comic books may have been the inspiration for pop art, but they are rather homogenous. By contrast, kids' comics in many other languages are varied, imaginative and often beautifully drawn. They are a major vehicle for conveying information and even literature. For example, *The Monkey King*, the great Chinese epic known by more Chinese than perhaps any other literature, is read most widely in a comic book of several hundred pages. Ask your book importer or traveling friends to buy some comic books for your child. Look for comic-*style* books as well. Larousse has, for example, a series of Spanish paperbacks in large format presented in cartoon form for the young reader, including *Robin Hood* and *Los Tres Mosqueteros;* Bilingual Publications issues *Juanita en el Bosque,* a colorful, involved Spanish-language fiction for the older child. In French there are the *Asterix* and *Tintin* series and also the popular stories of Bécassine. One German example is *Schabernack und Lesespasse*

Heute Dies und Morgen Das (Recklinghausen: Kunterbunter, 1973). *Tintin* and *Lucky Luke* comic-book albums are printed in many languages. For compelling historical drama in Italian, see the illustrated histories written by Enzo Biagi, a famous Italian journalist, for the firms of Mondadori and Rizzoli on discoveries and inventions, Rome, Italy (three volumes, Milan: Rizzoli, 1975), the Orient, Greece and so forth, in comic strip form. In Italy, many adults read comic books for relaxation; children and grown-ups alike adore Mickey Mouse.

With comic books I class historical paper dolls and coloring books. Your francophone five to ten year old, for example, will enjoy *Erte's Fashion Paper Dolls of the Twenties, Great Fashion Designs of the Belle Epoque* and *Uniforms of Napoleonic Wars* (all from Dover Books, 180 Varick Street, New York, NY 10014). They are in English but support the child's bicultural interest. These can be ordered by mail.

Joke books and puzzle books are other peripheral books your child will enjoy in his second language. Tobacco and stationery stores sell them abroad; so do the more visionary import booksellers in the United States. Thus, Continental Books (11–03 46th Street, Long Island City, NY 11101) has sets of puzzles and junior joke books in German, and Vanni offers *Manuele della barzelletta* and *Secondo manuele della barzelletta* (New York: Vanni, n.d.), hundreds of illustrated jokes and games in Italian for the child of nine to 13.

Magazines

A subscription brings the child the excitement of receiving mail. Each issue is new, to be discovered. A general children's magazine has something for everyone—games, stories, puzzles, projects, a reader's column, articles on nature, technology and history. You can even find special-interest magazines on such subjects as science or the movies for teenagers.

For an inkling of what is available consult Lavinia Dobler's 1970 *World Directory of Youth Periodicals* (New York: Schulte, 1970). To update its references, ask bookstores that import foreign books, for they often carry foreign magazines as well. Or write to the International Youth Library in Munich (Schloss

Blutenburg, 8000 Munich 60, West Germany). Include an international postal coupon of a few dollars if you wish to see sample pages of children's magazines that are available in one of the four major European languages. For help in acquiring Spanish-language magazines or magazines from anywhere in the Third World, write to the Information Center on Children's Cultures (331 East 38th Street, New York, NY 10016). Children's magazines from the foreign press are often graded, steplike, by age level. Whether you choose to follow the age recommendations or not, you will definitely want to graduate from preschool magazines such as *Pomme d'Api* in France or *Barba Papa* in Italy, to more advanced publications like *Corriere dei Piccoli* and *Topolino* (Mickey Mouse) in Italian (carried by Speedimpex Publications, 45-45 39th Street, Long Island City, NY 11104; a very friendly place furnishing any Italian magazine or newspaper available in America); or, in French, *J'aime lire* from Paris and *Passe-partout* and *Video-Presse* from Montreal.

Letter-Writing Guides for the Parent

Bernage, Berthe. *Savoir écrire des lettres*. Paris: Gautier-Languereau, n.d. Also in Spanish.

Larousse, *500 Lettres pour tous les jours*. Paris: Larousse, 1979.

Johnson, Mary. *Guía de Correspondencia Española*. Skokie, IL: National Textbook Company, 1978.

Domingo, Francisco. *Como Se Escribe una Carta*. Barcelona: De Vecchi, 1978. Distributed by the French and Spanish Bookstore.

For other titles, be sure to ask for a guide not directed exclusively to secretaries. You can also ask a native speaker to set up a little file for you of basic correct ways to open and conclude various types of business and personal letters.

If your child wishes to exchange letters with someone in the second language, he may at first need your help. You might start by dictating letters, but you should know when to stop being your child's amanuensis. Even a young child can make an illustrated "movie" on paper, describing a day or vacation with captions and can send that. Hear what Kaethe Crawford, a German-American now in her late 70s, says about the value of writing letters in keeping her German strong. "Since my marriage in 1940, I've had no opportunity to speak—but I have carried on extensive and very interesting correspondence with several cousins. They insist I write in German—although they can read English after a fashion. When I sit down to type a German letter, I automatically 'shift' mental gears, and immediately begin to think in the German idiom. Only rarely do I need to refer to my dictionary to find a desired word, and then I continue quite fluently from there. I have admonished my cousins to 'read with their ears'—in other words, to try to 'hear' me as if I were speaking, as they remember me from our meeting back in the mid-1930s. This they do—and we even share jokes and ironic incidents from our associations with other people, though we have not met for so long."

7
Finding Materials

How do you go about acquiring non-English materials? The first stop is a bookstore that carries your language. If you live in or near a large city, there may be a bookstore that specializes in foreign-language books, such as the French and Spanish Bookstore in New York City, and Schoenhof's in Cambridge, Massachusetts. Get to know the buyer. This person probably loves books and can help you select good titles.

Even if your town does not have a large foreign-language bookstore, it may have a smaller store that sells materials to an ethnic community. In an ethnic neighborhood in Astoria, New York, you can go either to a bookstore or gift shop for Greek books, magazines, cassettes and discs; and one of the candy stores even has a small paying lending library. Find out where children enrolled in Saturday schools get the books they use— often, there is a local outlet.

Bookstores

If you live within near driving distance of an appropriate bookstore, make regular trips. Taking a book-buying trip with your child to a city where there is a concentration of ethnic speakers of the language and a major bookstore is not only fun but helps you purchase wisely, note future books to buy and establish a personal rapport with the bookseller. Besides, making the trip can be as important as the content of the book itself. If possible, purchase it in the second language. A meal at an ethnic restaurant, *in italiano* or *en français*, makes the trip all the more informative.

Friends' Trips

Other people's trips are another source: you can ask friends to bring back or ship books to you. Emphasize that you are looking for books that will last through many readings, have texts (no wordless picture books, please) and are natively produced. (This can be determined by checking the back of the title page.) If possible, involve your child in writing the list of requests. Besides books, you can ask for a jigsaw puzzle with a local scene, word puzzles or games, activity books, a calendar, issues of popular magazines or children's magazines or cassettes of popular songs or spoken stories. The larger bookstore or department store can probably mail these purchases home. Remember to ask for books a year beyond what you estimate your child's current reading level to be—the books, sent sea freight, may take several months to arrive. Cassettes, of course, are wonderful—light, compact and appealing.

Our cheap French books were obtained from a Parisian friend whose son had outgrown them. Every hand-me-down book your child reads wears the "book jacket" of another child. A community of past child readers happily haunts my children's bookshelves. Let friends here and abroad know you are looking, and thank them with a new book in return. Consider advertising on a bulletin board or in an ethnic newspaper for hand-me-downs as well.

Mail Order

A third way to acquire foreign-language books is by mail, either stateside, from an importer, or from a dealer abroad. Whenever you do not know a specific title, you will have to rely on the judgment of a middleman as to whether a book is a good choice. The three rules of thumb in relying on book importers are: avoid a heavy surcharge, seek an importer who gives personal advisory service and be flexible about titles.

Certain titles, especially dictionaries and ultra-famous picture-books like the *Babar* series, are imported and kept in stock in the United States by international book dealers like Rizzoli's, in New York, with branches in Chicago, Washington, D.C. and Dallas; the French and Spanish Bookstore in New York and San Francisco; and Schoenhof's in Harvard Square, Cambridge. For Spanish, Arabic, Korean and Chinese children's books and records pre-kindergarten and up, contact Iacono, 300 Pennsylvania Avenue, San Francisco, CA 94107; for Spanish and French classics, there is the Children's Book and Music Center, 2500 Santa Monica Boulevard, Santa Monica, CA 90404; S.F. Vanni, 30 West 12th Street, New York, NY 10011, is a genial importer of Italian books; and families receive excellent service on Hungarian and German children's book orders from Kerekes Bros., 177 East 87th Street, New York, NY 10028.

For French, German and Spanish classics, Continental Book Company, 11–03 46th Avenue, Long Island City, NY 11101, has a good stock and handles custom orders efficiently. From Continental's catalog we chose our abiding favorite poetry book, *60 poésies et comptines* (Paris: Centurion, 1975), sight unseen. We find we can depend on their excellent list. Often a book chosen from it takes two months to arrive, but the service of book specialists for each of the three languages is impeccable. On the grounds that you are home-schooling your child in the foreign language, if you intend to do considerable business with your import bookseller, request a school discount. Note that books that have been ordered specially are nonreturnable, and the prices are subject to change.

Verify before giving a store your business that they will take special orders. Rizzoli's takes as much care in getting you a paperback of *Il Piccolo Principe* by Saint-Exupéry (Milan: Bompiani, 1978), as they would one of their prestige art books. Typically, Rizzoli's informs you of the cost once they receive the book (in a month if the title is available), and ship by UPS. If a bookseller is laconic, difficult or bored with your special order for children's books, go elsewhere!

When ordering through a foreign-language bookseller, also ask whether there is a surcharge. If it is more than nominal (or reasonable), ask the store to include your list of titles—ancient

Egypt, biography of Julius Caesar, a beginner's Spanish cookbook—in its general order. You may have to wait longer for your books, but you avoid the surcharge the bookseller is obliged to impose to make money on an order for a single, specific title.

Every music store has records featuring dances, music and songs from other lands. These are usually accompanied by explanatory texts. Like bookstores, music stores can find what you seek on special order. For many languages, such as the Eastern European, Greek, Spanish, Arabic, Japanese and Chinese, there exist ethnic music stores as well. To find these stores and their addresses, glance through the advertising in an ethnic newspaper. To take one example, the *Orthodox Observer*, published by the Greek Orthodox Archdiocese in New York City, and sent to the homes of church members, includes advertisements for books, records, tapes, games and videocassettes of films.

Don't underestimate what you will find published in the United States, by the way. Major houses that have foreign-language lines or selected titles in foreign languages include Regent's; National Textbook Company; French and European Books; Larousse; Little, Brown; EMC; Random House and Frederick Warne. Their addresses can be found in the *Literary Market Place,* a reference book available at your library. Special ethnic publishers are active enough to supplement the import sources. Check the listing in the *Subject Guide to Children's Books in Print* under the language desired and, for the ethnic publications, write to church or social organizations of the appropriate communities. R.R. Bowker Company's *Bilingual Educational Publications in Print,* 1983, in the collections of larger libraries, is another tool; instructional and audio-visual materials as well as fiction and nonfiction books are covered.

Catalogues

Here are a few examples of catalogues you can request:

National Textbook Company. (8259 Niles Center Road, Skokie, IL 60077.) Offers abundant materials in German, French and

Spanish, as well as worthwhile publications in Portuguese, Italian, Vietnamese and Russian. Especially notable are classroom editions of literature (simplified for students, or with glossary and vocabulary) and extensive series of fables and legends from Mexico, Spain, Latin America and Puerto Rico, and many imported pocketbooks in French.

Larousse and Company. (572 Fifth Avenue, New York, NY 10036.) Carries French and Spanish children's books. Other Larousse books—the foreign publications—can be special-ordered through them from France.

J.P. Lippincott Junior Books. (10 East 53rd Street, New York, NY 10022.) *Libros Lippincott en Español* are Spanish translations of distinquished books from the Lippincott list, including both fiction and nonfiction, for a range of age groups, in hardcover. Also available is the popular *I Can Read* series, translated into Spanish by Pura Belpre, former Spanish children's specialist at the New York Public Library; they include *Osito (Little Bear)* by Else Minarik and *Daniel y el Dinosaura* by Syd Hoff.

Bilingual Publications. (1966 Broadway, New York, NY 10023.) Has Judy Blume in Spanish and hundreds of other popular books for Spanish-reading children, young adults and adults.

A.R.T.S. (32 Market Street, New York, NY 10002.) Has a small list of unusual, low-priced and worthwhile books in Spanish and Chinese.

The Children's Television Workshop. (1 Lincoln Plaza, New York, NY 10023.) Intermingles Spanish articles and stories with English, as on their television program "Sesame Street," in several of their publications.

Alphabet Books

Alphabet books published in this country include:

Feelings, Muriel and Tom. *Jambo Mean Hello: Swahili Alphabet Book.* New York: Dial, 1974. Available in paper and hardcover; a word book rather than an alphabet book *per se.*

Fisher, Leonard Everette. *Alphabet Art: 13 ABC's from around the World*. New York: Four Winds, 1978.

Hamann, Bente. *A Friendly ABC, French-English Alphabet Book*. New York: Warne. Not in print but found in many libraries.

Lapine, Jennifer and Susan. *My First Hebrew Alphabet Book*. New York: Bloch, 1977.

Palandra, Maria. *Dalla A alla Z: L'Alfabeta Dei Bambini*. Illustrated by Giancarlo Impiglia. Bronx, New York: Northeast Center for Curriculum Development, 1978. Distributed by Lesley College.

Postman, Fredericka. *The Yiddish Alphabet Book*. Illustrated by Bonnie Stone. Palo Alto: P. Nye Press, 1979. Available from The Printer's Shop, 4047 Transport, Palo Alto, CA 94303.

Reese, Ennis. *Little Greek Alphabet Book*. Illustrated by George Salter. Englewood Cliffs, New Jersey: Prentice-Hall, 1968. Out of print but available in some libraries.

Rosario, Idalia. *Idalia's Project ABC/Proyecto ABC: An Urban Alphabet Book in English and Spanish*. New York: Holt, Rinehart and Winston, 1981.

Rosario, Ruben del. *ABC de Puerto Rico*. Poetry by Isabel Freire de Matos: Illustrated by Antonia Martorelli. Sharon, CT: Troutman Press, 1968. Order from: Las Americas Publishing Co., 37 Union Square West, New York, NY 10003.

Sasaki, Jeannie, and Uyeda, Frances. *Choco is For Butterfly: A Japanese-English Primer*. Seattle, Washington: Uyeda Sasaki Art, 1975. Order from: JACP, 414 East Third Street, P.O. Box 367, San Mateo, CA 94401

Spuridake, Eugenia. *Apo to Alpha, Os to Omega*. Illustrated by Giorgio Marina. Cambridge, MA: National Assessment and Dissemination Center for Bilingual/Bicultural Education (Lesley College), 1979.

Svec, M. Melvina. *My Czech Word Book ABC's*. Drawings by Jean E. King. Cedar Rapids, IA: Czech Heritage Foundations, 1974. Order from: Box 761, Cedar Rapids, IA 52406.

Wolff, Diane. *Chinese Writing: An Introduction*. Calligraphy by Jeanette Chine. New York: Holt, Rinehart and Winston, 1975. Hardcover or paperback.

Buying Directly From Abroad

I have left this method until last, and so should you, because this path is *mined* with difficulties. However, if you know which books you want, and don't mind the work of setting up your own mini-business, here's what you do. First write to the overseas publisher with your order. The publisher will send back the prices. You then send back an international bank draft for the correct amount in foreign currency, and the publisher sends the material. This can take several months to accomplish. If you cannot find a good dealer, try this direct method. Most publishers will also provide a catalogue of children's titles upon request. If necessary, you can write to most of them in English.

Lists of some children's-book publishing houses can be had from the libraries of the Goethe Institute, Istituto Italiano and French Institute/Alliance Française in New York City. For example, a prepared printed handout on French book sources from the Alliance suggests Editions Casterman, Hachette, Ecole des Loisirs, Larousse, and Nathan (an educational games company). The familiar Walt Disney books are available in many languages. You can inquire for them from the following sources:

French: Les Editions Heritage. 300 Arran, C.P. 8, St. Lambert, Quebec, Canada. Cloth books; workbooks.
Edi-Monde/Hachette. 23/25 rue de Berri, 75008 Paris, France. Story books; pop-up books; activity books

German: Ehapa Verlag GmbH. 700 Stuttgart 1, Postfach 1215, West Germany. Paperback books.
Delphin Verlag. Reichenbachstrasse 3, 8000 Munich 5, West Germany. Story books.

Italian: Arnoldo Mondadori Editore. 20090 Segrate, Milano, Italy. All kinds of books.

Spanish: Organización Editorial. Novaro S.A. Apartado Postal No. 10500, 53370 Mexico, D.F., Mexico. All kinds of books.

The International Youth Library in Munich (Schloss Blutenburg, 8000 Munich 60, West Germany), provides recommended reading lists of children's and young people's literature free of charge, not only to publishers and libraries, but also to parents interested in giving their children good-quality foreign-language literature. Lists for some of the world's major languages (French, German, Italian, Spanish, Russian, Japanese and so forth) are prepared yearly, based upon the 12,000 releases received at the Library from publishers throughout the world (other languages receive attention on a more irregular basis). Specify your preference for the English version of the annotated list.

Only a few minutes' walk from the United Nations in New York City is the United States Committee for UNICEF and its unique service, the Information Center on Children's Cultures. The subject of this center is children of the world, especially of the Third World. It collects educational and cultural materials about children of other lands, and also primary-source materials such as games and children's art. The Information Center (331 East 38th Street, New York, NY 10016) will send an up-to-date list of bookstores here and abroad that handle children's books in foreign languages. This list enumerates nearly 100 bookstores in half as many countries. This and the International Youth Library lists are essential research tools. Based on the Information Center's collection of over 20,000 books and periodicals and 10,000 filmstrips and other multimedia materials, the librarians can make authoritative recommendations, especially with regard to publications in languages of the Third World (Spanish is within their ken).

Once you have the titles, you can order from the book publisher or dealer abroad. I suggest you ask them to make a substitution if a book on your order is no longer available, according to parameters you describe.

Book Clubs. Some publishers and book associations abroad have book clubs, which you may find of interest. France, for example, has Collection Kilimax (four to seven years of age) and Minimax (two to four). Join a book club and a book wends its way to your child on a regular basis, often monthly, summers excepted. Here are a few such clubs:

Bibliothèque Arc-en-Ciel. 123 New Kirk Road, Richmond Hill, Ontario L4C 9Z9, Canada.

Six times a year the child chooses from 90 French books, at different levels of difficulty, and at considerable savings. This is one of Scholastic's overseas book clubs.

Edebé. Paseo San Juan Bosco, 24, Barcelona 17, Spain.
A book club magazine, designed to make children aware of new books and to distribute them at a discounted cost.

Barnposten. Order from: Läseklubben, Box 45070, 10430 Stockholm, Sweden.
Another reading club magazine; they also print a members' newspaper.

German Scholastic Book Club. Care of: Lesen & Freizeit Verlag GMbH, Marktstrasse 24, D-7980 Ravensburg, West Germany.

Borrowing

When you decide to raise your child bilingual, you will want also to borrow children's books from a variety of sources. Your local library may not have more than a few children's books in a foreign language, but your search for loans starts there. In the San Francisco Bay area, to take as a prime example, a city of diverse ethnic neighborhoods, Oakland Public Library has children's collections in their Latin American and Asian Community branches. San Francisco Public Library has in-depth children's collections in Chinese, Japanese and Spanish. In their Main Children's Room they also have smaller collections of children's books in about 25 other languages—more titles in French and German, smaller numbers in such languages as Arabic, Italian, Korean, Russian, Pilipino and Vietnamese.

If the local library does not carry your language, request books from the state library, or a large city library system. Librarians have become very aware of non-English materials and will exert themselves to help.

If the library cannot find good materials in your state, ask them to write to the North Carolina Foreign Language Center, Cumberland County Public Library, 328 Gillespie Street, Fayettesville, NC 28301. The Foreign Language Center's motto is "Use your library to learn another language." It has records and cassette kits for learning over 40 languages. Their materials are circulated out of state through your local public school, church or other library. Sound filmstrips and slide sets are also lent, one per patron, due back in four weeks. There are materials such as a set on Canada by the National Geographic Society, a filmstrip on German beer, 120 slides on Germany's geography, a filmstrip with a bilingual test on Italian restaurants, one on Venice and the Vatican and a simplifed *Don Quixote* in Spanish. There is even a filmstrip on "How to Conduct a Language Fair." The better children's materials are in Spanish, French, German and Italian, in that order, but the selection is so intelligent you are bound to find books of interest in almost any language.

The National Clearinghouse for Bilingual Education (1555 Wilson Boulevard, Suite 605, Rosslyn, VA 22209) gives advice and information free of charge and maintains a toll-free telephone hotline, 800-336-4560. Their primary concern is to answer questions about the transition of foreigners to English speaking, but they are helpful and truly national in scope. A subscription to their newsletter is free of charge, as are occasional focus papers. There are also Bilingual Education Service Centers around the country that handle local questions related to schooling and foreign language collections in libraries; these are especially helpful for languages uncommon in America (for example, Greek, Vietnamese, Turkish). The centers will even look for tutors for a family, to live in or out. A partial list of the centers and their specialties is as follows:

Asian Bilinqual Curriculum Development Center
  Seton Hall University
  162 South Orange Avenue
  South Orange, NJ 07079
  Chinese, Japanese, Korean

Arabic Materials Development Center
  611 Church Street
  Ann Arbor, MI 48104
  Arabic
  Offers social studies, science and math study materials, pic-

ture sets and alphabet books, beginning at the kindergarten level.

National Evaluation, Dissemination and Assessment Center
385 High Street
Fall River, MA 02720;

Lesley College
49 Washington Avenue
Cambridge, MA 02140

Core curriculum in Chinese and Korean; core curriculum and supplements in French, Greek, Italian, Portuguese and Spanish. A nonprofit center; sells books at cost.

National Materials Development for French and Creole
Distributed by the Department of Media Services
Diamond Library, University of New Hamphire
Durham, NH 03824
Some children's pre-readers, folksongs and social studies materials are among the listings. Also, rental of film and video of Radio-Quebec educational T.V. materials.

Evaluation, Dissemination and Assessment Center for Bilingual Education
3700 Ross Avenue, Box 103
Dallas, TX 75204
A series of textbooks in modern Greek that address topics of interest to Greek-speaking children.

National Asian Center for Bilingual Education
11729 Gateway Boulevard
Los Angeles, CA 90064
Chinese, Japanese, Korean, Cambodian, Laotian, Vietnamese
An array of bilingual books about American heritage, life and immigrant history; games, restaurants and folk tales of Asian-Americans.

Pacific Area Language Materials Development Center
University of Hawaii
2424 Maile Way
Honolulu, HI 96822
South Pacific and Oceanic languages

National Center for Materials and Curriculum Development
University of Iowa
North 310 Oakdale Campus
Oakdale, IA 52319
Cambodian, Laotian, Vietnamese

Anyone needing help in selecting lists of children's materials in languages that are not widely spoken or understood in the United States, such as Swahili, Portuguese or Hindi, can also write to the Information Center on Children's Cultures, mentioned earlier. Indicate what the specific need is, and age and skill level of the speaker and be sure to enclose a legal-size stamped self-addressed envelope. Note that the Center cannot supply selective lists in French, German, Italian, Dutch or the Scandinavian or Eastern European languages, although it can give information on national customs and the lives of children worldwide. Though most of its work is carried on by letter, visitors are welcome.

Various institutes lend foreign language books. We joined the French Institute/Alliance Française Library. From it, a mailing service to any address in the United States is available to all members who pay the modest annual membership fee. The library of 35,000 volumes includes many children's books and has a fine record collection. Applicants for membership should write to: The Librarian, French Institute/Alliance Française, 22 East 60th Street, New York, NY 10022. For German books, you can borrow in person or by mail from Goethe House libraries, the largest of which is the Goethe House New York (1014 Fifth Avenue, New York, NY 10028). Readers take home their pick of 16,000 volumes of literature, history, social sciences and the arts; of a small collection of new children's books; and from extensive spoken-word recordings. The Goethe House is closed from July 4 to Labor Day. Distant borrowers pay for postage; otherwise no fee is charged for use. The Istituto Italiano di Cultura Library (686 Park Avenue, New York, NY 10021) is another Manhattan cultural landmark with service to readers nationally. They have very few children's books but possess guidebooks to every region and city in Italy and art books are a forte; these too may interest your children. If you want information in depth on Italy's culture, or a popular novel or biography to try out, the Istituto will circulate what you need via your local library.

Additional cultural institutions with children's books include:

The Goethe Institute
170 Beacon Street, Boston, MA 02116, and

The Goethe Institute
530 Bush Street, San Francisco, CA 94108

Hispanic Society of America Library
Broadway and 155th Street, New York, NY 10032

American Swedish Institute Library
2600 Park Avenue South, Minneapolis, MN 55407

Polish Museum of America Library and Archives
984 Milwaukee Avenue, Chicago, IL 60622

Feehan Memorial Library (Irish)
St. Mary of the Lake Seminary, Mundelein, IL 60060

Shevchenko Scientific Society (Ukrainian)
302 West 13th Street, New York, NY 10014

8
Language Travel: The United States and Canada

No matter what your second language, you can have travel experience in it in *North America*. To speak Spanish you can shop in Miami. To speak Italian go to Boston, Chicago or Toronto—among other cities—especially at festival times. There are Chinatowns not only in New York and San Francisco but in Boston and several Midwestern cities. German is a little harder, because German-Americans to a large extent shed their language in the course of the First and Second World Wars. Still, there are several Midwestern communities where German is spoken conversationally and that hold annual festivities; and Chicago and New York both have neighborhoods where you can expect to hear German spoken, eat German food and, if you exert a little boldness, speak German yourself.

French is a particular delight in the Americas. It is the language of portions of Maine, and in New Hampshire, Berlin in the mountains and much of Manchester and the town of Suncook to the south; and is heard throughout the bayous of Louisiana. In Quebec Province and in New Orleans, French coincides with touristic high points. The accent varies but the language *is* French and comprehensible if you abandon the convention that only one French is correct. A detailed description of French-language travels in North America follows; similar trips can be arranged for speakers of many other languages.

At first, when I began to raise the twins speaking French, my sights were set on France. But gradually I became aware of French as spoken in Quebec, first because of the extraordinary children's books published in French in Quebec, and second because we could not afford the plane fare for an au pair from Europe. I put an ad in the Montreal daily *La Presse*, when the children were three. After three years of Quebecoise au pairs, the children and I can move in and out of the Canadian accent easily. Finally, we wanted to travel in a French-speaking area, to wrap the children in the language so they would see that more than *Maman* and a few friends spoke it. I am definitely not of the "Wait till they're old enough" school of thought. I am of the "If you like the tune, play it again" school. The teddy bear means a lot because it is hugged so many times. I wanted my children to gain an early appreciation of a French environment, so when they were almost five, we took our first trip to the "American France." We were also thinking ahead to one of those wonderful Quebec summer camps we had heard about. Of course, Paris has cachet; it is the hometown of Madeleine, and of the Red Balloon—beloved characters from books—but Quebec is nearby. From our au pairs, the children knew about Canadian syrup and smoked salmon. They sensed the excitement of the *feuille d'érable* (maple leaf) from delivering letters with Canadian stamps to the third floor. Our Quebecoise girls had gone home by train or bus for a weekend or week, to be with family, or even for an appointment at the doctor's or to play in a tennis match. Emma and Burton sensed that Quebec was foreign but "not too far."

We decided to enter Quebec the way my husband had as a child: grandly, with a short stay in Quebec City, the most French of Canada's cities, at the world-renowned Chateau de Frontenac. Centering the twins' first foreign experience on a famous hotel had a special appeal for me, remembering my own travels with my family abroad in Europe in the 1950s. It evoked the tradition of the Grand Tour. Moreover, a fine hotel is by definition filled with local people whose business it is to be courteous and helpful. The twins could get their bearings in the hotel, whereas to learn to know a city even superficially takes much longer.

On the outside, the Chateau de Frontenac is an imposing fortress, on the inside a cheerful village. The hotel has shops and restaurants, ballrooms and conference halls and wide promenades. We glimpsed several weddings and danced at a party in the lobby, to the music of a band of strolling players. The Chateau has its guilds of electricians and plumbers, cooks and bakers, launderers and locksmiths—tradespeople who work only there. Many speak only French, and were the principal, affable conversers with our children. We had no trouble understanding native speakers.

The children's first croissant occasioned an invitation to the hotel's bakery. There, croissant dough was proofing in long sheets, and the loaves for the night's canapés were emerging from the ovens. Emma and Burton had a hand at rolling out dough. They also grasped the four-foot paddle as a baker lifted the done loaves from the oven to a counter to cool. In French Canadian style, the bakers bid us *"bonjour"* instead of *"au revoir"* when we left.

The children were fascinated to find that everything in the hotel was in French. On the elevator they read their first French words in a public place: "RC" (*rez-de-chaussée*) and "SS" (*sous-sol*), on the panel of buttons. French really works, they discovered.

The excitement of the new environment definitely stimulated the twins' French. So did the smiling faces and the unhurried manner of life. When a high wind began spraying us with water, Emma enjoyed running with the other tourists from the Montmorency Falls. Burton called out the colors of the brightly painted farmhouses as we drove around picturesque Île d'Orléans. For the most part, though, their patience for sightseeing was short, for watching and listening to people long. The favorite event was the ferry ride across the St. Lawrence River and back. The boat was full of French-speaking children, and we met a friendly couple with a *chat tigre* (tiger cat) in a cage.

The first day in a new place, a traveler feels an exciting strangeness that is never repeated. It is like a perfume first inhaled. As a leading perfumer told me, next time you smell it you are smelling a memory. Northerners feel they deserve Tahitian weather when they go south. But New Orleans weather in late April was decidedly brisk, and the rain that fell for part of each day of the week Emma and I spent there pelted against the windows like hail.

The evening we arrived we traced the Vieux Carré (French Quarter) on a map and wandered around until we found a courtyard restaurant and had gumbo. Said Emma of the gumbo, holding up a leg of crawfish with the prongs of her fork, *"Ça me pique!"* She was being intentionally vague about whether she referred to the spiciness of the broth or the claw of the crustacean.

The gumbo, looking like a rich gravy, was predictably exotic for a child of five. But French bread and butter pats molded into shells were a version of the familiar bread and butter that Emma gobbled up. Never expect a gustatory adventure of adult dimensions when you have children with you. But this doesn't mean you can't have fun with new foods. I have seen families so discouraged by the waste children leave at dinner, that they give up "authentic" restaurants on a trip, and seek refuge in the McDonald's on the Champs-Elysées. The restaurant rule of thumb on a trip with children under 12 is one formal meal out every day. American children are unused to the many courses of a foreign meal. Breakfast in the hotel doesn't count—breakfast is never fussy or multi-coursed. Other rules: Ask the waiter to bring the soup and main course at once, then dessert. This adds up to no more than two courses. And if the children discover favorites, the way Burton discovered *jus de pample-mousse* (grapefruit juice) and croissants in Quebec City, let them order these foods as often as they can find them. Finally, do everything you can to encourage the children to order for themselves. Prompt them with a phrase in the foreign language like *"Qu'est-ce que tu prends comme dessert?"* ("What will you have for dessert?") as the waiter approaches, so the waiter hears the response *"Une tarte."* You can even learn and rehearse at ethnic restaurants back home useful phrases like "Water, please."

Another hint: Small departures from the familiar are safest. In Italy as children, my brother and I were disappointed at first that spaghetti was served with butter or a thin tomato sauce instead of a hearty meat sauce like our mother's. But the dish was familiar enough and we did eat it, eventually finding fresh, thin pasta delicious. I also remember apple juice on a British train that made us tipsy because of a slight alcoholic content—how we giggled! Mini-pizzas in Italy, in France dark, bitter-chocolate ice cream served with a triangular wafer, raw vegetables cut in pretty ways in the Netherlands, and breakfasts in Swiss pensions where the foods were familiar but added up to an elegant repast—these were the child-pleasers. We infinitely preferred cream of leek soup and crusty bread, the equivalent to soup and a sandwich in America, to more elaborate fare.

At the Gumbo Shop in the French Quarter, Emma was rapturous about a fountain in the courtyard. We sang a fountain song, "A la Claire Fontaine," while waiting to be served. Like me, she improvises lyrics blithely when she doesn't know them. This works fine when you sing for your amusement and not in a chorus. Emma enjoyed finding other bubbling fountains tucked into courtyards during our stay in New Orleans. I think it is because the twins' first tourist sight was of the huge pair of fountains that grace Columbia University's campus, that she loves them so.

I try not to point out views constantly, but often cannot resist. It matters little, because Emma will strike out on her own and turn to admire something else, seldom what I have tried to bring to her attention. The cagey way to encourage a child to observe and learn from the new or foreign-language environment is not to force it upon him. The French word for a child's response is most expressive: *entêté*, "according to one's head," is the word for "stubborn."

Spying fountains became one of two leitmotifs of our New Orleans walks. The other Emma fastened on was porch swings. We had ordered one from Sears for her father's birthday. In New Orleans, on several of the famous streets outside the French Quarter, we saw many people swinging on their porches in the bright spring afternoons.

New Orleans is a tired, regal lady with wrinkles in her cheeks and shadows under her sleepless eyes, yet she has a certain elegance, a *"je ne sais quoi."* As tourists, we were too new to her to regret what she may have been a generation or more ago. Cuisine and commerce of the French Quarter are the most intensely alive elements of the city's French heritage now. We wanted to be in New Orleans to absorb or ferret out French culture but not to be hit over the head with it. Emma was too young to learn history from the guidebooks, but very receptive to the city's French and Creole flavor. Also there were bits of history I could share with her, interpret for her, that did mean something to a five year old.

We walked along the *banquettes*. From lessons at home she knows that a *banquette* is a small bench. But the French Quarter sidewalks are also called *banquettes*. This is a carry-over from the days when the paved walkways had curved streetside edges, looking like low benches, to protect the pedestrians from the mud and sewage in the road.

We stayed away from the souvenir shops but enjoyed other boutiques, some of which had a decidedly French air. There was Fleur de Paris, an exquisite shop that sells lacy white nightgowns and cotton frocks, hats trimmed with beads, artificial fruits and flowers and sashes. There was fine lingerie, custom millinery, contemporary and antique clothing—who could say which was which. Emma's Boutet de Monvel book had hats like that! She custom-planned her own *chapeaux* in the store. We thought about crocheting lavender borders on her dress socks like those we saw.

There was Hové. Will Southern women someday bring back organdy and bonnets? If they do, they will surely wear perfumes like gardenia and tea olive to match. Emma liked the perfumes at Hové because she could recognize some of the flowers in the single-fragrance essences. The Hové perfumery is a business that has been in the family three generations. The original owner was a French girl from New Orleans who married a man in the cavalry and, as Julie Hové, her great-granddaughter and the present owner, puts it, "loved her waters." Wherever they lived, in outposts all over the country, the great-grandmother made her own scents. She grew up making cologne with her mother, as did Julie. "My grandfather, a retired Naval officer who was in investments, lost his money in the Crash, but Grandmama's perfume business didn't fail. She was a little unworldly. She had chosen a bank because she liked the color of the checks. It was the only bank in New Orleans that didn't fail!" The rose walls of the eighteenth-century structure that is Hové's are the color that the grandmother, who traveled widely to develop her art, recalled from Parisian perfumers.

Filles à la cassette will also catch the interest of visitors with an eye to French influence in New Orleans. Also called the "casket girls" (which sounds faintly ghoulish), these are the proud ancestors many New Orleanians claim. In 1727, six Ursuline nuns arrived in the French settlement to serve the hospital and to establish a school for girls. In France, marriageable young girls of good character were recruited for the colonies. They became wards of the Crown and were placed under the protection of the nuns until they could be married. Before their passage to New Orleans, each girls was given a small trunk, or casket, containing a basic wardrobe. It would be the only dowry that these girls from poor families could offer, but their reputation for skill in housewifely duties and their excellent character brought them many proposals. The first casket girl reached New Orleans in 1728, and they continued to arrive until 1751. Girls were also sent to the city from a Paris house of correction, but when native families of New Orleans trace their ancestry, they understandably emphasize the casket girls. Emma wanted to see the cassettes, so we ducked into an antique shop and saw a trunk of the right size and style to fit our idea.

No child can learn about French culture without encountering Napoleon Bonaparte. Emma did in this American city, at the Louisiana State Museum in the Cabildo, built in 1795-99 as the seat of the Spanish government. The Cabildo houses a Napoleonic collection and one of three surviving death masks of the Emperor, struck 40 hours after his death. It was a gift to Louisiana that was carried off during the Civil War on a refuse wagon, sold to a railway official, then eventually returned to the State.

At the Pontalba Historical Puppetorium on St. Peter's Street, we saw the legendary Louisianan gentleman-pirate, Pierre Lafitte, in action: refusing a British bribe to betray the Americans; Lafitte at the theater, falling in love with a fine lady; the pirate with buddies like Nez Coupé. Using the French-language guidebook from De Ville's bookstore in the city, I was able to read Emma the descriptions of the action in French, as we viewed the animated tableaux.

Promise them anything but give them a swimming pool, is my travel motto. Many of the hotels in the French Quarter that from the street look like guest houses do have pools. Ours was right on Canal Street and offered its own activities of cultural interest, as well as a place to swim. Tea was served from three to five, with jazz entertainment. Then a New Orleans jazz pianist, Ron Cribbs, played. He wore eccentric, jaunty clothes and said hello to everybody, remembering guests' names the following day. Because it was New Orleans, where you can always pick up some French if you have a good ear, Cribbs added French words to his songs for Emma: *"mon amie n'oublie pas."* He rendered the most sparkling "Frère Jacques" we had ever heard.

South central Louisiana, where the French heritage is strong, has seven parishes, of which Iberia, Evangeline, Acadia and Lafayette are the most traditionally Cajun—that is, of Acadian French descent. Small rivers are the parish boundaries. The center is the city of Lafayette, hub of Acadiana, a city thriving on industry, farming, oil production and food processing. Just outside of Lafayette is the Acadian Village and Gardens. Here Acadian dwellings, a church and period buildings have been created and restored on the site of an old settlement.

A town know as "Little Paris" is St. Martinville. Dating from the mid-eighteenth century, it is noted for the refuge it offered French-speaking exiles from Nova Scotia in 1755. Having developed a simple, pastoral culture in their home country, the immigrants found their way to rural areas of Louisiana, settling along the streams. According to legend, a number of French aristocrats left France during the French Revolution and settled near St. Martinville—hence its sobriquet.

Many of the towns celebrate the characteristic *Courir du Mardi Gras.* The "runs" occur on several different dates so you can attend more than one at Carnival time. The central event, men on horseback in masks and costumes, jesting and singing at farmhouses in exchange for a *poule* for the community gumbo, can be enjoyed best from a part of the road the riders will pass on the morning of Fat Tuesday. In a small town near Lafayette, at a bar of local fame, the riders practice their French the night before, repeating their songs and oral *récits.* The event is open to the public and this is as close to the *Chanson de Roland* as you are likely to get in the twentieth century.

Behind the CODOFIL program of French instruction in Louisiana schools is the philosophy that French is worth maintaining, a heritage in which Cajuns take pride. This signals a major change from the time when, as novelist Chris Segura writes in *Marshland Brace*, "French was forbidden, and its remnants in Gallicized terms and accents were discouraged, ridiculed, and displayed as ignorance." CODOFIL sponsors publications, write textbooks and guides French curricula in public schools. The staff will also advise families from out of state whose children speak French on noncommercialized ways they can enjoy French culture. The CODOFIL center is at 131 Chaplin Drive, Lafayette, LA 70504. Richard Guidry, an administrator of the bilingual program, passes on the following prescription for thawing the shyness of Cajuns about using their language with outsiders. "Go for a haircut. Or do something else that takes time and is a service tourists don't ask for. And when you ask, '*Parlez-vous français?*' say it with a Cajun lilt; that melts hearts."

Undisputedly the best town in which to talk and eat Cajun-style is Lafayette, but New Orleans is an exciting second choice. Chef Paul Prudhomme has opened a Cajun restaurant, K Paul's, that looks like a luncheonette and has gourmets standing in lines around the block for his authentic Cajun cookery. Having pored over photographs of Cajuns in Turner Browne's *Life of the Cajuns*, we found we could recognize Cajun hunters, fishers or farmers who had come into New Orleans for a job or a spree.

At the Café due Monde we ate beignets, sourdough crullers sticky with powdered sugar. When I asked a waitress whether any speakers of Cajun French worked at the café, she told me "Come back at seven," which we did. Emma recited for Big Steve the French version of the nursery rhyme about the Three Little Kittens, where, to punish their naughtiness, the mama cat says "*Pas de beignets.*" The exchange was a brief conversation and very encouraging. Big Steve said there were Cajuns working all over the Vieux Carré who spoke French, and gestured particularly to the drivers of the carriages outside.

Claude, one of the drivers, warmed to Emma's "*bonjour.*" He let Emma pat his mule. A husky, exuberant man dressed in country style, Claude spoke to us, making an effort to use the "French of Paris," a term other Cajuns in conversation with us had repeated. I don't know how self-conscious they were as linguists, how much they left out the Indian, Spanish and local words that are also a part of Cajun French to communicate with us. Claude seemed to understand us fine. "I'm speaking to you in the French of Paris," he said, "but I cannot make myself understood in the French of Quebec."

I said that we had French in the family, but were from New York. This vague explanation appeared to satisfy Cajuns we met. I think, if you have a forefather like our Huguenot from the seventeenth century, you should unearth him to make your French credible in Louisiana, where some Cajuns feel ambivalent about school-learned French, or sensitive about their patois. But if you want to be more forthright and say you love French and always wanted to come to Louisiana so you and your child could speak it there, this would probably be acceptable too.

The Lions Club held a state convention at our hotel during our stay. Their vests, men's and women's, were covered with pins they had traded with other club members. A whole group in the lobby's vast and handsomely appointed sitting area were speaking French. Emma had dressed herself in frilly white. We entered into conversation with a sofa-full of Cajuns who spoke to us entirely in French. Once they switched into French, they stayed in it. Dropping English was analogous to abandoning the *vous* for the *tu*—the polite for the familiar form. Once the friendship maneuver was made, I sensed, they would hardly retract it and return to English. The Cajun French that the group spoke had the cadence of a horse-drawn carriage rolling on an Old South road. Coming from the mouths of men and women dressed in a Western style, the language was fascinating to Emma and to me.

One Cajun Lion gave Emma a big kiss and pinned a club pin, enameled blue and in the shape of Louisiana, on her collar. Not only can you meet Cajuns and speak French with Americans to whom French is native in the city of New Orleans, you can do so in the lounge of your hotel!

Vocabulary

Certain French expressions will make you feel less of a stranger on your visit. Here are a few.

café noir; café au lait   black coffee; coffee with cream

andouille; boudin   two types of Cajun sausage. *Andouille* is made with beef, *boudin* with pork and rice. Sociologists recognize two types of Cajuns—the River (or *andouille*) Cajuns and Bayou (or *boudin*) Cajuns.

bayou   a sluggish stream, bigger than a creek and smaller than a river

comme ci comme ça   so-so

gallerie   porch or verandah

lache pas la patate!   Don't drop the potato; i.e., hang in there.

roux   What you make first when cooking gumbo or stew. A basic ingredient for many Louisiana recipes. Essentially, butter or oil and seasoned flour browned in a skillet.

A most helpful introduction to Cajun is Randall P. Whatley's *Conversational Cajun French I* (Gretna, Louisiana: Pelican, 1978).

Calendar of French Louisiana Events

La Grande Boucherie des Cajuns. The festival, patterned after the French and Cajun custom of the weekly *boucherie* (pig butchering), which provided fresh meat for rural families before refrigeration, features a variety of Cajun dishes made from pork. Cajun crafts and music demonstrated. Sunday before Mardi Gras. St. Martinville.

Louisiana Boudin Festival. The town of Broussard hosts an annual sausage festival with cracklin'-making, *boudin*-cooking, and eating contests, arts and crafts and carnival rides. *Boudin,* a favorite sausage in Cajun country, is made of ground pork, rice, onions and cayenne pepper stuffed into a casing. Second week in February. Broussard.

Mardi Gras. Mardi Gras means "fat" Tuesday, the last day of Carnival, when everybody lives it up before Lent. In New Orleans, Carnival spins out for two weeks of parades and balls. Each is lavish. Groups of families called krewes try to outdo each other with fancy floats and extravagant masked balls. For the parade, each krewe loads its floats with beads, fake gold doubloons and other favors called "throws." During the parade these are flung to bystanders in great showers.

While New Orleans celebrates Carnival with its legendary glamor, southern Louisianans (half of whom still speak French) focus on other traditions: on the *Courir du Mardi Gras,* French for "Mardi Gras ride"; on dancing ancient jigs; and on communal cooking and eating.

Thus, rural Louisiana has its own festivals: Several towns, like Mamou in prairie country, celebrate Mardi Gras in the old style with Cajun French music and *rigolade* (high-jinks). Costumed riders on horseback roam the countryside begging for contributions to a giant community gumbo. February, the Tuesday before Ash Wednesday. Ville Platte, Mamou, Church Point and other towns.

The Saturday before Mardi Gras, customs are reinacted for children in the Acadian Village on the outskirts of Lafayette. The Sunday before, masked, costumed riders follow *le Capitaine* on a wild ride through the Cajun countryside. At each farmhouse, the captain blows his cow horn and asks, *"Voulez-vous recevoir cette bande de Mardi Gras?"* The riders dismount, entertain and collect a food offering for a community gumbo. If the gift is alive, perhaps a fat hen, it must be chased and caught. After the 15- to 20-mile ride, riders return to town for a parade and street dance lasting late into the night.

French Acadian Music Festival. A program of Acadian songs and poems, dance contests and dancing until midnight. Second Saturday after Easter. Town of Abbeville.

Festivals Acadiens. Encompasses several festivals dedicated to Cajun culture, music, crafts and food. The festivals, some free, some with an admission price, are held in September. Located at various places in Lafayette.

Tournoi de la Ville Platte. The *Tournoi*, or tournament, which dates back locally for almost 100 years, is the ancient sport of the French knights. Mounted horsemen race over a circular course spearing rings. One of the few places in the world where the *Tournoi* is still held. Second week in October. Ville Platte.

All Saints Day. Traditionally, residents of Ville Platte set aside this day to tend the "cities of the dead," as the raised tombs in the church cemeteries are called. The vaults are cleaned and whitewashed and fresh flowers are placed on the graves. November 1. Ville Platte.

Fairs and festivals are an important part of Cajun life. For shrimp, sugar cane and rice festivals, *fais-do-dos* (street dances) and tours of marsh, swamp and cypress lakes, see the free guidebook, *River Trails, Bayous & Back Roads*, published by the Louisiana Office of Tourism, P.O. 44291, Baton Rouge, LA 70804.

Books on Acadiana for Children

Trosclair (James Rice). *Cajun Night Before Christmas.* Gretna: Pelican Press, 1974. Christmas on the bayou. The classic story of Old St. Nick placed in a Louisiana setting, with Santa in muskrat furs, riding in a skiff piled with toys and hitched up to alligators. One of a series of funny, animated stories and coloring books about Gaston the alligator, denizen of the bayou, illustrated by James Rice.

_____. *Gaston Goes to Mardi Gras.* Gretna: Pelican, 1978. An escorted tour of Mardi Gras and Carnival in New Orleans. En route, Gaston drops in on a *Courir du Mardi Gras* and *fais-do-do* in rural Acadian country.

_____. *Cajun Alphabet.* Gretna: Pelican, 1976. The abecedarium is Cajun French from A to Z. The short alphabet rhymes are a basic course in Cajun society, language, heritage. One of the more than 100 Cajun rhymes and phrases is as follows: "A is *au revoir,/* So long, not goodbye/ I'll see you *demain/ C'est amitié*, you and I." With glossary. Fun for children way beyond the ABCs stage.

Perales, André. *Fanfou dans les Bayous: Les Aventures d'un Eléphant Bilingue en Louisiana.* Gretna: Pelican, 1982. An elephant arrives from Paris and tours Louisiana with Paul and Louise. Written in basic French and presented in comic-book style. Cassette available.

For Adults

Tauriac. *La Louisiane Aujourd'hui.* Gretna: Pelican. Originally published in France, this is a complete, attractive guide to the state. Entirely in French, with maps and color photographs.

Whatley, Randall P. *Du Chicot.* Chicot Press, 1983. The author views Cajun culture as an old cypress stump, a *chicot,* that has lost its former majesty but still sprouts new life. This is a collection of syndicated magazine essays, in bilingual versions, of folklore, music, humor and commentary.

Write to Pelican, 1101 Monroe Street, P.O. 189, Gretna, LA 70053 for a complete list of French publications.

To whet your interest in French as an international language, here is a partial list of resort locations in our hemisphere that are francophone:

French Polynesia (Tahiti, or its closest island, Moorea)

The Seychelles

Guadeloupe

Martinique

St. Martin

St. Bartholomew. Not only is the eight-square-mile island of St. Bart's inhabited by descendants of Norman and Breton buccaneers, but the lifestyle is a cultural transplant from France. It is reached from St. Martin, the half-French, half-

Dutch island east of Puerto Rico. The yearly population of 3000 doubles at the peak of the winter season. Administratively linked to Guadeloupe and France, the island has a police force of a handful of *gendarmes* in *képis* (French military-style visors) and looks like an impeccable cameo of a French provincial setting.

St. Pierre de Miquelon, Canada. (Off Sydney, Nova Scotia; reached by ship from Newfoundland.) This tiny island speaks not Canadian French, but "Touranian," the French that is spoken in the heart of France.

Northern New Brunswick, Canada. The town of Caraquet holds an Acadian Festival in mid-August, and there is also a *Village historique acadien.*

For information on planning a vacation for your family to one of these spots, contact the French and French West Indies Tourist Board (610 Fifth Avenue, New York, NY 10020).

There are various ways to use your burgeoning new language while remaining in the United States or traveling just across the border.

Other Bilingual Friends

To this end you will want to find native speakers as locally as possible. Here is how. Listen when you are waiting for a bus, or in a shop, for the language your child is learning. When an acquaintance tells you, "My neighbor speaks that language," get a name and address. Put a classified ad in the local paper, or in the city daily or national foreign-language paper for a children's play group or book discussion club in the language. Post an ad on a church bulletin board in a neighborhood where you believe native speakers reside. Even if this neighborhood is downtown in the city and you live some distance away, maybe you and your child can go there for visits on Saturdays— and invite back. Also ask the grocer or druggist who sells foreign newspapers in that neighborhood: Do any families with children buy the paper? Do any friendly old people, who might have leisure time to meet you and your child, buy it? A local children's librarian is another source for referrals, because English story hours attract foreign-language-speaking mothers and children.

If you find an old person whose family has grown up and gone away, or who has limited mobility, you can arrange a weekly get-together like a tea-time or weekend lunch. If you find a family with playmates for your child, terrific. If a family has older children, maybe you can employ one as a sitter in the evening when you go out. Or take a young person along on a trip to an outdoor concert or family outing. What seems a drag with one's parents can be a pleasure with non-family if you are a teenager.

You may be able to "adopt" as a grandparent an elderly person whose native language is the one you are adding. If you explain your project and express an interest in the person's culture and life, the older person is likely to be complimented, not wary. Many communities have an adopt-a-grandparent program. Note that if you are seeing a person often, dialect is less a problem than if you see him or here rarely. If your language is Chinese, Arabic or another language where dialects differ greatly, don't overtax your child by bringing a foreign speaker of an entirely unfamiliar dialect on the scene, unless you intend to keep up the contact over time.

Holidays and Festivals

At holiday time religious leaders, cooks, musicians and crafts people are active in the community and happy to see you. Festive times celebrated publically in the language being learned privately are a joyous treat for your child. There are many more ethnic celebrations in America than you may have any idea of. Keep in mind that for children the small street fair can be as much fun as the mass event that attracts tens of thousands.

Several books give lists and inside information (though you will have to contact organizers in advance for dates and times). Among these are, for example:

Barish, Mort. *Mort's Guide to Festivals, Feasts, Fairs and Fiestas.* Princeton: CMG Publishing, 1974.

Filstrup, Chris and Janie. *Carp Kites on Main Street.* New York: Dodd, Mead, 1985.

The Harvard Encyclopedia of American Ethnic Groups. Cambridge, Massachusetts: Harvard University Press, 1981.

Exchange Visits

Put ads in newspapers, and contact churches, schools and ethnic organizations for chances for the older child to travel to interesting localities and stay with speakers of the second language. Growing without Schooling, the home-schoolers organization, has a hospitality list for exchange visits; a classified ad can be placed through them. Contact them at Growing without Schooling, 729 Boylston Street, Boston, MA 02116.

Hosting Programs

Nacel Cultural Exchanges: Summer Hosting Program. It is not necessary to speak French to host a French student between the ages of 13 and 19 through the Nacel Summer Hosting Program for American families. The student is received as a member of the family for a one-month stay. The French parents pay for transportation and insurance and supply their children's pocket money. Apply to Nacel Cultural Exchanges, 130 North Terrace, Fargo, ND 58102.

DIDAC. (3 Channing Place, Cambridge, Mass. 02138.) This agency places French visitors in American homes for a school year, semester or July or August. Host families specify preference regarding age of guests (ten to fifteen, to over thirty), and can be recompensed up to $10 per day.

The German-American Partnership Program. (Goethe House, 1014 Fifth Avenue, New York, NY 10028.) A non-profit exchange between groups of American and German high-school students. The German government subsidizes participating teachers with 75 percent of airfare, and each traveling student with between ten and fifteen percent. A four-week school term exchange includes a week of field trips.

Spanish. For a list of programs where high-school students come from Spain (and vice versa), write the Cultural Information Section, Spanish Consulate, 150 East 58th Street, New York, NY 10155.

9
Language Travel: Distant Shores

I would have a boy sent abroad very young into those neighboring nations whose language is most differing from our own, and to which if it be not formed betimes, the tongue will be grown too stiff to bend.

—Montaigne

Plans for my children's vacation abroad started with the word *boulanger* (baker). Emma and Burton didn't know what one was. Or a *boulangerie*. In fact, after nearly four years of speaking French among ourselves, they drew a blank at most of the qualities that make French bread French. "The French buy new bread every day," I explained. "They like it fresh. They couldn't imagine keeping it all week in the breadbox, or freezing the second loaf from the grocery store to be sure there's bread for Monday morning." I told the children about the crustiness of French bread, and how baby teeth are called milk teeth in French because they work better on soft foods than on the staff of life. I told them how well a *baguette* fits in a schoolbag or under an arm, and how surprised I had been as a child to see bread carried wrapped only in its own crust, not a paper package . . . . Suddenly it seemed very desirable to go to France, not to see the Rose Window at Chartres or the Petit Trianon, but for a *baguette*.

Far more than sights, a different language makes travel a foreign experience. The first contact with the foreign country *is* language. Everybody speaks so well! Before you bite into the *baguette*, you taste the talk in the shop and with the baker.

In *Innocents Abroad*, Mark Twain describes his first earful of French in Marseilles. At night, when he arrived by steamer from Quebec City, no planks were put out and he and two shipboard friends could not get onto the pier from the ship. They called to a boatman to convey them to shore. When the Frenchman didn't understand them, language shock set it. Wrote Twain, "He appeared very ignorant of French!"

The time to travel is before the tongue grows "too stiff to bend." Twain would have done better had he loosened his tongue on the French language as a child. Children naturally imitate local speakers. Unhampered by adult concerns and practicalities, they listen.

The temptation is always to delay—until the house is renovated, or your bank account is healthier; until you and your spouse can both take a month's summer vacation, until the children are old enough to appreciate the Alhambra. Or, this summer you yearn for a little R & R at a nearby lake. Robert Benchley's remark comes to mind: "There are two classes of travel—first class, or with children." But the time to start foreign-language travel is young. And children who already feel comfortable in a country's language are first-class travelers.

Long before they can recite the countries and capitals of Europe, children are receptive to the excitement of going there. Children who are learning Spanish may enjoy the taste of it they get in Miami or Houston, but what an exhilarating time they have developing their strokes in the language sea of Mexico or Spain! Abroad, your children meet native-speaking children and build sand castles with them, taste their daily bread, stroll the streets and learn all the vocabulary their little books mention but which, at home, referred to nothing they knew.

At five years of age, children raised bilingually are fully ready to wing it in their second language in the country where it is spoken. They are intellectually equipped to extend their curiosity to another culture, and poised enough to talk (especially about themselves!) to strangers. They understand that what is extra at home is essential abroad. They become leaders, reading signs, asking directions, reporting on today's weather as heard or overheard in local conversation. Having buttressed early curiosity with experience and competence, in later years (11 and up) the well-traveled child will retain a strong interest in the world at large.

Yesteryear's Grand Tour was intended to add polish to a young person's manners, mostly through firsthand contact with the wonders of continental Europe. Oftentimes, the young traveler's parents hoped for some learning of French, German and Italian as well and for that purpose, language masters were engaged under the auspices of hotels. But in other respects, natives remained part of the scenery.

Your Grand Tour is a language excursion. The point of the trip is less Culture with a capital C than interaction with speakers. After practicing at home, the children are ready for the international circuit. Your children will bring back stories of life and manners in a foreign tongue. Montaigne expressed it this way: "Conversation with men is marvelously useful and travel into foreign countries of singular advantage: not to bring back (as most of our young sirs do) only an account of how many paces it is around the Santa Rotunda, but to be able principally to take away the manners and customs of nations where he has been, and that we may whet and sharpen our wits by rubbing them upon those of others."

This really is a specialty tour, and one in which daily contact with the native speakers should be emphasized. You can plan an interesting trip without inflicting a slew of postcard-like scenes on your bored children. With this thinking you might, for example, choose the pebbly beaches of Dieppe in Normandy, where the "real French" go, over an international resort like Nice on the Côte d'Azur. When choosing a hotel in Paris, my first priority was that it be one described in a guidebook as friendly, my second priority, that it be very near the Jardin du Luxembourg, where my children would find playmates.

For children, conversation with living speakers, more than movies, theater and books, creates a language setting. This is very much to your advantage on the trip. Even if your child misses home cooking and his bike, the motivation to speak is there because of new friends. Young travelers who speak the language will, moreover, have an immeasurably better time because people welcome them. Their efforts are rewarded and applauded by the native speakers where they travel. When children speak the local language, even if it is not ethnically theirs, the voyage has the character of a homecoming.

Give your child manifold opportunities to use language skills without embarrassment. At first this can take the form of asking him to return the key to the hotel reception desk or request a glass of water from the waiter. Next he can take care of the transaction at the post office (children seldom meet the world of officialdom outside school, and feel very grown up posting letters in a foreign post office), or a commission at the pharmacy. The more you cover a city or town on foot and the more you loll in the cafés, the better is your chance for casual friendships where your child will join in the sociability.

Since this is a language-centered trip, let the children and the adult parent who speaks the language show off a bit. If your accents are reasonably good, people may think you hail from a far-flung territory or are émigrés—and native speakers. But with the all-American speaker whose use of the language is extremely hesitant or nonexistent, the situation may be a bit awkward, with the child pulling ahead in conversation and identifications. The best tactic is to let the child take over social and commercial situations whenever appropriate, or at least lead in the interchange.

Consider reducing your expenses by leaving the parent who does not speak the foreign language at home. If Daddy doesn't know a word of Greek and Mommy and Katrina are fluent, the trip may be less energetic in its itinerary but cheaper if Daddy stays behind. Such a trip is more child-centered as well as more language-centered. Sometimes a man or woman abroad with the children can meet new people more readily if not boxed in by the demands of both family and spouse.

There are other, less draconic ways to keep costs down. When you pinch francs, pfennig or lire, remember you are economizing in order to go back another year. Once you see how beautifully children develop their language proficiency from the trip abroad, you will want to try to make the *trajet* as regularly as possible. Take advantage of special airfares, of course. Go to Europe in September if you can, when the weather is still good enough to spend a lot of time outdoors, while rates for lodging have begun to come down, and there are fewer people touring (a factor that makes local people more interested in vacationers). Play up the *vie bohème* image with the family before embarking, so that you can live it to the most practicable degree: clothes dripping dry over the tub or shower stall; meals of bread, cheese, watercress and orange juice, on a bench in the park.

You will also spend less by discarding the notion that being abroad should entail night after night of extravagant celebration for the adults. You are on a tour not only language-centered but do-it-yourself as well. This attitude will benefit your children's grasp of the language. You may identify Rome, Paris and Munich with the *dolce vita*, the finer things of civilized life. However, if the children miss the Sistine Chapel in order to frequent the Rome municipal swimming pool, it is to the good. They have a whole life ahead of them for high culture, and their ultimate enjoyment of it will be increased by fluency. Other ways to save are house exchanging, renting and camping. You will find details about these arrangements at the end of this chapter.

The fact that the trip is more for language than for sightseeing means you don't have to be so organized for tourism. For example, you don't want to seal yourself into an automobile for the entire trip. People on foot or in local buses communicate more. You want to have a diverting holiday, but you also want to achieve the moments of serendipity that will utilize language skills. To counter the tendency to try to fit the maximum into your days and weeks abroad, try the following: (1) Go out some days without a watch; (2) For variety, instead of setting sightseeing goals, set the kind of goals you might on a Saturday at home, to repair something, revisit a person or place, go to a park and see what's doing; (3) Lounge more than it is in your nature as a busy parent to do, and pursue a leisurely activity of the natives, such as reading the local newspaper and comics with the children all morning at a café, or watching local television. (4) Take shuttlecocks to the park, with an extra set in case another family's child seems inclined to join. (5) Go to an untouristy place where there will be lots of animated talk, such as a produce market at dawn, a small church dance or an auction of postage stamps. Every daily activity is an adventure.

Furthermore, you can't know what your children's pace will be until you arrive. The spontaneity of your approach adapts to their travel stamina and savvy.

So resist planning too finely. On the other hand, talk up the trip itself beforehand. Enjoy the anticipation. The Indian writer Ved Mehta has a chapter in his autobiography called "Dinner-Table School" that epitomizes how significant trip planning can be. After the evening meal was cleared away, Mehta's father described life in the West to the young boy and his three older sisters, growing up in India. Gradually, the conversations at night turned into an imaginary tour of the European countries and America with all the family packed into a big imaginary lorry. "We would see the night clubs of France and hear the music festivals of Scandinavian countries and American jazz bands all at one time. Then we would imagine ourselves to be tasting Italian spaghetti, French wines and American hot dogs."

Mehta continues: "What had started out as a narration of interesting experiences and then transformed itself into day-dreaming, now had assumed the charcter of serious study. My father bought some pamphlets and books on Europe and India, and after our meal he would read aloud in English, stopping only to explain various points in Hindi and color them with his experience."

Look at books with pictures of the places you will visit and talk about customs the children have met in story books or in the homes of their foreign friends. Think aloud how it will be to travel and to live with less. Practice scenarios of buying tick-ets at a movie theater, asking the whereabouts of the restroom, and an exchange at the post office. Is there an aspect of the culture the children are keen on already? A writer, a sport or custom? Try to make your itinerary meet that interest in some way.

When I took the twins to France, I chose Paris over a seaside cottage for several reasons. First, on this maiden voyage, for its predictability. Language could, in that great city, only surround you. Second, to avoid the expense of a car. Third, because it seemed appropriate to recreate the old-fashioned Grand Tour for bilingual children using the traditional materials—Paris and a hotel—of the olden days, when European cities were a finishing school for English-speaking youth. Fourth, if you have been to Paris as an adult, it may surprise you how congenial it is for bilingual children in any season, including August. Ignore in your mental slide show of Paris, the busloads of tourists, historical and culinary monuments, the Louvre, Montmartre, and the Champs-Elysées, where you would be hard pressed to find someone to converse with in French in the peak tourist season. Instead, think of the silent gates that open into quiet inner courtyards, the little restaurants with a dozen casual tables, bare except for Cinzano ashtrays, the food shops where the owners know the patrons by name. Paris has been and remains a conglomeration of villages (with the exception of, to my mind, the 8th *arrondissement,* which includes the Champs-Elysées), and retains much of its neighborhood intimacy.

My own training for the trip came from having live in Paris twice before, once, temporarily, in a hotel as a child with my parents, and once as a working girl living in a *chambre de bonne.* (The top floors of Paris apartment buildings are often segmented into rented cold-water maids' rooms.) From these experiences, I had both an image (that it's best to go native) and a philosophy (that a big city quickly becomes a village, if you let it) to follow. However, I must stress that it is not necessary for the parents to be familiar with the country they are going to visit—all that's required is imagination and a spirit of adventure. Since in my case months of scheming turned out as radiantly as I had hoped, let me present a rough model of a hotel stay in a big European city for you to evaluate.

First of all, the financial angle: To stay in a Parisian hotel for one month you have to have a little, but not a lot, more money than if you are going to camp as a family of three or four: No matter how the exchange rate fluctuates, expect modest hotel accommodations and car rental to cost about what they do in the States. Europe boasts more comfortable, reasonable, well kept and "interesting" hotels than America (the adjective interesting eliminates motels!). Select a two-star hotel so that it will be clean, have a proper reception desk, and be a place you will want to return to on other trips. In France, choose from the chain of independent, mostly two-star hotels called *Petits*

Nids de France; for a brochure, write the Hotel du Mouton Blanc, BP 132, 59403 Cambrai, France.

I selected the Hotel Lindbergh for reasons that apply universally when selecting your family's hotel: First for its accessibility to the Jardin du Luxembourg, that splendid combination of park, children's playground, and formal parterre, with fountains and sculptures, that sprawls south of St.-Germain-des-Prés. Anyone staying in Paris with children for either July or August, the calendar months our 32 days spanned, will bring children under 12 to the Luxembourg. We bought sailboats at a kiosk in the park, but on fair afternoons you can equally well rent one of the noble, tri-sailed vessels that Burton called the pirate boats. There are swings for two and a wooden kiddies' carousel, as well as a challenging children's playground, all for a few francs. There are also free attractions—big sand lots, runways, and several clean little wading pools (closed off from Paris's abundant poches).

Moreover, the Hotel Lindbergh was described by Fodor's guidebook as friendly and pretty. The hotel's owner wrote me immediately in answer to my questions about accommodations for my family and lodgings for the young Canadian, Geneviève, a former au pair who had agreed to stay near us during her coincident visit to Paris, and to babysit. The qualities a hotel must have, if you are to succeed in your language-centered holiday in a large European capital, are as follows:

Smallness. In a small hotel (the Lindbergh has 26 rooms), even if foreigners are communicating in English at the desk, you won't notice them because there is little traffic. In a Hilton you pay for luxury and get along with it such problems as queuing at the reception desk, waiting for the elevator, and floods of English-speakers. In a small hotel, when the elevator is busy, you can duck up the staircase. Emma and Burton made friends with all the young people at the reception desk at our hotel and the *valet de chambre* left them jokes in the arrangement of their toys and shoes when he did the room.

A salon with magazines and television. At home we have no television. Not only do my husband and I believe the absence is superior to the surfeit but, as is explained in chapter four, television in English is usually detrimental to a bilingual effort. But television seen abroad is a language vitamin supplement on evenings when we stay in. When I attended a Goethe Institute in a Bavarian village as a graduate student, the intermediate-level course had me memorizing endless formulas, but watching German television with my host family in their little sitting room, while they kept up a steady commentary about what passed on the screen, gave me my best "language lab." And, while European television may offer fewer choices than ours, it is less violent, and made more appetizing by few or no commercials. A hotel sitting room is a good way station between the hotel room and the world outside. One day, when Emma and Burton were behaving as though they had acute cultural sunburn, I decided they were suffering from overexposure to things public. We walked to the Bon Marché store at the end of the block, bought the hardest available jigsaw puzzles for children their age (60 pieces), and high-tailed it for home. While I read a novel in our room, they roamed from the beds to the floor to the reception desk, the salon and the hotel entrance. There were no ill-mannered antics and the hotel staff remained unruffled. People could not have been nicer at Eloise's Plaza!

A residential/commercial neighborhood. The hotel doesn't have to be in a quaint part of town, so long as there is active pedestrian street life as well as cafés, small stores and a pocket- or larger park. This probably does describe an older section of the city. In any city it is well to avoid the outlying areas, where you must commute to sights and the nightlife is nil. By crossing the street from the hotel, we were at the metro or bus stop and were only a short ride from the Louvre and Eiffel Tower. The Lindbergh was a block away from *two* of Paris's half-dozen children's bookshops.

An interesting neighborhood. Neighborhood selection is important because you are looking for more than a place to lay your heads. You want to treat the city as the local residents do, as a village. This is how you promote your children's language immersion in a tourist capital. It meant a great deal to my children that our hotel was around the corner from a park (the Place Sèvres-Babylone) with jungle gyms, sand, benches and flowers, where they were likely to meet Suzie, one of the café-owner's daughters, after supper. My children soon knew what cars were missing from the usual line-up by the front door, because at the Lindbergh we had delightful French doors opening onto a balconette over the street. They learned the names of several local dogs and often had conversations, at the Parisian grocery across the street, with a concierge, and at the three cafés (including the renowned Brasserie Lutetia) where we spread our favors.

A room with a private shower and seated toilet. Reserve your room with private WC in advance. A tub usually costs more.

A breakfast room. All *auberges* and inns have breakfast rooms; this is desirable in a hotel as well. For my children, eating croissants and hot chocolate in the *sous-sol* was another fun link to "our" hotel. When packing for a language-centered trip, remember the following:

Extra batteries. These are high-priced items in many foreign countries. Bring plenty in the appropriate size for your cassette recorder and/or radio. You will be buying story-cassettes for your children, and don't want them left hanging in the middle of a great yarn.

A picnic blanket. You must picnic to afford your long holiday. Picnic spots are also prime places to meet local people. Especially handy is a light, big, washable quilt.

A picnic thermos. A big thermos is useful, but my first choice is the smaller liter-sized ones, which holds just enough to wet everybody's whistle, but is not cumbersome.

A stationery case. Writing in the language (or dictating, if the children are preschoolers) is part of your trip plan. I carry a packet which I call my Executive Travel Kit. It contains a dozen useful supplies, including Scotch tape, scissors, a small stapler and a pocket knife.

Art sketch pads, felt-tipped pens and colored pencils

A few plastic bowls and cutlery. Even if you aren't going to camp, these can be handy. Bring a good Swiss Army knife too, to cut bread and fruit.

Also consider taking:

Paper dolls and art coloring books. Two paper-doll books published by Dover, Tom Tierney's *Great Fashion Designs of the Belle Epoque* and *Erté's Fashion Paper Dolls of the Twenties*, introduced us to French fashions. Another, *Antique French Jumping Jacks* by Epinal, gave us hands-on experience in assembling a traditional doll we saw repeatedly in French shops. *Uniforms of the Napoleonic Wars* became meaningful after a visit to the Musée de L'Armée at the Invalides. You can find these and other fancy paper dolls and coloring books with a range of historic references in museum shops and bookstores. Or write for a catalogue to Dover Publications, 180 Varick Street, New York, NY 10014 or to Bellerophon Books, 36 Anacapa Street, Santa Barbara, CA 93101.

Transfer figures. We mounted these on paper and used straws for handles to make a toy theater on the side of the bed. The theater was then stashed in an envelope for future use. Also take along some extra packs of transfers and stickers; they are light and portable and make good gifts for friends' children and park playmates.

Playing cards. With cards, you'll feel native in a café; or you can play in a restaurant and the waiters will appreciate that you are keeping your children occupied. A game of cards makes a wonderful icebreaker between the children and their new acquaintances. Bring several packs, including the special-purpose games like Old Maid. Bring a book on simple card games as well, provided your children are old enough to enjoy them.

Brush up on nursery games for under-sixes, including Go Fish, Old Maid, War Solitaire and Concentration. When brains are tired, play Toss the Cards in a sand bucket or circle drawn with a stick on the ground.

Other games, puzzles and toys. Knowing a language means knowing the geography of the land. What speaker of "American" can't find San Francisco and Miami on the map? Most toy and school-supply stores abroad sell educational map games and puzzles. For a child going to France you can invest in Jeu Paris Metro. Players visit all of the city's monuments on their cards by choosing the most direct subway lines and throwing the dice. The game introduces students to the sights of Paris and teaches them the subway system. It is available through Continental Books. From Jeux Nathan there are Bonjour la France, a game for two to six players in which the map of France, with its departments and regions, is reconstructed (age 10 and up); and a lovely puzzle, called France par départements, for ages eight and up.

Deutschlandreise, a board-game journey through West and East Germany, is also distributed by Continental. The board is a map of the two countries, and the object of the game is to find the shortest route to a certain city through the throw of the dice and drawing of cards. The game is an aid to learning the names and locations of 280 German cities, as well as famous rivers and mountains.

Children like to learn other *jeux de société* as well, because they provide a bridge with strangers and with older kids. Travel checkers or chess, mah-jongg or dominos come in fetching portable versions. In the train compartment or pension, you'll find partners and time for these games.

Instead of a toy chest, a child can take along a shoebox for toys. Think of other icebreakers for your child to have around other children, such as toy soldiers, miniature farm animals, pick-up sticks, a big bag of marbles with shooters and a collection of balls.

Lastly, hide away a few treats in your pocket. If you're in a guided tour or at the theater and your child grows impatient, your magnifying glass, game of jacks or mini-croquet set—whatever—saves the day.

Going abroad with just a few toys also means you have space for new ones relevant to the language and culture in which you are traveling. My children found it fun to be away from the things they had at home. I thought Emma might miss the contents of her wardrobe, but she didn't. Instead she developed into a highly observant window-shopper, comparing styles, colors and displays, and cataloguing which clothing styles went with each period in painting. Burton, who plays with toys a great deal at home, progressed from doing 35-piece puzzles to working, over two days, 150-piece puzzles.

How much language your child will learn while abroad depends on how much the child knows prior to going. The better the child speaks before the family travels abroad, the more, in general, he learns. At first he will find it peculiar to hear familiar words in an unfamiliar context, but the mind works skillfully and rapidly to move from passive to active knowledge. If your child knows vocabulary, syntax and idioms, having had a shower in the language before being immersed in it, every conversation becomes an effective learning session. If he knows only words and phrases, you must not let him drown in discouragement. Bacon put it this way: "He that travels into a country before he hath some entrance with the language, goeth to school, and not to travel." A teenager or older child going alone *must* have some language beforehand, otherwise his trip is likely to be an experiment in international misery.

Going native is every good traveler's goal. But it is elusive. "We are getting foreignized rapidly, and with facility," boasted Twain, in *Innocents Abroad*. How does going native happen? Kipling's Kim learned to be equally at home in two cultures. Kim liked to slip out of the walls of his British-style school and wander, dressed as an urchin, through the streets and markets of Bombay. He managed this first and foremost by having an ear for language. "Going native" should signify to you and your child fitting into the landscape as Kim did. It will mean seeking out and frequenting local establishments and lodgings. It will mean walking. "There is never a better way of taking in life than walking in the street," maintained Henry James, and in the older sections of European towns, streets invite the visitor to ramble. Above all, it will mean blending with the culture.

There are tricks to accomplishing this self-camouflage. If you are going to a country where your racial stock is not radically different, wait for your haircuts until you arrive, and go with the local styles. Wait, too, to buy the shorts, shirts and dresses for your trip until you arrive, unless the country is in Eastern Europe, where good clothes are exceedingly expensive.

Going native with children along is both hard and easy— hard in that you require more equipment if they are very young; their legs and attention spans are shorter than yours in most situations; and you want to be careful about eating from street stalls (perhaps avoiding them altogether). You don't want to endanger their health, of course, or the charm of the adventure. But blending is easy with children too, because you must use laundromats and look for parks and playgrounds, as local people do. Traveling as a family, you are already a little different from most tourists, who tend to arrive in ones, twos and bus-loads. You are going to prefer cafeterias and small *trattorie* to glamorous restaurants, and parks with swings and pedal boats to posh art galleries.

I remember Rome as a preteen tourist. In the late 1950s, sellers of souvenirs were so insistent at sights like the Spanish Steps that they swarmed and blocked the way, waving their cheap wares at us until we felt dizzy in the sun. In the Colosseum my brother joked that we needed a gladiator to defend us. I remember wishing at every monument in Rome that we had lived hundreds of years earlier; I felt hostile to the tourist-plagued present—which is the glummest way a traveler can feel.

Maybe the tourist trade is less hungry in Western Europe now and the hawking less abhorrent. But if you travel as we did to famous spots, you want to look and act as much like native sparrows and finches, as little like visiting pelicans, as possible. And you want to take home glimpses and observations that transcend the standard postcard views. That means keeping clear of tourist traps and channeling the children's interests to make their trip constructive.

Let's continue with other touring tips, for wherever you go:

Start slowly. Remember that you will have jet lag to overcome and that your children are not accustomed to the rhythm of being with you abroad.

Know your way before setting out for the day. Children's *bête noir* is getting lost, or trailing after lost parents. They will moan and groan at a mistaken detour of a few blocks but be indefatigable in following a path traced in advance like a military maneuver on a map. Besides the street plans of a city in the guides, there are flash-maps and manuals like *Recta-folder* that describe the location of every street in a city and the best subway stop for it. Let the children find the way!

Include the kids in the decision-making. Let even young children know the part of the day's program that you have pre-planned and let them take part in the planning. The disposition of funds should concern them as well. My children shared with me the wise and foolish things we did with our daily budget. When, ten days into our month, I felt confident that we could live within our limits, we bought toys, fancy pastries and went to see Gérard Philipe's *Fanfan la Tulipe*, all in one day. Another day, in the heady aftermath of a fashion parade of Balmain's winter collection, seen free of charge, we strolled in the pricey Faubourg St. Honoré and blew an exorbitant amount on juice and croissants. We lived the rest of the day on the small change from that one big bank note. The children understood that playing in the Parc Monceau was all the budget would stand that afternoon.

Frugality becomes a game of the trip. Carry a thermos instead of buying café drinks. Do hand laundry first thing in the morning, so it has all day in the shower stall to drip dry. Pick up plastic sacks from the store to wrap sandwiches in. Local people know free and inexpensive ways to have fun; try to find out what they are. Where do they picnic, promenade, watch practice sports matches and rehearsals, attend street fairs? Go where people are *talking* since you haven't come abroad to commune with the trees. We stepped out of the Louvre one Sunday (free admission day) with eyes full of treasures but ears whirring with a dozen languages. By lining up at the cordon where the

Tour de France was awaited, we enjoyed two convivial hours of sports talk and jokes with French cycling fans. Thirsty and with charley horses by the time the gleaming bicyles passed by, Emma and Bruton were also lively friends with a henna-haired, neat-ankled old lady who wore eye-catching Art Deco jewelry.

Here are some further practical suggestions:

Do amusement parks and children's parks on weekdays to avoid throngs.

Abide by the law of three. If it would take you one day touring to ascend the Arc de Triomphe, stroll down the Champs-Elysées and see the exhibit in the Grand Palais, spread these over three days and fill up your free time with child- and language-centered activities. Most cities have cartoon shows, revival films, children's libraries and (for older children) lectures and guided tours—all good language practice! In Europe, guided tours to craft workshops, artists' studios, historic homes and bakery kitchens are patronized by natives with a passion for history. (You meet a lot of provincial and out-of-town school-teachers, for example.) Listed in weekly entertainment guides, they offer something for everyone. And they don't feel like school, they feel like field trips. In Paris, the walking tours are advertised in *Spectacles de Paris* and *Pariscope,* the weekly pair of guides to entertainment, sold at magazine kiosks. Be adventurous! I had intended to take Emma and Burton to the zoo in the great park of Vincennes, at the eastern end of a metro line, but we got off a stop too late. I warned them the Chateau de Vincennes, where we found ourselves, was unfurnished and military in appearance. But our tour of the *donjon* was a hands-down success. They saw a moat, a daring escape plan and a winding staircase leading to where the king's children had lived at the top of a tower . . . because heat rises. Speakers of English only stay clear of guided lecture tours in a native language. You can take them! On the better tours, a guide unlocks a theme from the past, and the children identify historic persons and associations with the sight before their eyes.

Go to more films than you would back home. There is no other form of passive immersion like them. They are so easy! Go to theater and puppet shows as well. Choose the spoken arts over concerts, ballets, sports matches and circuses. Museum exhibitions are top priority only if the children can read labels or you have, for at least part of the visit, a non-English guide. To a child, buildings and picturesque spots become all too easily, as Eloise's Nanny would say, "Views, views, views." On this trip you want to maximize the *spoken word*.

Keep to the rule of doing nothing American. I was tempted, one day, to take the children to see *Pinocchio*, dubbed into French, which would have been fine, but am glad we went to *Tintin et le roi du soleil* instead. Before leaving Paris, we were able to buy a *Tintin* book and a cassette tape of the movie. Good! Tintin had never struck my funny bone, but my children are ready for it to strike theirs.

Frequent places where there are other children. Remember, your child will learn the most of a language in a playground or on a beach, listening and chatting. Children love a playground. One day, when the wind was too strong for our model sailboats, we walked back towards the hotel from the Tuileries. We went the long way, by the Invalides, with a stop for a *citron pressé*. The children were too tired to speak, after their long walk, but suddenly perked up and skipped through the gate of an unexplored playground. They "played off" their fatigue. Talk to parents on the park benches, so that when you go back you know a few habitués your own age. By the third evening of going to the park near our hotel with Geneviève, my children (who sometimes form an island of twinness when they feel strange) knew a child named Suzie, and, through her, several cousins. When Burton won a green paste ring at a fishing game in the Jardin d'Acclimation (at the Bois de Boulogne), he presented it to Suzie the next evening. The souvenir Burton asked for repeatedly was a tall shovel that, he explained, would do double duty in the sandboxes of Paris and gardening back home. That is how Emma and Burton experience their French too—as a handy tool for both sides of the ocean.

Hunger definitely loosens a child's tongue. Meals are an important part of your trip, and can be either a problem or a pleasure. Even if you are camping, it is a good practice to eat out once a day. Think of it as what the rabbits call "silflaying" in Richard Adams' animal fantasy *Watership Down*—going above ground, outside, to feed. Silflaying takes on vibrant meaning when you are making inroads in a new culture. Go back to the same restaurants if you can. Become a regular. Your child will rally to speak to the waiters and proprietor.

It is essential that you take your children to small, family-run eateries, where local people will take an interest in them, and engage them in small talk. One mother recalls handling the absurd food whims of her daughter (now grown and with a sophisticated palate) abroad. "Every summer we went to Europe for a month. When she was seven and at the stage of eating only a few things it was—¡caramba!—plain chicken and canned peaches in Spain." Learn to scan menus for what the child likes, regardless of its unconventionality: order a plate of roasted potatoes and two bowls of soup, if that's what he likes. European restaurants tend to be understanding of parents who order one *plat* for two children, so go ahead and do so, if you wish, rather than order more than they can eat. Still, it's part of the program to introduce them to a few native dishes, and to avoid advertising that you're foreign; if your children expect ketchup on meat, fish and potatoes, ask for a dish of tomato sauce on the side, instead of Americanizing a meal unmistakably with ketchup.

Order simply for your children. Ask waiters for small quantities. Even the way a hardboiled egg and the long, slender slices of French bread, decorated with tiny curls of butter, were served was a gastronomic adventure for my twins. We frequently made a dinner of eggs, bread and orange soda in Parisian brasseries. Then, as we might at home, we occasionally dressed up and dined out in good family restaurants—those the children discovered with me on our walks. La Cigale, next door to the hotel, led them to recite La Fontaine's fable, "The Ant and the Grasshopper," because of its name. Another, Le Récamier, faced onto one of the prettiest, least known little parks in Paris.

The children's eyes popped to see tuna fish, that old standby, artistically garnishing their omelettes at Brasserie Lutetia. The sauce chef, however, hung up his apron when he saw us coming!

Spend a part of the day quietly together. Take a siesta or have a slow breakfast at the hotel, and don't trek out until 11 o'clock. Tourists are so dogged: You should not imitate their frenzy on your quite different trip. Being a foreigner you are also a natural spectator. Emma, Burton and I often lingered to watch old men playing *boules* (French outdoor bowling), and chose cafés where people were playing *jeu de sous* (pinball). At one café, the children were riveted by an intense lunch-hour competition between two well-dressed government workers. After a while they parted, but within minutes the better player had slipped back into the café to practice for, we guessed, a follow-up match, thus affording us a great deal of amusement.

Give your kids a treat; splurge at least once on an unusual ride around the city, like the three-hour boat trip on canals and through locks in Paris (less touristy than the legendary bateaux-mouches, free for children under 10), or a horse-and-buggy ride in Lucerne. You can pay a taxi to show you sights in a smaller city, and children enjoy this kind of overview. If Henry James had a glorious recollection of the Place Vendôme from age two, as he claimed, I can only imagine it was because he was looking from the vantage point of somebody's comfy lap.

Wherever you are going to spend a protracted stay, write to official authorities, such as local, city or national tourist offices, in advance, requesting information about private and civic sports activities, day camps, library programs, and babysitters. The magazine *Loisirs-Jeunes* (36 rue de Pothieu, Paris 75007) can be checked for up-to-the-minute information on Paris events for children. The big September issue covers computer clubs, painting clubs, parks and sports that children can enroll in during the school year, while summer arts and crafts, dance and cooking lessons for children are publicized in the *Paris Free Voice*.

Moments of great or increased fluidity happen once or twice to a child when he is gaining his sea legs with a language. It is like switching on the ignition key that suddenly turns the engine motor over. In Iran on an exchange program when I was 16, my Persian progressed through sitting at long family parties and joking with the five children in my host family. I was tacitly expected not to answer the phone that rang in the office of the spacious Tehran house. But one day, six weeks into my eight-week stay, and feeling increasingly at home in the language, I dashed for it. The person at the other end of the line obviously thought I was one of the daughters. I took and wrote down in English translation a complicated message. After that phone conversation I was so elated. I felt confident that if the conversation had gone on I still could have held my own. It was as though the light had suddenly shone through a forest of words. I might yet stumble but if I proceeded carefully, I would never be in the dark in the Persian language again.

A moment like this lifts the student to a new level of fluency. A teenager from San Diego, camping across Europe with his parents and a 10-year-old sister, reported: "We liked a camp on a lake at the German-Swiss border and decided to stay an extra week. Then it rained. Every day my sister and I went to the spa and talked, swam and played ping-pong with German kids. My German, learned from listening to my grandmother, got strong. One day when my sister and I arrived back to the trailer camp where our minibus was parked, my mother said, 'Won't Grossmutter be glad to hear you're speaking German!' My sister and I were *jolted*. Neither of us had realized we *were* conversing in German. We were just continuing the conversation we had been a part of at the spa. German flowed in like a wave up a beach—we didn't have to measure out sentences anymore."

Learning a language is like pushing back and forth across a hill on skis until your ankles ache and your breath comes in puffs, then finally flying down the hill with eyes stinging pleasantly from the bright snow. That is where the sense of achievement and exhilaration comes in. The training runs are over, although the child must still work to keep his balance and negotiate the slopes. In *An Autobiography*, Agatha Christie describes the happy day when she found she could speak and read French fluently. She picked up a copy of *Memoire d'un Ane* and as she turned the pages, the book seemed to read itself aloud to her. "Great congratulations followed, not least from my mother. At last, after many tribulations, I knew French. I could read it. Occasionally I needed explanations of the more difficult passages but on the whole I had arrived."

A travel journal helps a child sort out all his new impressions. It also draws his focus away from souvenir-hunting and gives him a way to share with relatives, friends and classmates the high points of his travels. "I was there" becomes less important than "What I did, saw, thought and experienced there." If at all possible, the child who is bilingual should keep the diary in the foreign language. It can be written or you can dictate it. It can be translated orally later to share with friends who do not speak the language.

There are several different ways of keeping such a book. First, you can buy the old-fashioned kind of travel diary, with a page for each day and pages for keeping track of hotels stayed in, restaurants dined at, gifts and postcards sent home and so forth. There is something commanding about the headings on the pages, and the diarist tries to make an entry each day. Sheaffer Eaton markets various styles from plain to fancy; if you are unable to find them in your area write to Sheaffer Eaton Textron, 75 So. Church Street, Pittsfield, MA 01201. The Smithsonian Institution, the Metropolitan Museum in New York, and small leather-goods departments of fine department stores have handsome leather-bound travel logs. The Smithsonian's is illustrated with color reproductions of art works on a travel theme that come from its collections. A simple faux-leather log in burgundy with gold-edged pages can be had from Lilian Vernon Corporation, a mail-order firm, 510 South Fulton Avenue, Mount Vernon, NY 10550. Travel logs are small, usually about four by six inches, and generally conservative in appearance.

Alternatively, you can buy a blank book covered in fabric, and let your thoughts or your child's spill over from page to page. It is still important to keep the children to a daily habit of writing, say, before breakfast. The children's "What *did* we do yesterday?" is a good way to get them started, and a way of getting the most out of what fun you have had. The log-keeping gives your little gypsies a gypsy's *memory*.

A notebook bought locally, of local school paper, is amusing to use but may fall apart quickly unless you buy an unusually high-quality one. A local art store can sell you something better. You may like to have notebooks small enough to tote all the time. Should something interesting happen or be overheard en route, it can be entered in the log.

If you combine prose with drawings or photographs, you will come home with souvenirs that will be much admired by friends and can be brought to show-and-tell at school. Illustrations and captions can go on one side, text on the other, or they can be intermingled. A looseleaf is useful because it can be expanded as necessary. Buy the looseleaf beforehand and the idea is set. The writing can be done on the trip and the photographs filled in later. Children may enjoy decorating the borders only of the pages, or writing captions as well with a calligraphic marker. Even if most of the trip book is in English, the captions at least should be in the foreign language. We found that a spiral artist's sketchbook made a good trip book. We used fine, long-lasting sets of Eberhard Faber calligraphic felt-tipped pens for the written entries and a set of 24 medium-point watercolor markers (Marvy markers) for the drawings. Eberhard Faber also has sets of 24 colored pencils packed in hard plastic boxes, suitable for older children. For the photographs, even a young child can operate an automatic self-loading 35mm camera like a Minolta. All these give good depth of field and range of exposures, and are small. Or trip book photos can be taken with a Kodak disc camera. (35mm film can be developed anywhere, the discs in larger European cities.) Quality of the felt-tipped pens varies, so ask for these by name at your art or stationery store.

Tell the children to write the most important thing that happened each day. If they want more guidance, suggest they tell about someone they met, or a conversation they had. Open-ended ideas from you will elicit more thoughtful and enthusiastic writing than "Describe the balloon seller on the Rialto Bridge." You can explain the journal as a "letter to yourself," paraphrasing if you like, the Argentinian writer Julio Cortázar:

"Write for yourself, and when it's finished, sleep comes and the next day there are other things rapping on your windows, that's what writing is, opening the shutters and letting them in, one notebook after another" (from "Return Trip," in *We Love Glenda So Much*). Make clear criteria for which language is to be used. Encourage them to use a dictionary but impute no shame to tucking in the odd English phrase or word.

Nelly Sidoti, a linguist who specializes in the designing and teaching of Spanish afterschool programs for children (see Groups, chapter eleven), has her New York students from the second grade up write essays in Spanish. By the spring of their first year (after two lessons a week, followed up by the classroom teachers), the children are assigned to write on the same kind of themes they might be given in English, only briefer, 150 words or a page in length. They are encouraged to write their best Spanish but they may also fill in English as needed to express their thoughts. In a trip book, your child should do likewise. By being allowed to mix in English, the child will gain use of the foreign language. He will try to express important thoughts that in some cases outdistance his command of the foreign language, or require a technical word, he knows only in English. Remember, there is a tension in writing which the child does not experience in speech—not so much self-criticism concerning content and style as hesitation over penmanship, neatness, legibility and spelling; this can slow the travel-book writing down. It's as though an adult wrote with a quill that he had to dip into ink every few words. With the expression of their thoughts slowed down from speech, it is natural, not a sign of laziness, that children fill in with English more than when speaking.

A trip book can take another form if your children's exuberance does not lend itself to writing. John Holt, founder of Growing without Schooling, in Boston, wanted to share a trip he had taken to Sweden with American children who have never been there. "I have many young friends in the United States, friends that are children," he explained. He taped accounts—everything from sounds at the airport to greetings in the language he wanted recall—and sent the tapes back home to a family with whom he was close. I wish Emma and I had composed an aural "trip book" like this when we went to Louisiana. New Orleans was for us more a listening and speaking experience than a sightseeing experience or visual memory.

John Holt makes no attempt to romanticize or polish his recording; but tells it like it is. How did he know a tape diary would have such appeal to children? In part it is the verisimilitude of details that draws the listener in. Hearing sounds of the environment is *interesting*—one is stimulated by them. "I have heard everything," thinks the adult, "but imagine, this is the siren of a *Swedish* police car." "The man is going to fasten his seat belt now, and that foreign language must be Swedish," thinks the child. Asked point-blank what Holt's cassette taught him, Burton said, "*Ça me fait penser que je suis en avion*" (It makes me think I'm on the plane).

The last type of trip record I suggest is one sewn: a needlework appliqué or embroidery design, worked as a flat piece for hanging or to cover a pillow. This project suits particularly when you go to one place to stay for a long period of time. It can be done with less or more elaboration. Banners, wall hangings or bureau scarves appeal to children of all ages who can wield a needle and thread. The fabric is purchased locally, which is fun and good language practice. The taste in prints and colors and fabrics among countries is heterogenous, so the bits of fabrics and notions will serve as a permanent reminder of the trip.

Choose a lap-size area to work, and a plain nubby cloth such as sailcloth as a background. Cotton pieces are then turned under to make a hem all around and stitched on to make buildings and bodies of water, lamp posts and people. Younger children from eight to ten can make an appliqué with felt, buttons and ribbon, which do not need hemming. The child may find it most satisfactory to work from several postcard views. I have two appliquéd pieces like this. One shows the harbor of the island of Jelsa in Yugoslavia, the other a section of a Persian bazaar with yellow terrycloth chickens strung up, and a big pile of watermelons, included because just the right zigzag green fabric was found. A tube-shaped border with open ends, of a matching color, is sewn at top and bottom, and dowels are pushed in to hang the appliqué from the top and weigh it down at the bottom.

You have seen how people gather around an artist and easel set up at some picturesque spot. But they usually don't disturb the artist unless he is cleaning brushes or on a break. I have found that when working my appliquéd hangings many people stop to ask about them—not only other foreigners. The stitched souvenir becomes a conversation piece when the person making it wants it to be.

Guidebooks

You should read about the country you are visiting in a guidebook in *its* language. This may mean waiting until you go, since foreign-language guides are not readily available in the United States. If you do wait until your arrival, make a pointed effort to get a guidebook with considerable cultural information and also a children's guidebook (or geography). Nevertheless, by buying your guidebook when you are starting out, you can begin to peruse it during the trip from the States. Buy at least your road maps in advance, and set the children to routing the places they would like to go.

Michelins are a best bet if you want a guidebook in any of the four languages emphasized in this book, or in Dutch, because you can buy them in the United States. There are paperback editions of the Michelins in French for many European countries and capitals, Canada, and for all the regions of France. We find the New York edition wonderful for touring our home city. It supports the vocabulary I need to do it in French. You can take a German Michelin to Spain, the Loire Valley, Provence, the Riviera and Italy, as well as to German-speaking countries. There is an Italian edition for Italy, Spanish for Spain, and Dutch editions of *Belge-Luxemburg* and *Nederland*. There are Michelin camping guides as well, all available from French and European Publications (115 Fifth Avenue, New York, NY 10003) or from Michelin, P.O. 1007, New Hyde Park, NY 11042.

Nagel's guides are encyclopedic and will give you the greatest information on contemporary art, literature, industry and folkways, as well as sightseeing, theater, restaurants, hotels and music. French and German editions can be specially ordered from Hippocrene Books, 171 Madison Avenue, New York, NY 10016. *Blue Guides* to parts of Italy and France, are also meticulously researched and written for visitors who want immersion in history, art, archaeology and architecture. Write: Guides Bleues, 11 boulevard de Sebastopol, 75013 Paris. Baedekers are the other ultra-serious guidebooks, available in French, German and Spanish from Baedeker, Rosastrasse 7, 7800 Freiburg, West Germany. American edition *Baedeker's Travel Guides* to a vast number of countries are available in English here, as are the *Companion Guides,* which give detailed background information and entertaining stories on such popular places as the Loire, Normandy, the south of France, Florence, Rome and Venice.

Since traveling at a gentle pace is the only way to meet and talk with people, look (either in *Books in Print* or at the library) for guidebooks slanted towards walkers. *Long Walks in France* by Adam Nicholson is a magnificent eyeful and a balanced view of the French countryside. In the great tradition of British travel books, it neither praises nor damns but illuminates. With maps, selected list of restaurants, cafés and shops, a section of information and advice and one of chronology, the New Republic series, including *Pariswalks, Jerusalemwalks* and *Florencewalks,* walks you through the city's "private" streets, leaving typical tourist attractions to other kinds of guidebooks, and outdistancing most of them on both history and modern trends. Take advantage of the fact that your children have no preconceived ideas of what *must* be seen, and make a specialty of out-of-the-way touring.

Staying in One Place

A very good way to increase your options for a low-cost, linguistically intense trip abroad is to stay in one place. You spread the net for your children's friendships wide, and incise images of the trip more deeply in the memory. Your whole family can go abroad in a friendship program. Your children will adapt well; ask yourself whether you are as flexible as they. Some means of staying in one place are outlined here.

Staying with a Family Abroad

Travelers Home Exchange Club, Inc. (P.O. 825, Parker, CO 80134). Families can act as hosts for travelers abroad or arrange for exchange visits between their young people. Duration of exchange is up to the family.

United States Servas Committee, Inc. (11 John Street, Room 406, New York, NY 10038). Servas (which means "serve" in Esperanto) is an international system of hosts and travelers established to help build world peace, good will and understanding by providing opportunities for personal contacts among people of different cultures. Stays are of two or three nights but can be as short as a day. There is a small annual contribution to cover organizational expenses. No money is exchanged between travelers and hosts.

Chez des Amis (131 West 87th Street, New York, NY 10024). Publishes a directory of French families receiving paying houseguests through France.

Renting

Renting offers real savings on accommodations. You can stay in a near-luxury rental home or cottage off-season for far less than you would pay at an indistinguished hotel.

Villas International (213 East 38th Street, New York, NY 10016). Offers a wide selection of European rental properties, listing over 20,000 villages, cottages, apartments and chateaux. Separate brochures and fliers published on their properties in desirable resort locations in countries including France, Spain, Portugal, Italy, Switzerland, Greece, Austria, Germany, Yugoslavia and the Caribbean islands. In France, for example, housing is available not only the Riviera but in Chamonix in the French Alps. In Greece, a windmill in Rhodes, a villa in the Dodecanese Islands or an apartment in the Peloponnese can be had. Fully furnished apartments are offered in Paris, Florence and Vienna.

Price reductions are often available on rentals of one month or longer. Bookings are made through the New York office. Booking as far ahead as possible is advised since rental properties are frequently booked three to six months in advance. They also assist with flights and local car rentals. There is a choice of accommodations between luxury and budget. In Italy, thus, there are rural cottages near Florence, Pisa or Siena, or palatial apartments in Venice, on the Lido or near the Grand Canal.

Fédération Nationale des Gîtes Rureaux de France (35 rue Godot de Mauroy, 75009 Paris). A *gîte* is a room or cottage to rent, a private, self-contained unit, usually part of an individual's country home or, less frequently, a separate lodging on private property. *Gîtes* are all approved by the Federation and ranked as normal (at least a shower and water basin), comfortable (has in addition kitchen equipment and more stylish furniture) and deluxe (superior kitchen equipment, antique or more stylish furniture and a courtyard or garden).

Allo Vacances (163 rue St. Honoré, Paris, France). Lists real estate agents specializing in apartments, holiday cottages and villas.

For renting in a town you fancy you can also contact the appropriate civic authority. In France, for instance, you would write the Syndicat d'Initiative. Newspapers also carry ads of properties for summer rental; in France, notably *Le Figaro*.

Bellaglen Villa Holidays (62 Aldermans Hill, Palmer Green, London N13 4PP England). A villa-rental company that specializes in medium-priced rentals in two destinations on Italy's Mediterranean coast. Marina di Pietrasanta is close to Pisa and two hours by car from Florence on the Versilian Riviera and Principia a Mare is on the Riviera della Maremma farther south, halfway between Pisa and Rome. What is unusual is the naturalness of the settings and the untouristic quality of the resort and environs. The beaches of Principia are sand and set in a natural landscape of pine woods extending down the broad shore. Sitters are available, tennis, horseback riding and sailing. Bicycles can be hired to get about the quiet, flat towns.

House Exchange

With people curtailing and budgeting their vacations, this strategy for international travel, once a novelty, offers an important option for families. Even a modest home with a good location in the States can get you a resort apartment in Nice or mountain bungalow in the Austrian Alps. You can swap for two weeks or several months. You can become fast friends with people from the foreign culture where you lodge, or keep the arrangement more strictly a business one. You can go to a resort destination off-season—a second home that is unoccupied—or to a location so un-touristy that you will truly be immersed in the culture.

Homes are exchanged between two parties for a prearranged period of time. The understanding is that they are staying as invited guests. The more flexible you can be about travel dates and locations, the more chance there will be for a good match. Many exchanges are made between members not only of homes but of their automobiles. The responsibility of a home-exchange service is limited to publishing listings and mailing them to members. Don't be shy about contacting the owner of a home that seems superior to yours: they will be visiting your rented home or property, not purchasing it! Mail letters of inquiry as far in advance as possible. Write in *their* language and involve your children in the whole process. For example, the children can decorate the photocopied letter with a drawing or map that gives added information, or make a montage of photographs on the back.

There are no perfect formulas for success, but you should try to exchange the most complete letter of agreement possible about animals to care for, payment of utility bills, guest fees at the swim club, insurance and responsibilities. Your house is more idiosyncratic than you think. Leave notes on how everything works, and doesn't. Specify in advance anything—your stereo, the contents of the liquor cabinet—you don't want to "exchange."

Among organizations offering home exchange services are the following:

Hideaways International. (P.O. Box 1459, Concord MA 01742.) Puts out a directory of home exchanges that also includes rentals and yacht charters. Annual subscription for three issues.

Home Exchange International. (22458 Ventura Boulevard, Suite E, Woodland Hills, CA 91364; or 130 West 72nd Street, New York, NY 10023.) Arranges home exchanges in Europe as well as the East and West Coasts. In addition to the registration fee, there is a closing fee paid when the exchange agreement is signed by both parties. This is not merely a listing. It specializes in one-to-one home exchanges arranged on a confidential basis. The company has offices in New York, London, Paris, Milan and Sydney.

International Home Exchange. (P.O. 3975, San Francisco, CA 94119.) Publishes a directory of exchanges and rentals each spring and updates quarterly. Annual subscription includes the subscriber's listing.

Loan-a-Home. (2 Park Lane, Apt. 6E, Mount Vernon, NY 10552.) Offers a directory with supplement, listing rentals or exchanges primarily for academic families. Here is where to find the longer- than-a-month-or-two swappers.

Vacation Exchange Club. (12006 111th Avenue, Unit 12, Youngstown, AZ 85363.) Prints directories twice a year. Linked with Intervac International. Directory's symbols are time-consuming to read but the international representation is impressive.

Travelers Home Exchange Club, Inc. (P.O. 825, Parker, CO 80134.) Brings out a yearly directory with April supplement. Several possibilities are offered by this service: Home exchange; rentals (all rental agreements and exchanges of money are handled by members involved); rent or exchange listings (you advise you are interested in either type of transaction); foreign travel companion; vehicle exchange of motor homes, caravans and camping trailers; hospitality exchange (you offer your home to the club members you select and act as their host;

then, during your travels, you stay with them as their guests); youth hospitality (you act as a host for a visiting youth, whose family in return hosts your youth).

Worldwide Exchange. (P.O. 1563, San Leandro, CA 94577.) Arranges rentals and exchanges of homes as well as of yachts and recreational vehicles. A home exchange costs each party a finder's fee.

InterService Home Exchange. (Box 87, Glen Echo, MD 20812.) Has lots of European listings—claiming the most favorable exchange balance for France—and includes helpful guidelines for home swappers in their directory.

Pensions

Pensions are the most reasonable accommodations in Italy and every town and city has them. Through the Italian Government Travel Office, get addresses and make a reservation in advance. In the summer months it is essential to avoid the major cities that tourists favor if you want to speak Italian. To find a rental for several seasons, make a reservation in a pension in two areas where you might want to stay, a few days in each. Then explore for the rental in the following ways:

1. Through a real estate agency (agencia di proprietà immobiliare).

2. Ask at the local tourist office for a list of real estate brokers (agenti di proprietà immobiliare).

3. Get a map and walk around a neighborhood you like, looking for "For Rent" signs (the sign will probably say "*Da Affitare*" or "*Affittasi*").

4. Talk to the proprietors of small shops and restaurants.

Austria is a favorite travel spot for many Americans. For a booklet of small hotels in this German-language playground, write: Zentrale Buchungsstelle, Landes-Fremdenverkehrsverband, A-4010 Linz, Postfach 800, Austria. Request a list of those with child-care available, or kindergartens. For example, Salzkammergut in central Austria has numerous lakes, and the biggest, the Attersee, has several hotels with *Gastkindergärten* and *Kinderaufsicht*.

Another hotel that caters to families is the French Hotel Hameau (Les Ages, Chartier Ferrière, 19600 Larche). Their year-round, family-oriented program includes bread baking and *foie gras* making weekends, with courses taught by local farmers, along with lessons in horseback riding and tennis. Friday evening through Sunday afternoon. For the bread weekend, students prepare bread in the village oven. For reservations, write to Hotel Hameau, 218, rue St.-Jacques, 75005 Paris.

The French Consulate or National Tourist Office can alert you to other weekends that offer intimate contact with the French countryside and traditions, in which guests become temporary members of a family.

Study Opportunities

Opportunities for your older children to study, live and work abroad have increased dramatically in the last 25 or 30 years. In addition to using this list, consult the embassy or cultural organization for the country where your children's second language is native, for scholarships, group trips and study abroad programs. Your children, because they speak the foreign language, are the pick of the crop. There is no reason not to send a child off at 13 to a well-supervised program abroad. It should not be an extended first experience away from home, however. Can a parent go at the end of the child's stay to meet his or her new friends and possibly accompany the child home? Absolutely. It means a great deal to the young person in relating his new experience to home if the two worlds can meet.

American Field Service. International/Intercultural Programs, Inc. (AFS, 313 East 43rd Street, New York, NY 10017.) Homestay program to many countries. There is usually a fee but it is subsidized considerably by the nonprofit organization. Year (11–13 months) and summer (8–10 weeks) programs. Ages: 10–

12th grade at time of application. Existence of chapter in community no longer required.

American Heritage Association. (AHA, Marylhurst Education Center, P.O. Box 425, Lake Oswego, OR 97034.) Asia, Europe, Canada and Mexico. Group programs for students grades six through twelve in the Northwest. Summer and spring programs led by teachers with language and cultural orientation.

American Scandinavian Student Exchange. (ASSE, 228 North Coast Highway, View Suite, Laguna Beach, CA 92651) For Denmark, Finland, Germany, Norway and Sweden. Year or six weeks in the summer. Ages: 16–18, year; 15–18, summer. B and C+ grade average respectively required. ASSE provides cultural instruction on arrival.

De France. (P.O. Box 78, Choate, Wallingford, CT 06492.) A high-minded, extremely well-conceived program of French studies in Paris, while living with a Parisian family. This is combined with a choice of two three-week vacations *en famille* with French families, or one family stay followed by a bicycle camping trip. The three-hour morning course in Paris includes French performing arts, classes on ballets, plays, films, concerts and operas that can be seen in Paris during the season; a history of French civilization and French cultural life. Classes are devoted to helping the students use their time well outside the school context. Another unusual feature of the program is that it offers three courses at different levels of French language competence.

The Experiment in International Living. (312 Sutter Street, Suite 412, San Francisco, CA 94108; Brattleboro, VT 05301.) Summer and semester, ages 14–21. One to three years of Spanish or French required for countries where these languages are native.

Future Farmers of America International Programs. National FFA Center, P.O. Box 15160, Alexandria, VA 22309.) Three-, six-, and twelve-month agricultural work experience programs. Around-the-world (two five-month placements, six to eight weeks travel). Ages: generally grade 12, ages 18–24. The Work Experience Abroad program (WEA) is open to high-school seniors and college-age FFA members and alumni. As it is a work program, participants receive room, board and a stipend.

Iberoamerican Cultural Exchange. (13920 93rd Avenue N.E., Kirkland, WA 98033.) Guatemala and Mexico. 6-, 12-, 18- and 24-week programs; 12 weeks or more may be in one locality. Ages: High-school age to 30. Requirements of two years Spanish study or the equivalent. Six days of intensive conversational Spanish and cultural orientation are provided participants upon arrival in Mexico City.

International Summer Stays. An agent for North American Cultural Exchange League (IS/NACEL, 923 Southeast 26th Avenue, Portland, OR 97214). Programs to France, Germany, and Spain for the month of July or August. Ages 13–18. Two years of language study required. Program departure point is Chicago.

Kosciusko Foundation. (15 East 65th Street, New York, NY 10022.) An organization that promotes understanding between Poland and America. The foundation offers programs in Poland for Polish-Americans and sponsors many fellowshps, scholarships and so forth for Americans to study in Poland, and Poles to study in America.

Lions Club Youth Exchange. Has programs to Europe, Japan, Mexico and South America in the summer. 16–21 years of age, preference to 11th-graders. Recommendations needed from school officials.

Pacific Intercultural Exchange. (1356 Sunset Cliffs Boulevard, San Diego, CA 92107.) Host country is chosen by the participant, from a choice that includes Austria, Brazil, France, Germany, Japan, Mexico and Spain. In French-, German- and Spanish-speaking countries a language background is required.

Youth for Understanding. (International Student Exchange, 3501 Newark Street, N.W., Washington, D.C. 20016; 400 Dayton, Suite C, Edmonds, WA 98020.) Year and summer options are offered to a wide variety of countries. The host country is decided by the applicant. Scholarship and financial aid are available. To qualify, individuals must have good academic records and meet language requirements where applicable.

Language Camps in Canada and the United States

Annuaire de l'Association des Camps de Quebec.

This is an easy-to-use directory of about 125 camps for boys and girls, family camps and group facilities, with full information, including current prices. A map shows where all camps are located. Free from Canadian Camping Association, 1806, Avenue Road, Suite 2, Toronto, Ontario M5M 3Z1 Canada. Selections from it follow:

Camp Edphy. A summer and winter camp for children six to sixteen; with a strong sports program. Children and parents can also lodge together at the inn. (For brochures write to Edphy Inc., 100 boulevard des Prairies, Suite 103B, Laval, Quebec H7N 2T5 Canada.)

La Manoir Pinoteau. (Mont.-Tremplant, Quebec JOT 1Z0 Canada) A year-round family resort with a lodge and cottages in the Laurentians.

Les Chalets Française. (Box 62, Deer Isle, Maine 04627; Winter address: Box 6102, Fremont, CA 94538.) A camp for girls with a long tradition of offering an opportunity to learn French while camping in the spruce forests along the rockbound coast of Maine.

Institute Francile of Canoe Island Camps. (P.O. Box 185, Eastsound, WA 98245; Winter address: 2549 Sycamore Canyon Road, Santa Barbara, CA 93108.) Boys and girls from ten through fifteen come for two weeks to the San Juan Islands of Washington State for French language and culture and the usual arts and crafts and sports programs. French is taught at different levels of proficiency, and the program includes French cooking, folk dancing, singing and fencing in the morning.

L'Ecole des Ingénues. (3252 Peach Tree Road Northeast, Atlanta, GA 30305.) The school's summer program, Ingénues de Taos, is a unique summer camp-finishing school with sparkling accommodations, archaeological excursions, cultural events, sports, beauty and fashion classes and French cooking (roasting escargots on a stick and French pastries to eat with tea). This exclusive camp is linked with Directrice Anne Oliver's well-thought-out trips abroad. A native Frenchman teaches individualized French, especially vocabulary for travel, cuisine, fashion and greeting friends.

International Language Villages. (Concordia College, Moorhead, MN 56560.) Seven language villages sponsored by Concordia College, where children ages seven and up learn to live a language and its culture. Program includes a one-week session for seven- to eleven year-old beginners, two-week session for beginners and intermediates, and a month-long session. Each village has games identified with its culture—French *boules,* Danish *gymnastik,* and Finnish *pesäpallow,* for example. Folk dancing, cooking, drama, folk singing and the publishing of a village newspaper involve more use of the language. The languages of the villages are: Danish, Finnish, French, German, Norwegian, Russian, Spanish and Swedish.

Language Camps in Europe

Ask for a book on summer-camp possibilities for children from your book importer. The French one is Jacques Bonnet's *Guide du Mercredi en France et des vacances scolaires* (Garmier Frères, 19 rue des Plantes, Paris). Here are some possibilities:

French:

Brillantmont International School Summer Course. (Avenue Secretan 12-18, 1005 Lausanne, Switzerland.) A Camp on Lake Geneva having half days in French conversation and the study of civilization, culture and cooking, as well as sports. For girls 13-18.

Chevallet. (Contact Cecile Arnett, Director, 675 Water Street, New York, NY 10002.) Chevallet, Madame Arnett's family home since 1595, is set on a 600-acre estate. She provides 18 French and American children with an educational and recreational adventure including hiking, field trips, horseback riding, tennis, swimming, traditional cooking and—naturally—speaking French.

Loisirs de France Jeunes. (30, rue Godot de Mauroy, 75009 Paris.) A system of *"centres de vacations"* on the seaside and chalets in the mountains: for children 6-12, 9-13, and also for adolescents. The centers tend to be small—40 to 80 beds, and a family atmosphere is stressed. There are also winter camps of skating and skiing near Grenoble.

Prealpina International School Summer Camp. (1605 Chexbres, Switzerland.) For girls 11-18, in a village near Lausanne on Lake Geneva. Intensive study of French for foreign students is combined with a program of excursions and sports.

French/German/Italian:

TASIS Summer Language Program. (American admissions office: 827 Promontory Drive W, Newport Beach, CA 92660.) Summer programs conducted by the American School in Switzerland (TASIS) of two four-week sessions of intensive French, German, Italian and English on the TASIS Lugano campus. Art, theater, activities and travel in multi-lingual Switzerland. Le Chateau des Enfants is their international summer camp for children ages six to twelve. French and English (whichever is the foreign language) are learned.

International Camp Counselors Program/Abroad. (YMCA of Metro New York, 422 9th Avenue, New York, NY 10001.) ICCP/Abroad is the outbound portion of the ICCP of the YMCA. Youth are placed in holiday camps throughout the world for a several-month period. The American counselor pays travel costs and the camp provides room and board during the session. Some camps also provide pocket money, domestic transportation to camps and other benefits. The French camps require all counselors follow a special one-week to ten-day training course in late June, called *la stage*, before counseling. Applications are submitted between January and March for the coming summer. Camps are in Austria, Colombia, France, Germany, Greece, Hong Kong, Israel, Italy, Netherlands, Portugal, Switzerland, Tunisia and the USSR. Speaking ability in the language is required.

Nacel Cultural Exchanges. (130 North Terrace, Fargo, ND 58102; 923 Southeast Avenue, Portland, OR 97214.) Besides its Summer Hosting Program (see section above on visitors in the home) for American families, Nacel has since 1974 had a Summer Discovery Program for American teenagers. It is open to teenagers 13 to 18 who wish to spend four weeks with French families. There are chartered trips for July and August, departing from Chicago, Preference is given to those whose families have participated in the Summer Hosting Program by hosting a French teenager. A working knowledge of French (two years of instruction is indicated) is required, confirmed by a recommendation from a French or German teacher. On the trip to and from Europe, the young people are accompanied by American teachers who serve as chaperons. The chaperons stay in France during the month-long stay. Students call chaperons if they need advice or help in adjusting, or may also call the Nacel office in Tours.

International:

NRCSA. (National Registration Center for Study Abroad, 823 North 2nd Street, Lower Lobby, Milwaukee, WI 53203.) Arranges a wide variety of academic, sports, cooking, camping, riding and other study and vacation experiences, most with language immersion. Some schools in their network accept students as young as 13 or 14, but most are high-school age. The agency works with schools in Latin America and Europe, representing a foreign institution and publishing directories about schools. Length of abroad time varies form one week to one year, and normally includes tuition and living with a family with half or full pension, or in a hotel. Eighty percent of their business is in Latin America.

TASIS Summer Programs. (The American School in Switzerland, CH 6926 Montagnola, Lugano, Switzerland.)

Language Programs. Two four-week sessions of intensive French, German and Italian for students 12-18. Students select one language per four-week session, at the beginning, intermediate or advanced level. Students also participate in art, drama or music in the language in addition to classes. Well-developed program attracts an international community. Many excursions and optional weekend trips take advantage of the school's southern Swiss location.

Le Chateau des Enfants. An intensive educational summer camp offered in two four-week sessions for children aged 6-12 from many nations. Conducted by American and French bilingual teachers, the program aims to give children experience in international living and acquaintance with a foreign language. The children hear English and French all day and also study it (two hours of daily lessons in the foreign tongue). Language is reinforced through drama, arts and crafts, sports, games and activities. The children are taken on excursions, including visits to castles, funicular rides, boat trips and overnight camping trips. Expensive.

International Language Villages. (Concordia College, Moorhead, MN 56560.) Biking adventures for ages 16-20, departing from Minneapolis. French Abroad program takes place every summer. Spanish, Swedish and German Abroad, every two years. Winter travel to Russia likewise every two years. Knowledge of the language is required. The backpackers and Russian travelers are encouraged to speak their respective languages whenever possible. At the end of the bike trips to France or Spain a Peugeot 10-speed touring bike or Beistegui Hermanos bike comes home with the student on the plane as a souvenir of his or her accomplishments. The tours include two four-day family stays and a big city tour. The Russian trip is scheduled for the winter at a time when fewer tourists are in Russia and cultural life, such as the Bolshoi, is in full swing.

Goethe Institute. (c/o Goethe House, 1014 Fifth Avenue, New York, NY 10028.) The Goethe Institute has since 1983 offered two three-week programs of trips, sports, games and language study, in July at the castles of Mossingen Schwab, Altensteig-Schwarzwald, near Stuttgart, and Bieberstein, near Frankfurt, and on modern premises at Versmold-Teutoburger Wald, near Hanover. Course members are 14-18. The Goethe Institute provides accommodations for course members but not for members of the family. The idea is for students to go alone. As in other Goethe Institutes, placement tests put students in appropriate levels.

International Courses of Modern Languages

Courses for Young People in Spain. Accepts children from 9 to 19 as boarding students. Combines language study at a beginning to advanced level with other cultural activities, such as theater, folk music and excursions. It is held at the Duperier Youth Institute in Avila, one hour's drive from Madrid and Segovia, and is sponsored by the Ministry of Culture. Classes are mornings, 9 o'clock to 12, and afternoons from 5 to 6 weekdays, and Saturday morning, with an excursion Sunday. The month-long session occurs twice, in July and August. Four levels of instruction, 200 students. Write the Spanish Embassy in Washington, D. C. , or Institute de la Juventud, Calle Ortega y Gasset, 71, Madrid, Spain; also, Residencia du Perier, Avenida de la Juventud, S-N, Avila, Spain.

Spanish Language Courses for Children. Organized by the Parvulario Mickey (Mickey Nursery School). Conversation, sentence practice, songs and games. 30 children maximum. No previous knowledge of Spanish required. Classes are 9 o'clock to 1 o'clock, in an attractive chalet. Pupils are lodged with Spanish families who have children the same age. Every week the parents are informed about their children's health, behavior and eating habits. Mothers take them to school and fetch them home. Most host families have children who attend the Parvulario during the school year. For ages 8-12. Address: Calle Impresor, Jose de Orja, 8 (Chalet), Valencia, Spain.

Atlantis Kingdom America. (AKA, 43865 Lakeview Way, P. O. Box 777, Foster, OR 97345-07777.) Programs to Japan for one year; also, sister school program. For high-school age students with good academic record.

German-American Partnership Program. (GAPP, 1014 Fifth Avenue, New York, NY 10028.) Group exchanges of high-school classes for four weeks in Germany. A sister school program established by the Goethe Institute. Some grants are available.

World Experience. (W. E., 14627 East Los Robles Avenue, Hacienda Heights, CA 91745.) Year and semester placement for 15-18 year olds to Latin America and Europe.

Au Pair Positions Abroad

This is for a child who is at least 18. He or she agrees to stay a minimum of three months (but usually no longer than 18 months), and can take language courses for foreigners during her stay. In France, and some other countries where au pair jobs are regulated by the government, her duties must not exceed five hours a day and her work schedule must allow her enough time for her studies. (See chapter three for additional discussion of this.)

Even though she is required to take language classes, an au pair is expected to have already a working knowledge of the language. She receives an allowance and is expected to pay for her trip to and from the country. Request from the Embassy or Consulate of the target country a list of agencies that place au pairs. The agencies can also help by making arrangements for language classes before the person leaves the United States.

Camping

Europe is well organized for camping trips. Since this is a popular way for Europeans of all classes to travel, camping is in effect a way of going native. There is no better way to meet non-English speakers than to spend a week at a continental campsite. Tents and the relaxed pace of living make good neighbors. You don't have to limit yourself to the boonies—even Rome has a laudable campground (Tiber Camping, Km. 1; 4000 Via Tiberina).

If you want to travel in a mobile home, Cortell Holidays arranges rentals. Cortell also arranges car rentals. Contact them at 3 East 54th Street, New York, NY 10022. Check the 800 listings of the telephone directory for regional offices in Atlanta, Chicago, and Los Angeles.

The number of excellent guidebooks to camping sites reflects the high status of this kind of touring in Europe. The British Automobile Association publishes a biannual guide, *Camping and Caravanning in Europe*. This covers 4000 sites in 18 European countries and gives detailed information on facilities. You can order this from the British Tourist Authority, 64 St. James Street, London SW 1A 1NP, England. From the Camping Club in England comes *Where to Camp in France* and *Where to Camp in Spain*. These can be ordered from K. Spencer Agency, 1 Warwick Avenue, Whickham, Newcastle-on-Tyne, England. In the United States, Prentice-Hall puts out *Europe under Canvas*, another comprehensive guide.

In Europe, Michelin publishes *Camping, Caravanning France*, and ADAC Verlag (D-800 Munich 70, Baumgartenstrasse 53, Postfach 700 126, West Germany) offers both *Campingführer* and *Familien-Ferien*. The latter describes places to stay with your children that have planned activities. They separate into categories of mountain and seaside. Eight prepared postcards are provided to fill in and send to the holiday accommodations that attract you.

10
Living Abroad

Whither, O splendid ship? . . . Whither away, fair rover,
and what thy quest?
—Robert Bridges

Two Worlds

Opportunities to live abroad abound. Recognizing the advantages of working in the "global village," many corporations have manufacturing and/or retailing units in other countries. Banks, oil companies, computer manufacturers and export-import firms are just a few of the private sector businesses that send staff abroad. In the public sector, international agencies, the State and Defense Departments, and universities often require living abroad.

If you have an opportunity to live abroad, take it. Setting up in a foreign land touches a person for life. If you remain abroad for more than a year and enjoy it, part of you never wants to return stateside. Immersion in a foreign culture brings bilingualism to full fruition. As we shall see, partaking of two cultures can raise a problem as well as incur rich rewards, but it is the problem of individuation—of a duckling who is *sure* to become a swan. Children returning to the United States have acquired new manners, a different way of doing things, and perhaps a different point of view about the world. They are oblivious of television shows, peel an apple with a fruit knife, prefer a fountain pen to a ball-point, and have a beautiful accent in a language previously unstudied in school. What's more, these young people with a *je ne sais quoi* are likely to be rather indifferent to the conformist impulses of peers, to make friends across age and clique lines, and to pursue clear-eyed their own futures. We are made resilient, broadened, intellectually awakened by living abroad: Thus it is a "problem," an opportunity and a privilege.

People in the entertainment business have often benefited from living abroad, so let's turn the spotlight onto two film stars. First, the dancer Gene Kelly. He learned French working in France, because "I had to, in order to communicate with my Parisian colleagues" Although Gene Kelly is not an example of a bilingual upbringing, he became bilingual as an adult. He says, "I can assure you that just the learning of another language has opened many doors of knowledge and experience to me—plus enjoyment." He quotes a French adage for what it has meant to him to work in France using the language: "*Si on connait la langue de son voisin, on possede le clef de sa maison*"; to know the language of your neighbor is to possess the key to his house.

Another star who feels at home almost anywhere is Charlotte Rampling. She was the daughter of a British army colonel, moving from base to base throughout Western Europe. One of her father's postings was at Fontainebleau, outside Paris. Here, in three years, she learned to speak fluent French. "I was a reserved child," she recalls, "but, with all the uprooting, my sister and I had to make new friends—and speak their languages." Married to Jean-Michel Jarre, the French composer, Rampling is raising her own children to speak French and English. "The reason is not an intellectual exercise," she says. "It reflects more than a personal desire on my part and Jean-Michel's to have the children speak our native languages. I see my children's bilingualism as a monumental flexibility, preparation for the cosmopolitan existence I recognize as the best legacy I had."

Although most families manage to live abroad because an employer sends them, if you have no such billet you might consider fashioning your own job exchange or unofficial sabbatical. The Mackenzies, high-school teachers, "invented" a sabbatical year to Switzerland when their children were two, five, and seven. They look back on 1965 as "the most romantic year of our marriage. Granted, we lived close to the bone," John Mackenzie says, "but we do the same at home. The hard part is to detach yourself from home for a year in the first place." Another family, a medical librarian, his wife and their nine-year-old son, "took off" when they found among the American Library Association's job listings a chance for a two-year job exchange in Germany. "It was a nearly seamless exchange," the librarian says. "The other librarian had a Volkswagen too, many of the same books and the same awkward but usable knowledge of English that we did of German by the time we arrived in Frankfurt."

At 21, Judith Bastanelli, graduate of a New England college, went to live in Paris, where she met and married a Corsican photographer. He being as curious about her homeland as she was enthralled with his, six years later they moved to the United States. Pierre became a hospital photographer and the Bastanelli daughters, Irene and Christine, were born in this country. "I was determined that this 'misfortune' should not rob them of their French heritage," says the mother mischievously, explaining why, even though now far from contact with France, she spoke only French to the babies. Later, after the parents' divorce, when Christine was five and Irene seven, Judith thought English "was crowding out their French," so she took both daughters to France for a year. "This was probably the final reinforcement, which had the lasting effect I now enjoy," says Judith Bastanelli. "We lived in Bordeaux, where Irene and Christine went to the 'cours préparatoire' and 'C.E.1' (equivalent to kindergarten and first grade), and suffice it to say, the year was fun and a success." Where did the adventure money come from? "I went on sheer determination," replies Judith immediately. Although I now work as a nurse's aide and give sewing lessons, during the girls' elementary-school years I did not even earn a salary. My success is obviously due to my total commitment to the cause. And I know how to live on nothing! When I took the girls to France I sublet the house, we bought no clothes, and ate very economically. When we traveled, it was with a backpack and tent."

If language is the gift you give your child, customs and manners of the second culture are the wrapping and the ribbon. In that other country, what makes people laugh? How do they conduct themselves on the commuter train, at the butcher's, at a neighbor's for tea? This is grammar too; through culture language achieves many dimensions. Living abroad as a child is a glorious beginning to world citizenship. It has great staying power and is extremely formative. Dr. Mary S. Calderone, the well-known psychologist, relates: "In Paris I spoke English to my parents (Clara and Edward Steichen) and French to everybody else. I was ten years old when the war broke out in 1914 and we were refugees to this country. At the time I left France, in my village school, I was just finishing the "times-eight" tables. Presently I find myself dreaming in French, and there is no question that I multiply in French up to the 9's after which I automatically switch to English!"

Growing up bilingually by dint of living abroad means becoming intimate with two cultures, that is, bicultural. Children who have lived abroad are shaped by the different world within them in unseen ways. Paul Chattey, a young archaeologist attached to the Alaska State Parks in Anchorage, grew up fluent in English and Spanish, in several overseas American Foreign Service colonies, where his father was in the diplomatic corps. "I don't remember learning either language," he says, "only having experiences in each." Being bicultural is Paul's most prized experience, one that, he says, continues to fascinate and perplex him as a grown man: "It is something like being ambidextrous. I have a preference, determined by my parents and my education, but am generally comfortable in either."

Paul understood early that, as a child, considerable freedom would be afforded him as a non-native speaker: "I made the effort to speak Spanish without making it seem difficult." He sensed people's pleasure when he spoke in Spanish on the streets. English was the language of responsibility. Grammar had to be studied as well as spelling. It was the tool that he used to learn other lessons. His Spanish was more freeflowing. A spate of lessons came only when he was eight or nine, when his parents recognized that he was illiterate in Spanish, except for what he had been able to teach himself and transfer from

English. He describes his dismay at having to suffer through verb drills, conjugation exercises and spelling lists. "I really preferred to speak and hear Spanish and experience its soft melody and subtle inflections, which were impossible in English. While English was for use at home, with friends and in school, Spanish was a street language."

While Paul's parents attended the receptions and cocktail parties of the diplomatic corps, Paul spent "a good deal of time in a warm kitchen or on a back porch at sunset, learning how to cross myself, sharing my coloring books, hearing stories of neighborhood heroes and finding out about our servant's families. As a Protestant I had some fascination for our Catholic maids and cooks. Their stories of saints and the power of confession entranced me. I heard their gossip about other households with patent relish. I learned quickly to get up early for a black-beans-and-rice breakfast with the milkman, who brought our milk supply on horseback, in a pair of five-gallon cans. Sometimes he would even let me ride his black horse around the house. By the time I was nine or ten, I learned to enjoy going to large markets alone or with a friend. The color and excitement made me fee as if I'd come to a circus. Everyone seemed to have mysterious things to do; there were exotic things for sale, like meat cooked in front of me, and the people selling their wares seemed to belong to a greater unity."

English was for use within Paul's family. An only child, he drew upon whatever came his way to flesh out the American culture upon which his English was built. He read *The Ladies Home Journal, McCall's,* his father's engineering journals, *Time* and any children's magazines that were sent him from the States. American comic books were not available in the house. Nor did they listen to the local radio stations, and there was no television. The language Paul favored for reading was English. Because English was his more literary language, he became very concerned about writing and spelling correctly.

Vacations in the States came every two years. Paul visited his uncles' families scattered in the American South, and spent several weeks at his grandmother's, whose small Texas town, Paul recalls, "was made even more curious to me." The boy on home leave developed a certain determination, striving to relate his two worlds. "Language often failed me at these times. There were wonderful things all around but I had to reckon with little local interest in the language or country from which I had lately come." He learned to keep his thoughts more or less to himself, but far from being fettered, separateness made him sensitive to other people's feelings, "because my own seemed impossible for them to relate to." Returning from stateside vacations, Paul found his experiences equally impossible to describe to his Hispanic friends and contemporaries. The United States was a mystery to his Latin friends as it was, on a certain level, to Paul.

Eventually the two cultures did blend together in a comfortable proportion, Paul believes, that leaves him "room to navigate experiences in each". He adds, "Only in moments of extreme stress do the Latin and American cultures assert their own identity. Shock and hurt, insofar as I deal with them internally, are not completely soothed until they are understood in both languages."

Because Paul's parents gave him the freedom, encouragement and stimulation to explore both cultures, he eventually incorporated in himself good points of each. Moreover, through exposure to them, Paul was able to find the footing of his career path—anthropology and teaching. Says Paul, "I treasure both sides of my culture. They provide an edge to my life and provoke and stimulate me. I would miss either to the core if it were not there."

Jonathan Wylie lived in Roussillon in southeastern France from 1950 to 1951 because his father, Laurence, a Haverford College French professor, wanted to find out at first hand about modern French country life—the basic culture in which the language is embedded. He also wanted to help Americans understand the French, and to that end wrote a book about Roussillon, a great and original classic called *Village in the Vaucluse*. There is a picture of Jonathan at age five in the book. A photograph of David, the younger son, is on the cover of the later, paperback editions.

All children who live abroad learn the language, but they respond to the stimulation differently. Laurence Wylie marvels at the great divide between how his sons, two years apart in age, took in the French language. The younger son, David, was more adept in nonverbal routes to communication. "David learned with any means at his disposal," where Jonathan "is an academic type and always has been." David started speaking from the first day in the French environment, when his communication was almost all mime and nonsense ("He hardly knew what he was saying!"). David was more open to people, less academic in his language acquisition approach. Jonathan was more methodical and purposeful about it. "When I asked Jay [Jonathan] when he would start speaking French, he said as soon as he had learned one more word—and that is just what he did."

By the end of the year, when they were three and five respectively, and again, after a second trip, seven years later, the boys preferred French to English. Back home they maintained French fluency differently too. "With David it was easy come easy go," Professor Wylie recalls, "When he didn't have contacts anymore there was no point. But Jay, who learned in a bookish and thoughtful way, retained French. After they came back at ages ten and twelve, they had good friends left behind in the village. Once a month they corresponded with them by audio tapes. I could see David's fluency going. One day he couldn't talk. It had disappeared. Whereas Jay read, talked about French and in it with me—and hung onto it. This was a personality difference. We shouldn't expect all children to do alike. If we want to reinforce their maintenance we have to think of personality too."

The family's return to France occurred in 1957, when the father had another sabbatical. Jonathan was then 11 and had just graduated from sixth grade. Professor Wylie now wanted to study a contrasting sort of village, devout in religion and to the right of center in politics (Roussillon had voted Communist). He chose Chanzeaux in Anjou.

Now a professor of anthropology at M.I.T., Jonathan Wylie has written an engaging, unpublished essay about living abroad as a fieldworker's child. Generalizing his own experience, he suggests that "a child's initial sense of *dépaysement* is worse than an adult's, since it is unbuffered by such intellectual constructs as 'another culture' and by such exercises as keeping a journal . . . . But things are easier for a child when the initial shock is past. Without really understanding them, I internalized French ways rapidly and thoroughly, learning French culture without having to learn much about it."

The Wylie boys were not merely the only foreigners attending their local Catholic school in Chanzeaux but the only Protestants. The father had to get permission from a bishop for them to attend. Yet they moved into the radically different school environment well. Because they were living a comparison, they developed a critical edge on schooling. Jonathan recalls, "As the initial shock wore off, I came to like the Ecole St. Joseph better than the Friends' School. The rules were clearer, for one thing. In Haverford, if you misbehaved by getting too rowdy in class (just how rowdy was that? It was hard to say) you would be warned that you were being unfair to the other kids . . . . In Chanzeaux there was no rowdiness—unless M. Bédoin left the room, of course; and then if you chose to talk or pass notes or even leave your seat you did not have to fear a classmate's betrayal later."

At first David and Jonathan were seated with the youngest of *"les grands."* Jonathan's ambition was to be seated with the boys his own age. This took several months, and of course required learning French. "Whatever the grown-ups said, my command of French did not come back magically from the year in Roussillon. I worked hard at it, and took the grammar lessons seriously. (Assiduous reading of *Tintin* comic books helped a lot, too). David, being a gregarious soul like my father, at once began speaking something that gradually approximated French more and more closely. As in Roussillon, however, I said as little as possible for weeks, wanting to speak correctly if I spoke at all . . . . By the end of the year our French was fluent and accentless, but sometimes awkward . . . . David has forgotten a good deal of his French. I remember most of mine. Probably because I was just old enough to retain in an adult way a language I was just young enough to learn in a childish one. This must be one of the few advantages of puberty."

Even if a child does not grow up to be an anthropologist, living abroad bilingually teaches him to size up human situations, gives him moral discernment. Mary Vreeland's mother was an American college student working at a summer resort in California when she met a Dutchman returning from work in Indonesia. They fell in love and off she went with him to Europe. English being the language they had in common, when Mary and her sister were born, that was the language spoken at home. Until 1939, when Mary was 14, home was Hamburg, Germany. Therefore it was German they spoke with all their playmates, and when they were school-age, both attended German public schools. But Mr. Vreeland was a Dutchman; perforce Dutch was viewed as a necessity too. Mary was induced practically by royal command to strengthen her Dutch. She says, "When I was visiting my grandmother in Holland one spring, I came down with the mumps. The rest of the family went off for a walk in the park, where they saw Princess Juliana riding on horseback. I was so jealous of their luck that I embroidered a silk hankie and sent it with a letter, in English, to the Princess. Several weeks later I received a thank-you note from a lady-in-waiting, asking why a little Dutch girl would write a letter in English and hoping that the next letter would be in Dutch. I never did learn to read and write Dutch as well as English, but had I tried, I doubt the lady-in-waiting would have detected that I was a little American girl, as well as a Dutch one." Fluency in German and Dutch gave Mary insight and a sense of being unique; it did *not* fill her with foreign ways; to the contrary. "You feel an immediate kinship with anyone who is a foreigner like yourself," Mary stresses. "You feel a healthy detachment from the mainstream of the society in which you live. In my case it was a detachment from Nazism, which dominated the society of Hamburg when I was growing up."

If you can, go abroad with your children for the first time, as these families did, while the children are young. Only in the last year or two of high school, should you weigh carefully the consequences of sending your daughter or son to a native foreign school. Tutoring, home study or a bilingual or English-language school may serve this young person better. If possible, delay your move abroad until her or she graduates so that the first year of your adventure becomes a fruitful break before college.

There is a great advantage in taking a child abroad when young: the younger child takes to a second language far better than a teenager. Heidi Mastrogiovanni, the child of a German mother and American father, spent most of her childhood and early adulthood in Connecticut. Most of her mother's relatives were in Germany, so her connection to her native country remained strong. As a result, Heidi lived with her grandmother in Regensburg, a city in Bavaria, at two separate times when she was growing up. Now a professional actress in Manhattan, Heidi describes how much easier it was to don her German cloak when very young than in later childhood. "The first trip, when I was two, I picked up the Bavarian dialect in a matter of days from the cousins and other children I spent my days playing with. My father came to stay with us for a few weeks during his vacation, and the story is that I greeted him at the airport by crying and saying 'I want to go back to grandmother's' in German. It seems I had forgotten most of the English I had learned up to that point. When we returned to the States, I promptly forgot German, and then relearned it when we returned to Germany three years later, again picking it up rapidly from the other children. The *next* time I went to Germany was on a family visit a number of years later. I distinctly remember wondering why it seemed that I was having difficulty relearning German. It didn't happen overnight, as it had the other times." The younger child is vastly more apt to become fluent at the developmental level rapidly and achieve a native accent, by "osmosis" in the new surroundings. It is also true that upon the young child's return to American his second language leeches away more quickly if not reinforced, but that problem can be dealt with, and will be addressed at the end of this chapter.

If you are lucky and have relatives abroad, an alternative is to send your children off on their own for a year's visit. This too can often happen before the children reach their midteens. If the child speaks some of the language already, there is little risk that people will condescend; he will be accepted as "one of us," not only ethnically and by family ties but linguistically. In addition, the child feels less like a stranger. If you start your children off on the right foot with kin by giving them the means to communicate, they *can* (*pace* Thomas Wolfe) go home again. Beautiful reunions are made possible by the ethnic American's bilingualism. It is as though the young person speaks flowers, or brings a hug across the sea.

Each of Kathy Snow's four children, all bilingual in English and Spanish, became so, not in her own home, but through a foreign home-stay. Each was sent to Mexico for a year at around 11 years of age. Mrs. Snow outlines how the unusual pattern occurred: "When I was very young, my mother died and I was sent to a convent boarding school. Many of the Hispanic families from south of the border used to send their children there, and thus I met a lifelong friend. We made plans to exchange our children when we ourselves were about ten. She was the first to send her daughter to me and had I not seen how marvelously and rapidly she adjusted, I might not have made the move myself. It is not easy to send a young child off at an age which is generally quite delightful, but my husband and I talked ourselves into being unselfish. Both families decided on that age because, generally speaking, the youngster has not yet become aggressively independent, is still a child, fits into a family scheme of things and pretty much takes everything as it comes. You know how it is later on. One could offer 14 year olds a balloon trip over Switzerland and they would rather stay home and meet their friends at the beach!" As for homesickness, Kathy Snow denies that it laid low any of her four children or her friend's three or her brother's three: "Perhaps it is no compliment to us, but I think we were barely missed at all! People probably forget how easily children adjust."

Even without consistent subsequent practice in Spanish, the facility never left the Snow children. As expected, their vocabulary was that of any 11 year old when they returned, Mrs. Snow notes, "but the use of ordinarily exasperating concepts like the subjunctive gives them no trouble even today, in their 30s and 40s." The Snows and the Hernandezes are now into the next generation of private child exchange, with the Snows' grandson haveing returned from Mexico "just last September," suddenly bilingual. Arrangements like these are not easily made by everyone, but I have heard from many bilingual families who have succeeded. So can you, if you choose to take the plunge.

Let's assume for a moment that your child Bobby speaks only English and that your employer has asked you to move abroad. Will Bobby pick up the language automatically? Not necessarily. America's streets are not paved with gold; nor are Italian, Spanish, French or German streets a guarantee that your child will gain fluency.

To begin with, you have to help your child overcome the loneliness and isolation he will feel when you live abroad. Bear that in mind when you choose living quarters. Instead of looking for the equivalent of a suburban American house, take a place in a lively downtown area. The Langhaug daughters learned Parisian French faster than many other American Embassy children because they lived on the busy rue Victor Hugo over a cheese shop instead of in the suburbs of Neuilly or Saint-Cloud, behind a gated fence. Immersion begins in the neighborhood. The more contact your child has with neighbors, the better. This informal curriculum is all-important in getting a child going.

If you want your children to take to the language happily, be positive towards the local scene. When there is a change of milieu and culture, your attitude is paramount. If you growl about those crazy foreign drivers behind the wheel, your child may, in imitation, let off similar (unsociable) sparks on the playground or in the schoolyard. Your values are in place, but your child's are forming. Some national stereotyping is fairly innocent, a way of organizing our understanding (for example, that Latins are fun-loving or Belgians dote on children), while others are damaging and block learning. Encourage your children to pose intelligent questions about their surroundings. When it comes to life's little irritations, such as those crazy drivers, hold your tongue.

Give the child independence in the language. This is how Pearl Buck took on Chinese as a second skin. She calls her life story *My Several Worlds*. Try to give your children as much space to evolve their contiguous, second world as the famous novelist had. Buck writes of China, "In the spring there were kites made in every imaginable shape, and sometimes we made them ourselves of split reeds and rice paste and thin red paper, and we spent our days upon the hills, watching the huge and intricate kites that even grown men flew . . . . We went to see the troupe of travelling actors who performed their plays in front of the temples far and near, and thus I learned early my Chinese history and became familiar with the heroes of the ages. Such occupations and pleasures belonged to my Chinese world into which my parents seldom entered with me, for they remained foreign, whereas I was not really a foreigner, either in my own opinion or in the feelings of my Chinese friends."

Learning a language is a private experience. Says Suzanne Alejandre, who has lived for several years in Dortmund, Germany with her husband and two sons, all four Americans, "Too many times, parents try to control what should be the child's experience. They want to know what the child knows in order to evaluate the child and make certain her or she knows 'enough.' In my mind, it is often none of the parents' business. When children—or adults—are in control of their own learning, then it will meet their needs, and that should be enough."

Mrs. Alejandre continues: "We still don't know how much German Niko or Lee know. They don't speak German with us. Our home language is American English. We only hear Niko and Lee speak German when we overhear them at the park, or when they have their German-speaking friends over or when we are involved in conversations with them with Germans. We never quiz them or try to evaluate their performance."

Giving the child a measure of private responsibility and experience abroad can be daunting. Being in charge of a child in a strange land triggers all our protective urges. But you can loosen up without being foolhardy if you let the children act on their initiative to communicate, not on your desire that they achieve fluency. The Alejandres are true to their understanding when it comes to their sons' language exposure. Suzanne knew when they moved into their apartment building that one of their neighbors had a child. She made, however, no attempt to "force" a meeting. "If I had wanted to meet the child's mother and arranged that," Suzanne explained, "then for me that would have been acceptable. But to set up meetings for Niko and Lee so they could learn German was out of bounds as far as I was concerned. We felt it was their business to learn if and when they were ready, and it would have been meddling if we busied ourselves with this learning." Parents are advised to help their kids overcome loneliness and isolation with minimal interference—and no overprotection.

How does Suzanne's minimalist attitude work? First of all, the family chose to live in the heart of Dortmund. They rented an apartment in a building that shares a courtyard with two others. There is a park half a block away. You can visualize the possibilities for contact with other people; so did the Alejandres when they chose their quarters. The family arrived in winter. For a time the boys made scant progress in German. Then, in late May the weather turned sunny and warm. Suddenly, the neighbor child was playing out in the courtyard. Once Niko and Lee began going down to play too, he would call for Niko every morning. In forming a friendship with the neighbor boy and his mother, Niko steadily increased his German. About ten other neighborhood children regularly came to the park, and both Niko and Lee made friends with them too. The Alejandre parents responded, whenever possible to the boys' requests for special jaunts to the swimming pool, the big park and so on. They selected a summer vacation spot in North Africa popular with German vacationers. Nevertheless, the rate and degree to which Niko and Lee learned the language was left unconditionally up to them.

It didn't take long. By the end of June of the first year, "as far as we could hear," Niko spoke very well. His new-found friends spoke no English, so Niko had no alternative but to find a way to say it all in German. The speed and vocabulary of his German increased and his accent improved amazingly each day. At first he improvised freely when he didn't know a word that was needed. He would express himself in a roundabout way, or mime or point. Never did he use any English. As soon as Suzanne started taking the boys to the park the next spring, Lee joined his big brother and his friends in play. These friendships resulted in his communicating in German as well. Suzanne Alejandre underscores the fact that all four family members have approached learning German in the same way, according to individual need. "Rich and I have occasionally strayed by bowing to the adult pressure to learn grammar. Otherwise we, like Niko and Lee, try to learn by responding to our own needs." Even among members of the family, fluency progresses at different rates. As the case of the Alejandres suggesting, learning a language abroad is a by-product of developing relationships with other people. That is why learning the language cannot, or rather, should not be forced. "A parent can set up all the situations and motivations in the world," says Suzanne, "but unless children are allowed privacy to investigate individually what this new culture and language are about, then, whether the language is unknown or partly known, they won't speak it."

Watching two children who don't have a common language play together, you can't help but marvel at their solutions to the problems of communication. But this is play in an intimate setting where there isn't, perhaps, a great deal of conflict, and motivation is strong. The child abroad may need your assistance. The help you give him can take may forms. Mrs. Alejandre, despite her strong feeling that children should form their own friendships, gives them a leg up by taking them to the playground regularly. Children are always anxious to "fit in" with their peers. Not knowing the local forms of behavior, your child may not know the sensible ways to conform. Does he shrug his shoulders to "I don't care," stand with hands on hips, or make a *tssk* sound from the roof of the mouth? The child observes the local manners while making his first tentative friendship gestures. Children pick up signals with amazing rapidity, as they do language, through close attention, curiosity and a rapport with one or two other children. Don't be surprised if your child's first friend is younger that he. Being the older one will put him in a confident position.

Resistance to learning and speaking a foreign language is social. Children who feel they can hold their heads high will make every effort to communicate. If you can remove the social stigma from foreignness then you have half the job done. You may be wondering, "What stigma?" Let your thoughts range to . . . . sneakers. Without the right black-and-white sneakers in your sixth grade, probably you couldn't have scored a basket. You could never have braved a dance without the footwear the others girls had on (even if the high heels came off on the dance floor). Likewise, your children will be self-conscious about their differences. Be sure they are dressed for success. Outfit your child with the same kind of lunch pail, socks, shirt, and haircut as the local kids. A few American touches are fine, but the basic child should feel that he is of the same species as his peers.

You should think that with the peer exposure they offer, schools would be a language-learning heaven. But schools subject children to the battlefield of suspicions about being different. The tongue, even if you have spoken it back home in the United States, can conceivably sound more outlandish here. For example, Suzanne White tells how her bilingual girls, born in France, resisted speaking a "foreign tongue" when at eight and nine she took them to live in the United States (returning to France when they were both 13). "They resisted when they met with prejudices and taunts. In the States they were frequently called 'Frenchy' for the first year. They had little plaid skirts and knee socks and handknit and cotton-crochet sweaters. The younger came home from school one day in mid-semester and said to me, 'Mom, can I have some freak clothes?' Not knowing exactly what 'freak' clothes were, I took her to a discount store where she pointed out a nylon T-shirt with JAWS written on in blue and red, a pair of blue jeans and sneakers. She didn't go back to wearing chic clothes until she returned to France in 1979 with her American tattered jeans, and so forth, and everybody laughed at her. It really was capital to change her spots once more. Now she's chic, but when she goes to camp in the States in the summer, she goes back to tattered jeans."

Daisy White, the older sister, lives in New York City now, where she is a model with the asset of being able to talk "boutique" with the French fashion trade. The younger daughter, Autumn, is a French rock singer near the top of the charts, and goes to a bilingual school in Paris. "She loves it," says Mrs. White. "All the kids are like her, not always English and French speakers, but at least bilingual. It's a comfort at that age not to be different."

Another way of dressing the children for success is to encourage them to watch television, read magazines and attend films in the language. An immersion in "teen life" helps comprehension by providing a conversational link with the topics discussed by peers. Says Mrs. Rodner, mother of English/Spanish bilinguals in Caracas, Venezuela, "Many American families here make the mistake of permitting their children to watch only videotapes in English. For this and other reasons, many American children who are here for two or three years do not learn to speak Spanish fluently, cannot cope with the local schools and feel left out of the life, bored and resentful. This is especially true of teenagers."

At Home

One way to bring the language into your home is to employ servants. Whether you do so will often depend on the local mores and economy more than your disposable income. If you can, do, primarily for the extraordinary boost they can give you and your children in learning a language; second, for the cultural information they can give you: reflecting opinions, passing on shopping tips, extending your view of the place you live in and which you may see only with the shallow vision of a newcomer.

Before you employ servants, prime your children to appreciate their role. When my husband and I, just married, first arrived in Tehran to live, we stayed with my former American Field Service host family. After a hairy search (there was a crippling housing shortage), Chris found us a palatial sublet apartment, and took me to see it, but neglected to tell me that a manservant came along with the digs. Coming from the stark, desert-white sunshine into the front hall, I tripped over the elderly gentleman, seated genie-like at the threshold. "This is Hassan," the landlord said to us, in a tone somewhere between a command and an introduction, "a faithful friend of the family, at your disposal." Embarrassed and unprepared for the idea of a servant, I rejected the apartment out of hand, only later to learn a great deal of my Persian from Fa'ighe, our vivacious housekeeper. In case you are worried that an apartment does not have space for household help and your privacy, remember that trained servants will, by their example, show you how the separation works.

Maximize your children's exposure to the foreign language in the home by giving lots of child care responsibility to servants. Impress on the children that the servant can guide them into fascinating aspects of their new surroundings. Explain as well that paying the servants proper respect means not demanding menial personal services of them ("It's how you lose a friend"). Just because you are in Kashmir doesn't mean your children have to ring for the maid when the mango juice needs a new ice cube. Such behavior is bad for a child as well as insulting to the servant. Also, in Europe, where so many household jobs are done by "guest workers" (non-nationals with working permits), be sure your servant, driver or housekeeper use the language you want your children to learn. This point is essential to clarify before engaging someone. While an Algerian babysitter may be able to speak a beautiful French with your child, the Turkish/English bilingual driver is not going to improve a child's German. Servants, finally, should be requested to use their own language and not (out of a sense of courtesy) English.

The Rodner daughters, in Caracas, learned all their Spanish from servants before entering Spanish preschool, since by decision only English is spoken at home. The elder two, now thirteen and ten, are fluent and the youngest, Mrs. Rodner says, "is coming along." Enthusiastic about the role of servants in creating a good language environment, Mrs. Rodner also offers a note of caution: "Be careful, if you have servants, with their vocabulary. In Caracas there are servants from a neighboring country who spice up their speech with expressions that are sometimes quite coarse. These phrases may mean little to your employee but incorporate words that children will later be punished for using at school, or that will cause them misery and confusion in general society." Take care that your children pick up slang that helps them cope, and that if they also pick up scatology they understand that it's use must be highly circumscribed!

Long-term Life Abroad

I recommend that at least one parent speak English in the house during a sojourn of over a year abroad, when you are the important link between your children and the English-speaking world. Parents of bilingual children remaining abroad must content themselves with a rough idea of their children's competency in the language of the environment. If the parents are not themselves fluent, one can draw an analogy to a non-musician who hears a violin sonata but does not realize that the player is improvising certain passages, or flubbing a note. This book is primarily concerned with raising your child to know a second language as well as English, but the issue is *being bilingual;* and that means, during a long residence abroad, not letting your child's English slip.

Although the Ramadoris, a Brahmin Indian and American couple, embrace the culture of the Dominican Republic, where they are raising a son and daughter, English consciously dominates their home. The Ramadoris live at the site of a gold mine, where the company provides housing and other comforts; Santo Domingo is two hours away by car. "In a sense," says Mrs. Ramadori, "language separates us from the Dominicans. They never forget that we are English-speaking. At the same time, being able to speak Spanish brings us closer together. It gives the Dominicans more of a sense of our humanity, and helps us to appreciate them and their lives. The one catch in a bilingual home is that one language must take dominance over the others. In our case, English is dominant. Our son, who is seven, has been taught to read and write only in English until now. Last year he was at home with me, working on materials sent by my mother in English. In addition, his father has been teaching him Tamil, but this is a casual evening activity, and the alphabet is utterly different from English. Michael now has a firm grip on written English, and is ready, slowly and carefully, to take a few classes in Spanish. This was not the case of his friend of the same age. The boy was sent to a Spanish school, where he began reading, and he spoke mostly Spanish at home with his nanny. This year his troubles in starting to read and write at home in English have been tremendous."

Don't worry that you will hold a child back from absorbing the local language if, during a protracted (again, *more* than a year) residence abroad, you speak English at home. Charlotte Gemundson reports on the experience of a group of American wives of Europeans in Switzerland that the better adjusted the parents are in learning the foreign language and joining in local customs, the less bilingual is the child. Quips Mrs. Gemundson, "Actually, a truly bilingual child who attends school in the foreign country probably has a mother who has not learned the new language (and must be pretty lonesome too!). Some choice!" If you are remaining in the foreign country for *only* a year, foreign-language learning should take center stage. However, in the life of a family overseas for years, English-maintainence is the issue, and to avoid losing English it must be spoken by *at least one parent* at home. Children thrive on creating bridges from one culture to the other, but don't try to redig the Panama Canal between them!

If you are married to a non-American or living abroad for long, speak English (a) because it feels right to raise your child to be fluent in your mother tongue as well as the language of his environment, and (b) lest stormy scenes ensue when the children discover that their English is inferior. In the fifth-grade class I taught at Tehran International School were Sikh and Parsee Indians and children of mixed Iranian and Eastern European backgrounds who went about learning science and social studies and writing book reports in English, their third language (Persian was second). Oddly, several half-American children wrote English poorly. Either their mother had decided to throw herself wholeheartedly into living the language she had wed, or the children were tended mostly by servants or the parents lacked adequate determination to raise a bilingual child. In any case, they neglected to provide their children with the extra learning skills in English that others gave.

With hindsight and regret, a Catalan-speaking mother in Switzerland has this to say about raising her daughter to speak only French in French Switzerland: "I spoke to my infant in the language that was spoken to me by my mother, without having premeditated it, instinctively. At that time we were living in French Switzerland, and French had become like a second native language for me. But the Catalan of my youth in the Pyrenees came back. For me it isthe soft, gentle language of mothering. My husband encouraged me to speak Catalan to the baby, although he understood the language but little. He

was all the happier because his own father had brusquely forbidden his mother to continue speaking Russian to him from
the age of four. But when we consulted a psychologist about a
separate matter, he declared that a child should never be addressed in a language the father doesn't understand. A member
of my husband's family whose opinion we sought seconded
the psychologist's without hesitation. With suffering and internal violence I changed to speaking French with my daughter.
She was five months old. Much later, she often reproached me.
Now I am convinced that theories shouldn't intervene. We
should do what feels right at the deepest level of ourselves. To
another person that might have been to adopt French, but not
for me."

As Suzanne White, raising her daughters bilingually in Paris
sums up: "You really do have to mandate that your kids speak
another language. It's nice to make fun, but it's forced none-
theless. My daughters spoke French with their babysitter in our
building and English at home with me. There was a rule. If you
walk through the door at Mom's house, you have to speak
English. They used to stand outside the and say, '*Bonjour, Maman.*' Then they would step inside and say, 'Hi, Mom.' It was
a game, but it was also being obedient."

School Days

The foreign school is the acid test of a child's ability to cope
with a language. Going to school in that language is also a way
to learn it fluently and quickly. It is up to you to see that your
child speaks enough of the language before starting school so
as not to feel inept—"enough" being as little as a few key words
and expressions for a child of three; enough to perform at
within a year of grade level, in the case of a 15 or 16 year old.
By outside lessons, by delaying enrolling the child for half a
school year after your arrival, or by enrolling your child in a
"package" of special-interest courses (such as the children's
courses in sports, crafts, history of art and sciences of the French
Association pour le Développement de l'Animation Culturelle, 27,
quai de la Tournelle 75005 Paris, France). The idea is to mini-

mize the period of noncommunication with peers, because any foreign school is hard for a child *at first*.

Try to find a school that has been recommended by other foreign families who have gone through a similar experience with their children. Choose a school whose teaching staff, even if they do not speak much English themselves, have had some experience with children who speak very little of the native language initially, and where the teaching staff (most important) have the patience and understanding to deal with the possible timidity and loneliness of a child thrust into an alien environment, and unable to understand everything that is going on. Try to prepare the child, before school begins, with some rudimentary words and phrases of school talk. What is the procedure for asking to go the W.C.? The nurse's office? The school telephone? What are the words and phrases used about the curriculum? Are there etiquettes taken for granted for which your child will need additional vocabulary? Be sure the director is someone of sympathetic mien who doesn't condescend or set your child rigid standards.

Some time will inevitably be lost before the child can follow lessons as a matter of course. A year may have to be repeated if the child is beyond the preschool stage when entering the school abroad. But the advantage of sending a child directly to a local school is that he will be immersed in the new language in work and play, will find friends who speak it exclusively and will thus be very much encouraged to communicate. The child will pick up the vernacular, will speak idiomatically, rather than in the stilted manner of textbooks. The child who already speaks the language will grow comfortable in extended and natural use of it, as opposed to the usage he encountered in your stateside home, where it was publicly foreign.

"We have three girls who all entered Spanish preschool with a minimal understanding of the language," writes Felicity Rodner from Venezuela, "since I am English, my husband is American and we only speak English at home. The oldest girl (now 13, born in the united States) is perfectly bilingual. The second, now ten and born here, has a trace of an English accent in her Spanish but also speaks fluently. Our third started preschool one year ago, and for the first half year understood some Spanish but refused to speak it, despite an exceptionally sympathetic and encouraging kindergarten teacher. She is a very independent-minded child however, and came around to the idea of Spanish when she felt like it." Because the Rodners' two older girls have adapted well to the Venezuelan school, they decided to be patient with the third's "stubbornness, fear or slowness—we are not sure which."

Nevertheless, some children cope better with bilingual school, where English is in use as much as a second language. The bilingual school abroad gives the child a chance to shine in English, while studying in the second language as well. A relative rarity in America (but see in chapter eleven), bilingual schools abound in Europe, Latin America and Asia. If you anticipate wanting to take your children out of school now and again in order to profit from living abroad by interesting trips (which may not fit into the school vacation-period), look for a bilingual school, which will tend to be more flexible.

Let the conforming aspect of school work in favor of your child's language mastery. Professor Laurence Wylie did his investigations into French small-town society with his older child (age five) as a research assistant. The boy gave the Professor a view of school life—and loved kindergarten. He went half-days until he *requested* to stay for the full day like the other children. Explains the father: "To us it seemed cruel to ask a five-year-old child to sit at a desk for six long hours a day listening to a language he did not understand, so we sent him at first only in the morning. After a few weeks, however, he asked if he might attend both the morning and afternoon sessions. He said he liked the Peyrane School much more than the kindergarten he had attended at home. 'At home we always had to keep playing all the time. Here we can learn real letters and numbers and things.' "

Of course, moving to a new school in a new language is an enormous leap. The risk is that the child will sink, not swim. If you have some lead time, or even if your child must begin school quickly, focus your help on the myriad little details that can make the difference between success and failure. When the Chaixes decided to live in Switzerland, they immediately bought a record of German poetry (Goethe's *Alder King*) to have their children hear some beautiful German. Once in Zurich, they cast the boys into the waters of German. The children were five, eight and eleven. The first day of school, the oldest came home saying he needed an eraser. "Go buy one," was Mr. Chaix's reply. "You say *Gummi*." The boy went, with some trepidation, and came back with his new eraser—the first obstacle was past. As for the second son, he made his own discovery and passed it on as advice, radiating good sense, to the third. "There is one word you must know and that is *Grüezi* (greetings)." "The child went away, joyously saying 'Grüezi' to everybody," relates Mrs. Chaix, "which won him many friendships in return."

Your child's strongest motivation to master a second language will be thirsty necessity—that is, being in a situation where he or she can't communicate with others without it. Parents should do their best to arrange this kind of situation, and leave the rest to fate.

Jean Carse Mitchell's father took his family as well as his journalism with him when he traveled. Almost three of the first six years of Jean's life were spent in the south of France, in the course of three separate trips. Mrs. Carse maintained that Jean learned French out of "fury and frustration" at being the odd kid out. "I wore what was then probably one of the first ski suits seen in Europe. It just so happened that there's a unit of the French army called 'Les Chasseurs Alpins,' a mountain unit. Mommy claimed that the little French kids would point to my ski suit and laugh and giggle. She said the steam was just boiling out of my ears, so I had to learn what they were saying." *That* is necessity! (Mr. Carse made French a necessity at home too, when they returned to the States. At his insistence, the family spoke no English together for the next 25 years.)

Preparing children for school may involve hiring a tutor. When diplomat James R. Bullington was assigned as chargé d'affaires at the American Embassy in Benin, there was no English-language school in the country, and the children (then monolingual) were put into a French-only school. For two months before school started, the daughters, then seven and nine, had lessons with a French tutor for two hours a day. The French system had no provision for special classes or even special attention for non-francophones. The Ambassador notes, "It was a simple question of survival."

The tutoring gave the girls words and phrases to cling to on those first days of school. When the father had to request the intervention of the French ambassador to induce the school authorities not to make the girls both start out in first grade (they had completed second and third, respectively, in their American school), because of the language handicap, the presence of an extracurricular tutor argued strongly in the girls' favor. Says the Ambassador: "After about three months, with the help of two hours per day of tutoring after class from one of the teachers, whom we hired, both girls were able to comprehend and speak enough French to get by in school. Perhaps just as importantly, from the linguistic point of view, they began to have French playmates. The older girl was soon moved ahead to the grade equivalent to where she would have been in the States. The younger girl probably could have moved ahead as well, but she was happy where she was, and not significantly older or bigger than the other children in her class, so we decided to leave well enough alone. By the end of our second year in Benin, both children, although not at the top of their classes academically, were doing better than average. They were essentially bilingual. The experience was a bit difficult for them during the first few months, and worrisome for us, but in no way traumatic (as far as I can tell) and has left no psychological scars."

Returning

American schoolchildren generally suffer less academically than other nationalities when they spend a year abroad, because American schools are often less structured than European. A French, Italian or Japanese elementary- or secondary-school student might be unable to catch up with his peers upon return to his home country. Professor Lambert's own children lost a year in their French secondary school in Montreal when their father spent a year at Stanford University. Rosemary C. Salomone, associate professor at the Harvard Graduate School of Education, suggests that mathematics be studied with an

American textbook at home, if the child is in local schools while abroad. "If you are going to move around a lot, make sure the approach is consistent," she advises.

When the time comes to pluck the plums from the pudding, how will your children keep up the language on your return home? Some families are lucky and can sent their children to a bilingual school on American soil. For example, between assignment in Benin where the Bullington daughters became bilingual and the appointment of their father as Ambassador to Burundi, the Bullingtons were in Washington, D.C. for one year. In order to prevent their losing French, the children were enrolled in a school that uses both French and English. "Thus they now have completed three years in French schools," says the Ambassador, "and they will have at least two more years here in Burundi. We very much hope that by then they will have become permanently bilingual."

Your choice, if a bilingual school isn't convenient, is either to insure, in various ways, your children's opportunities to continue using their second language informally, or face its rapid decline. What planning can a family, while they are still living abroad, with regard to their return?

Roberta and Jim Law moved to the Netherlands in 1981, when Charlie was one and Jimmy four. They maintain English in the house as purely as possible, by reading books and "talking about things" together ("We talk about the stars, the Space Shuttle, flowers, magnets, what Daddy does all day and so forth") and have allowed the teachers and children on the street to teach the boys to speak Dutch. For Roberta, alone with the children most of the day, the necessity of maintaining and developing their English while they lived in a totally Dutch-speaking environment has admittedly cramped her own study of Dutch. "I have had to learn the Dutch language outside of my time with the children," says Roberta, "and can only rarely share that language with them."

For a month at the beginning, Jimmy could not stay awake in the afternoon program of kindergarten. After every morning session he walked the three minutes home and immediately fell fast asleep. But after three months, he was chattering away in a small vocabulary, with a perfect local accent, comfortable and happy. At the graduation of his *kleuterschool*, it was Jimmy who was asked to give the farewell poem—because, one of the other mothers told Mrs. Law, he speaks clearly and memorizes quickly. Charlie was in the Netherlands nearly two years, staying at home and speaking English with his mother, before she arranged to exchange playtimes with a neighbor who had a daughter his age. Charlie had learned some Dutch from his brother and his brother's friends, but this regular contact with Anne-Marie was the turning point in his Dutch development. In a month or two he was chatting confidently with her, Jimmy's friends and Roberta's grown-up friends. The boys speak much English, but more and more Dutch. "When they played with Jimmy's friends a year ago, Jimmy used to translate often for Charlie," Roberta comments. "But now they are comfortable talking to each other in Dutch, English or a sliding mixture. In the mixture it is mostly the verbs that are Dutch." Next year the Laws are moving back to Tampa, Florida. Then they will be faced with a new problem, the issue at the end of any family's experience living abroad: how to maintain the second language at home.

If you have spoken the extra language in the home situation prior to leaving America, your return will be linguistically hassle-free. The use of the foreign language merely shrinks to within the family circle and occasional conversations with foreign friends. But if, like the Laws, you were using English abroad in the home (to maintain it), your command of the extra language may not be sufficient for exclusive home use. "We've been thinking about it more and more," Roberta muses, "and here is what we plan: To have Dutch students in our home for a summer or year at a time; to join the Dutch Club of Tampa, make Dutch friends and see where that leads; bring back Dutch books and magazines of various levels and arrange for friends in Holland to send us new materials from time to time; return after a few years for a vacation; and send the boys to spend a year with a Dutch family. It's all at the speculative stage. Someone abroad even asked us why we bother to maintain a language as 'useless' as Dutch. We have to be ready to answer that one, too."

The Laws have planned a rich fabric of approaches to Dutch language maintenance. From this packet of ideas they will bring back to America with them, any one of several seeds could produce a golden bloom. However, one in particular is the kind of hardy plant needed to effect the transplant, for the continuity of Dutch to be unbroken—and that is to have a Dutch-speaker in the home. For this they must arrange for an au pair from the Netherlands, or perhaps find a Dutch student locally, in Tampa, who has the time to be the regular companion of the boys. (For more about the au pair arrangement see chapter 3). For a smart family like the Laws, it isn't enough that their children come back from the years away "broadened" or "enriched"; they want their English/Dutch bilingual sons to keep and hone their special language skill.

11
Groups

Children love to teach one another. My son stayed overnight at a French-speaking pal's. At four, Burton had been speaking French to me and a few adult visitors, but rarely to other children, for two and a half years. After the overnight, the French mother repeated this telling conversation to me: "I like Burton!" Baudoin had said. "And he speaks French too." "Of course," his mother had replied. Said Baudoin quickly, "Yes, I taught him." Peer relationships, either a friendship or through group exposure, are the best way for a child to keep up or pick up a language at the age of four and above. In *The Promised Land*, an account of a Russian immigrant's experience in America from 1894 through the early years of the twentieth century, Mary Antin describes the successful method by which she learned English, as one of the older "green children." "There were about a half a dozen of us beginners in English, in age from six to 15. Miss Nixon made a special class of us, and aided us so skillfully and earnestly in our endeavors to 'see-a-cat,' and 'hear-a-dog-bark,' and 'look-at-the-hen,' that we turned over page after page of the ravishing history, eager to find out how the common world looked, smelled, and tasted in the strange speech. The teacher knew just when to let us help each other out with a word in our own tongue—it happened that we were all Jews—and so, working all together, we actually covered more ground in a lesson than the native classes, composed entirely of the little tots." The mutual help society, adds Miss Antin, helped the immigrant children learn so rapidly under a good teacher and was so simple, "that I only wish holiness could be taught in the same way."

Several states in America before the Civil War had German-English public schools, where the instruction was divided between the two languages. French-English programs existed in Louisiana and Spanish-English programs in the Territory of New Mexico. In the same period, Norwegian, Czech, Italian, Polish and Dutch were taught through the grades in American public schools. Furthermore, bilingual instruction flourished in private (mostly church) schools established for immigrant children from Eastern and Southern Europe. The wave of xenophobia that swept America in the late 1800s and early 1900s closed the doors of many bilingual and foreign-language schools. In the view of educators who promulgated English-only instruction, the role of schools was to assimilate, not perpetuate differences—including foreign-language knowledge. Gradually foreign-language instruction was granted a fifth or less of the high-school curriculum, and its end was for students to complete a course's text, not achieve fluency.

But foreign-language day schools and afterschool programs have continued to the present day. Religious and ethnically affiliated institutions remain their chief sponsors, but there are also independent high schools, and extra-curricular language programs, one of which, in New York City, includes 30 different languages in its course offerings to the young. All these schools—the excellent and the passable, the all-day and the sort a child attends for two or three hours a week—share a solid virtue lacking in foreign-language instruction in an English-language day school: everything, from the faces of classmates to roll call to the calendar, is experienced in the second language. In the group situation, children suspend their disbelief that languages other than English are a necessity. This chapter summarizes the options for group formal language instruction and informal play settings available in the United States today—group programs that can complement the home.

Sample Day-School Programs (French)

Throughout the United States, we are growing conscious of a shrinking globe because of the presence of thousands of families working here for international corporations, banks and businesses, as well as the traditional immigrants. In Westchester County, New York, to take a prime example, the new German school in White Plains, founded in 1980, uses German only and is for German nationals, providing a continuity with their school program back home. By contrast, Westchester County families who speak no French at home, binational or bicultural, have a new alternative for bilingual private schooling in the French-American School of New York. The school weds two educational methods, the structure and discipline of the French system (poetry is memorized; copy books must be tidy and handwriting good; math is accentuated) with the individualized program of the American. Imagine your child learning the fine calligraphy that even the retail businessman and doctor have in France.

The feature that makes our children's first school experience different is its two languages, woven into their school day as they are now woven into their lives. The idea of flexible modes of communication is a reality in the school day. Even locker- and lunchroom-talk and forming a line teach my children something— all their activities reinforce the second language. Because native speakers of French and English mix at the school, both languages are used informally. Education occurs in dead time; everybody is challenged.

The French-American School states its goals up front: "A thorough understanding of at least two cultures and two languages coupled with an ability to communicate well in each one will enhance the pupil's access to a world of interdependent businesses and government." Most bilingual schools will take older children only if they speak the second language but, the French-American School of New York, will take preschoolers who speak only English. In fact, the school welcomes American families. There are special English and French classes at all levels for those who need them. Three-year-old Nicholas' mother and father spoke no French when they enrolled him. At six, he converses in French or English at school, and English at home, although his parents hear him use French in solitary play and he sings French songs for them learned at school. The parents themselves eventually enrolled in a French course at the Alliance Française "so we would not be left behind," and look forward to a summer trip to France when Nicholas is a little older.

The staff believes that the school cannot be a Tower of Babel, not even a "creative chaos," if dual-language learning is to take place. They are trying to create a more disciplined environment than an English-speaking American school would have. Even the smallest children have to greet visitors politely, listen and take turns, stand in lines and sit down with the others. Most of the day is structured. More structure, Katrine Watkins emphasizes, is not merely the French way but is tailored to the bilingual nature of the program. "We have to get the two languages going. At the age of three you are not motivated to learn another language per se. It's virtually never 'Wow, I want to learn French [or English]!' The child has to be in a situation where the people speak a language they don't know, and where that language is needed to have concourse with them." Mrs. Watkins noted that, even a few weeks before the child starts spouting the new language, he or she babbles confidently in something that *sounds* like it.

The idea is not to Frenchify children but to give them another window on the world. Mrs. Watkins speaks for the school's philosophy: "American parents sometimes say, 'I'm afraid my child is going to become French.' That's not what happens. I think with a language comes culture, and with a new culture comes a new way of seeing things. It doesn't mean that you become French, but you learn that the French do things in one way, and we do things in another, and maybe there are a lot of ways and they're all just as good. I think a lot of understanding comes with living a language or living a culture as a very young child." An effort is made to introduce children to French customs. They are shown pictures of the flat, almond-covered French birthday cake, the *galette*, and practice their early orthography on the finely lined graph paper that children in France use for compositions. At the end of the year, the younger children perform brief songs and poetry in both languages, while the older may present an English skit they have written themselves, and, in French, several rollicking scenes from Molière. In a bilingual school, in myriad details, the distant culture is brought closer.

The French lycée system operates in most major capitals internationally. The student body of the Lycée Franco-Américain in San Francisco (one of the city's three day schools where French is used) is drawn from many parts of the world, as well as from a very wide spectrum of the San Francisco community. The lower school was opened in 1962, the bilingual high school 14 years later. Grades nine to twelve are heavily French. Kindergarten through grade five take non-French-speaking children. At kindergarten, most have never spoken French. The emphasis is heavily oral, and if they persevere in the bilingual program they are prepared to enter colleges and universities here or abroad upon graduation. The predominant language I hear on the playground and during recess is French, despite the fact that most of the student body is American. The stars of the French curriculum, director Dr. Bernard Ivaldi told me, are Americans. "Personality is most important for excelling. We screen for intellectual ability, use full immersion, and the kids who connect best with friends handle the French beautifully."

Oyster Elementary School in the Adams-Morgan neighborhood of northwest Washington, D. C. is one of the new bilingual public schools in the nation having dual-language instruction for all students. Its pupils come from a neighborhood that in the last decade has accommodated a heavy influx of Central and South American immigrants. Spanish movie theaters, a dozen Latin American restaurants and corner groceries with Latin products dot the vicinity. Instead of turning its back on this cultural component, as is usually done, this school system capitalizes on it. Classes are conducted in English and Spanish by native teachers. Each of Oyster's classrooms, kindergarten through sixth grade, is taught by two teachers, one English-speaking, one Spanish-speaking. Students learn to respond in either language, depending on which teacher is at the blackboard. Spanish isn't part of the curriculum—English isn't a second language—but the languages form a dual curriculum.

The model for early immersion school programs comes from Canada, designed imaginatively to raise bilingual citizens for an officially bilingual land. In Canada, immersion schooling implies a classroom situation in which all instruction is in French by a native speaker or person who has acquired idiomatic fluency in French. The program is tailored to children who are English-speaking, to teach them French as a second language. The curriculum parallels the English curriculum in a comparable school.

Sara and David Wright, nine and seven, are in French immersion school in a suburb of Ottawa. They have attended schools where French is the language of instruction ever since kindergarten and will continue to do so through high school. They never speak French at home or on the street, and hardly ever speak English in school. "Besides giving our children the advantage of another language and improving their prospects of employment, the French immersion really stimulates the kids and makes them use their minds," reports Ellen, the children's mother.

A ten-year survey completed by Merill Swain and Sharon Lapkin found that immersion students find better occupations than those who study in English. Particularly interesting is a shift in the sort of children who enroll. Ronald Lynch, the principal of the First Avenue Elementary School, another French immersion school in Ottawa, claims that the elitism that originally attracted many to the program has ceded to a more general enthusiasm for the immersion program as it has proved itself. "At first we were getting the children of liberals and politically active people," he relates, "but now we are getting all kinds of kids." Students who complete immersion programs are expected to be able to accept a job in a French community or go on to further education at the college level.

Immersion may also begin in the later grades (four to seven), in which case it is labeled "late immersion." In late immersion, French is the language of instruction for 80 to 100 percent of the time during the first year of the program, and in subsequent years French and English are used about equally. Although, as with foreign-language learning in general, early immersion is most effective, the late-immersion students (who enter with some formal French study) are able to achieve at the same level as native French peers by the time they reach high school.

Many Ontario and Alberta students are now enrolling in a partial second-language immersion program, known as "extended" French. In addition to the core French class, the children are taught one or two subjects in French, such as social studies, math or art. This has the effect of increasing the amount of instructional time in French as well as giving students the chance to use French in a meaningful way. Canadian Parents for French (Terminal P.O. Box 8470, Ottawa, Ontario K1G 3H6, Canada) issues various materials relating to the immersion programs that are of interest to any school that wants to make its foreign-language program a more integral part of the school curriculum and life. Among the materials is a guidebook for parents and a booklet on extended French, *What about Core?* So, if you persist in the notion that your children should learn a second language well within the school system, familiarize yourself with the approaches and results of the Canadians, who have been there first.

Sample Preschool Play Group (Yiddish)

Immigrant Jews at the turn of the century created schools with dual programs, the English language component expanding as parents saw a need for greater cultural integration. The schools had begun to decline by 1970. That trend appears to have reversed since 1980. Nearly 200 day schools in New York City and Westchester, Nassau and Suffolk Counties of New York State have an enrollment of 60,000—20 percent of all Jewish children of school age in the region. The pattern of Jewish day schools, yeshivas, is representative of religiously based bilingual schools. All yeshivas require students to learn Hebrew, although secular courses are taught in English. In Greater New York, the number of students attending yeshivas increased nearly 15 percent from 1980 to 1983. The schools devote half the day to teaching Jewish studies and half to a secular curriculum of math and science, social studies and English.

Many parents are impressed by their babies' language-learning and are interested in a special play group that will link their children with social peers. A language play group can be as simple to organize as finding other child native speakers and gathering together, or as subtle as a good teacher initiating children through group activities into a new language. Pripetshik, located on Manhattan's East Side, is a preschool Yiddish language-enrichment program for parents who are raising their children either entirely in Yiddish or bilingually (one parent speaking Yiddish to the child, the other English or some other language). Four out of five children taught in Pripetshik come from homes where the latter situation is the case. The preschool, therefore, serves an important function as a Yiddish-speaking situation outside the home.

Pripetshik meets every Sunday morning from ten o'clock to half past twelve at the Park Avenue Synagogue. The children range in age from two and a half to five and a half. Although the age difference does account for certain gaps in ability and interest among the children, the classroom is set up in such a way that each child is free to use the materials on his or her own level.

The room itself looks like any other nursery school or kindergarten. There is an art table supplied with paper, crayons, watercolors and occasionally special projects like collage and printing. There is a block corner, a dramatic play area consisting of a "kitchen" (dishes, plastic fruits and a wooden Sabbath set of candlesticks, "wine" and *challah* bread) as well as dolls, a doctor's kit, a purse filled with pennies and pieces of colorful material for the children to use as they please. A bookshelf is filled with Yiddish picture books and story books. Finally, there is a "word corner" consisting of lotto games, Yiddish card games, Yiddish alphabet stencils and three-dimensional letters, lined primer paper and pencils. The children choose their own activities for more than half of the two-and-a-half-hour period. They are encouraged to play together and to express themselves in as many ways as possible. There is only one rule: *Do redt man yidish* ("Here we speak Yiddish").

Despite the short span of the class in the child's week, Pripetshik imposes no formal grammar lessons. Its director, Mrs. Rukhl Schaechter, finds the children learn best simply by speaking and living Yiddish. "In educational terms," says Mrs. Schaechter, "this is called a language-experience approach. The children learn by doing, rather than passively receiving a teacher's lessons. They learn in a context that is familiar, developmentally appropriate, and initiated by their own interest. I do try to expand their vocabulary by repeating in Yiddish what they may initially say in English, for lack of knowledge of the Yiddish word."

The children often take part in preparing the snack. This gives them a chance to use vocabulary like "cutting," "slicing" and "peeling." Explains Mrs. Schaechter, "Snacktime is a good opportunity for sitting around the table and sharing what happened during the week, or just talking about anything that comes to their minds. After snack I take out the guitar and we sing Yiddish songs. I encourage the children to use hand movements and dramatics, in order to really get into the songs. I also read them a story or tell them Bible stories, which they seem to find fascinating, and usually get us into some heavy discussions in Yiddish, like 'Why did God like Abel's gift more than Cain's?'"

Pripetshik also celebrates all Jewish holidays, occasionally with the parents as well, so that the children have a chance to see their two Yiddish-speaking (in some cases) environments come together. Parents and other Yiddish speakers sometimes come in and lead an activity with the children, "so that they will see for themselves that there are many more Yiddish speakers than they've seen at home and at preschool."

In the peer group there are ways of cajoling and causing a child to speak Yiddish who seems to take less easily to two languages than other children, or is in a mixed-language stage. "There have been occasions where a child has openly rebelled in our class," Mrs. Schaechter admits, "for example, asserting with a mischievous grin that he can't speak Yiddish because he doesn't know any, or unconsciously slipping into English while playing with one other child. I find the former situation easier to handle because of its directness. I might respond jokingly, 'Well, if you can't speak Yiddish, answer me in Spanish!' Or else I smile and ask him a question on a different matter. For preschool, this method of distraction seems effective enough— after all, why make a big issue out of it? But as the children grow older and their rebellion becomes more serious, I would encourage them to air their views so that we could get into a discussion of values, thus letting them explore for themselves why keeping up Yiddish is so important, in the context of who they are, where they come from and what their roots are. As for the more unconscious form of rebellion, in which a child keeps switching to English apparently unwittingly, I usually wait to see if the child reverts back to Yiddish. If he doesn't, I may remind him that 'We speak Yiddish here.' If that doesn't work, I may explain to the second child that 'Leah sometimes forgets that she is speaking in English, so can you please remind her?' "

Afterschool Programs

There are after school programs that teach languages, usually Spanish or French, as an extra subject to exclusively non-speakers. They can, for example, be identified in New York City in the book *Afterschool*, a publication of The Resourceful Family (490 Riverside Drive, New York NY 10027). Elsewhere, ask your librarian for an education information hotline, and check with the public school guidance office. At an afterschool, instruction must be very structured, with the teacher keeping the language lid on, creating and sustaining the spell that "Here we speak predominantly in Spanish." Look for a class where children are, all the same, interacting a lot, and doing manual tasks, among them writing, as the class goes on. Singing is another mark of a good afterschool because the teacher and children are involved simultaneously, no one has to wait a turn to use the language and the child can take the language home. Japanese and Europeans often send their children to afterschools so they can enter or re-enter school back in the home country, without having fallen behind. American parents who find a language afterschool either have a child who has expressed curiosity and interest, or are dissatisfied with foreign-language instruction (or maybe there isn't any) in the child's daytime school. These programs are also useful for a crash exposure of a child to a second language before a visit to a Norwegian grandmother or a parent's job assignment to Vienna.

The consistent drawback to all these afterschool programs is the compression of exposure. The class takes up so little of the child's learning life. Typically, the Spanish Institute of New York has classes for ages eight through twelve in beginning Spanish, one hour a week for twelve weeks. The French classes offered by Mme. Françoise Bennet in Westchester County, New York are an afterschool or Saturday hour, regrettably brief, even though she uses considerable crafts and storytelling.

Nelly Sidoti, who has collaborated on research with Dr. Wallace Lambert, heads an organization called Native Intelligence Children's Languages, Inc., that has a viable solution to the problem of keeping alive the language from week to week, when the class is a low-dosage in-school or afterschool program. The regular classroom teacher, when the program is in the elementary school curriculum, or the parents, when it is an afterschool, realize a potential to be coteachers. Extracurricular sessions (once or twice a week) are first presented by a foreign-language teacher and then reinforced with specially designed materials. The child learns content about the seasons and the solar system, along with language. The parent or regular classroom teacher must attend the class with the children if he or she is a beginner like the children. The adult is thus given an opportunity to "learn as you teach" a foreign language. The minimum time needed for the accessory adult to carry the program is 15 minutes a day. Imaginative homework involves drawing, coloring, reading and writing. Six comic coloring books, for example, include Food, Sports, Family, Solar System, Dinosaurs and School. Between formal sessions, the children recall and extend what was done with the foreign-language teacher.

Using the Native Intelligence materials for Spanish, French and German, you or a teacher can conduct an afterschool with children from first grade to sixth, for a period of several years. When Ms. Sidoti teaches using the program, children review in second grade what they did in first, and so on, until they have truly internalized the material. If you are setting up a small after- school group class, and hiring a teacher (rather than relying on the knowledge of one of the parents), commit families to the short term, no more than three months, and keep the fee as close to babysitting rates per child as possible. Seek a motivated teacher who relates well to your children; the declaration "I adore the young" is insufficient evidence of a teacher's interest. Expect to obtain the enticing materials yourself. A nearby home is the most plausible location for the group. Treks to a nearby city for sessions must be made into easy, fun events by combining them with larks like a visit to a place of interest, lunch at a restaurant or a picnic in the park.

Today, a new search for roots has engendered a new reason for learning languages. People want to discover their whole identity without splitting off from the mainstream, and they perceive language as perhaps the greatest of all the legacies of home. As a Hungarian immigrant song, recorded by Michael Kraus in *Immigration: The American Mosaic,* expresses for all peoples, "We yearn to return to our little village/ Where every blade of grass understood Hungarian." How are families and quiet programs at Greek Orthodox and Armenian churches and Hungarian community centers passing on their languages? Chiefly via rigorous afterschools.

Where there is a concentrated ethnic group, afterschools are the logical solution. The child does not have to choose between an ethnic school and the public or nonsectarian system to accomplish the goal. They are voluntary, sociable and ambitious. The afterschools also have a tendency, as good as they may be, to bite off more than they can chew.

Japanese afterschools are designed to meet the needs of Japanese families whose children are expected to return to Japan. Competition is fierce for admission to higher education in Japan and parents fear that if their children do not keep up at their grade level, their educational chances will suffer later on. At the Japanese Supplementary School in White Plains, New York, *kanji,* a set of 10,000 Chinese characters used in Japanese, is the main subject. The school is large enough to have 18 classes that include diagraming Japanese sentences, interpreting a Japanese poem and learning *kanji.* Hiei Ando, a chemical engineer who teaches sixth grade afterschool, says the children's differing levels of Japanese fluency make it very hard to teach. "What makes it worse," he says, "is that we must do in a few hours what they take three to five days to do in Japan." To overcome this, motivation on the part of both students and teachers must be strong.

A rigorous afterschool that stresses achievement without anxiety is the Independent German Language School of Connecticut. In 1983, German Language School students became the first private language school (Saturday school) in the United States to take the *Sprachdiplom I* examination of the German government. Previously, the examination was only taken by students attending officially sponsored German Day Schools for diplomatic and other career individuals' families (in Washington, D.C. and White Plains, New York). Many of the students at the Connecticut school do not speak German when they enter, although they may come from German backgrounds. Tuition is kept low by help from the German government. There are school fests and an end-of-the-year show, in which every grade participates with a performance of songs or theater. Children can, if they wish, have their grades transferred from the Saturday school to the regular school: some struggle for good grades but students don't have to. Certain children, who come at age seven or eight, speaking no German, are able to do nicely on a second-year high-school German examination by the end of high school. Renata Ludanyi, the director, stresses that the school's aim is not to foster German-ness. "I reject all of that! But there are traditions that run with language. We create an awareness of them in our students." Homework depends on the teacher, situation and mood. For the teenagers, an assignment to read a book in two weeks would be typical. In part reflecting the decrease of German-language instruction in American secondary schools, enrollment in German afterschools is on the upswing. They exist in over 50 towns and cities across our map, and, states Mrs. Ludanyi, standards too are on the rise.

Not all the afterschool programs are so structured with formal language lessons as the two I have just described. To be a Hungarian-American scout, for example, and benefit from wonderful programs, trips and summer camps, you must master enough Hungarian to get along in the peer group. Some of the scouting activities double as language enrichment. One of the Hungarian scout vows is, "No English during scout meetings." The scouts sponsor programs of puppets and songs on December 7, St. Nicholas' Day, for example, the big Hungarian children's holiday of the year. According to Hungarian tradition, on this day the children's saint passes judgment on the good and bad acts of the scouts (ages eight and up) and younger children who have come for the festive and theatrical fun.

Nicholas enters dressed in crimson, with a long beard, bishop's mitre and crook. Accompanying him is Black Peter, a devil rattling lengths of chains, adding fear to the children's excitement. This cultural event carries gentle but firm propaganda for the use of Hungarian, like the activities of many religious or ethnic language-related children's activities. St. Nicholas has been tipped off by parents and as the children come one by one for red sacks of tangerines, chocolates and nuts, he compliments or prods them about their Hungarian. He tells a set of twins, "You don't speak enough Hungarian with each other. This year, speak more!" To a new immigrant child he says, "I won't ask you whether you speak Hungarian, but whether you speak English. Never forget Hungarian; it will never come back as well."

Private Tutor

Private tutors are not born and bred but made—by you! It is up to you to advertise and canvas your community for one; select on the basis of suitability, not experience (few will have it); and set forth clearly what you want your child to do and accomplish. The tutor can be as young as 13 or as old as 70. In fact, it is at the younger and older ends of the age range that you should seek: someone with time, who can tutor for a modest fee and stay with the job, and who speaks, reads and writes the language now (rather than just remembering it). The young tutor who comes from a family where the language is spoken will take this job (perhaps his first) seriously, and win your child's affection. If your child's tutor is an older person, he or she will pass on a great deal culturally together with the language. (Children's voices are fainter than adults'. Draw your chair away from the older person during your interview, to check that he or she hears well enough to be a feasible tutor.) Extend your search accordingly, to senior citizens' clubs, church bulletin boards and high-school guidance offices, as well as local shopping newspapers, where ads cost little.

In general, parents hire tutors for their children for remedial work, and the relationship can be rather tense. But that between the language-learner and native-speaking tutor can be more relaxed, and take on a sportive mood. Neither need the arrangement necessarily be as expensive as the traditional tutor employed by a wealthy family. The idea of one-on-one in an instructional situation is elite, but the reality (cost effective, untaxed and with no overhead) can be quite low-budget.

When we wanted a German tutor, the sequence of events to find one was as follows. First I inquired at two high schools in the area where German was taught for a teacher-tutor. The fees ranged from $20 to $30 an hour for lessons at the house. The price was prohibitive. I asked high-school guidance offices to let me know if a German-speaking student turned up who might like to tutor for the going rate for student tutors, $4 per hour. Meanwhile I asked the 13-year-old daughter of the owner of a small German restaurant in town if she wanted to tutor "for three-quarters of an hour, while you walk your dog." In this case, the children ended up having two German tutors because they like them both: a weekday afternoon tutor and a Saturday morning tutor, for one and a half to two hours of beginning German conversation a week. Even if one of the girls can't come, or we have other plans, or a child falls sick, there is German tutoring at least once a week. The total fees, as you have probably calculated, start at one fifth what I would have paid a professional teacher. In compensation, I have let the girls know they need do absolutely no preparation for the lessons. I pile up books, tapes and writing materials on the couch, where the children curl up on either side of the tutor in afghans. Or, in warm weather, they have their lesson on the porch swing or a blanket outdoors. It doesn't feel like school! The only rule is that the children must stay for a good while with the tutor. If one doesn't like a book that's being read or tape being heard, it is permissible to go play, and check back later to see what "better" entertainment is in store. With an older child, alighting, leaving and alighting again would perhaps be rude, but there are other ways of keeping the session low key. The children could go on a German walk with Sandy and her dog, or play Parcheesi with Ulriche. If you listen unobtrusively while you write a letter or fold laundry, you will know better what materials to lay out for next time, and can help call a halt if everybody seems fatigued with the lesson before "time's up."

The techniques a teen or other amateur tutor can handle famously fall into the category of "serious play." A lesson plan is not necessary, but a starter idea for each session guarantees a well-spent hour. Some starters I have set up for my teen tutors are:

• A foreign magazine to cut up and read from.

• An interesting letter the tutor has received in the language, or a Christmas or birthday card, which she shares.

• I roll up two dozen funny or vivid words written on little pieces of paper, and hide them around a room. The children make up sentences with the words as they find them.

• Each child learns to tell a secret in the language.

• Play telephone.

Especially in the first weeks, you should suggest to the new tutor activities that can be centerpieces of the tutoring session, too. Here are the two core activities I recommend.

A superb activity for any age is Dual Story Books. The tutor reads a story in English, then in the foreign language, or reads a part in each language and proceeds little by little. The older child can match up sentences on the page, or play translator, leaving the details up to the tutor. Repetition of the same story in two languages facilitates comprehension and builds vocabulary, the known text hovering like a friendly ghost behind the unknown. The child is immersed in a story instead of starting from scratch at every lesson. The stimulation of the story lets the children relive in the foreign language an experience understood in English. The books (or poems, or passages from a Bible or other text) should be an equation. If they exist in the language you need, use the *Bilingual Fables* from National Textbook Company (see page 144 for address). My children used the French to learn the German. Or you could use the English to work through the Spanish, Portuguese, German or Italian. Stories available include some of everybody's favorite fairy tales: Hansel and Gretel, Tom Thumb, Jack and the Beanstalk, Aladdin, Rumpelstiltskin, Sleeping Beauty, Snow White, Red Riding Hood, Pinocchio, the Elves and the Shoemaker and the Ugly Duckling; and fables such as Lion and Mouse, City Mouse and Country Mouse, and the Tortoise and the Hare. Note that *The Cat in the Hat Dictionary*, though it comes in various English bilingual editions, or English and equivalent foreign-language versions of one of the ubiquitous Richard Scarry word books cannot substitute for the bilingual stories. A story takes a child by the hand, drawing him over hill, dale and rocky slopes to the action's climax. By contrast, dictionaries, even cute ones that have a place in your child's foreign-language learning, are no page-turners. Would you rather your first steps in a new language be into a fairy castle or a roomful of bricks?

For the tutor's second core activity I recommend Sing-lingual. Like all great techniques, learning the beginnings of a foreign language through singing is simple. Uwe Kind, a musician and educator at the New School for Social Research, has developed Sing-lingual, an ideal core activity for a private or group tutoring program. This is where the language labs, those cemeteries of grammar drill, should have been in the first place. "This is an old recipe for passing on information," says Mr. Kind. "Our parents passed on transmitted poetry—the whole history of a people has been passed on in song." The Uwe Kind books and tapes are door-openers to Spanish, English and German. With the songs in the program, students can get into the language quickly. They are ingeniously designed to pass on grammatical information and teach conversational "functions" that can be used immediately. A familiar melody like "Oh Susannah" teaches the conjugation of a tense, while other melodies teach adjective agreement, indirect objects or the imperative.

To use this method, it helps to have a sense of fun. "You have to shed self-importance to enter in," Mr. Kind notes. Various international corporations are using the method to train executives in English, and in Japan, Sing-lingual is a bestselling home-study kit. For your child it can supplement a tutor or language afterschool. By perking up their sense of fantasy, imagery and play, singing the unfamiliar language relaxes both learner and teacher.

Several Sing-lingual series exist. *Tune into Spanish, Tune into English* and *Eine Kleine Deutschmusik* (Langenscheidt) concentrate on function—they are skits of communicative skills. Available in the same three languages, *Oh Susannah* (Regents) is more grammar-oriented. *Dich und Ich* is a comprehensive German program especially for children.

Versions of Sing-lingual in other languages must be homemade. If you want to open a language to your children who are past babyhood, and you speak well—or rustily—you or a tutor can devise several songs of your own. Mr. Kind, generous with his original idea, would like nothing better than to see "Old MacDonald" teaching the imperative in Slovak. If you want to try, take a look at the samples that follow. But don't drive yourself loco trying to think up lyrics. Sit down and plot them out either with a friend who speaks the foreign language, or with your children's tutor. Remember, this is by no means a complete program. Some grammar skills learned through Sing-lingual, like dependent and subordinate clauses, or adjective endings, may approximate those covered in a conventional first- or second-year high-school course, but the vocabulary acquired is more limited. What the student using Sing-lingual learns impeccably are language patterns, which he can draw on later. He is motivated by success to learn more, and the tongue is *working*.

Choose a specific scene of communication, such as introducing oneself to a new friend, asking directions, finding a good restaurant or arranging a picnic or trip to the beach. Jot down at this stage a simple, rough sketch. You should construct the situation as a question/answer dialogue: Each sentence alternates between speakers in a duet, so the child can sing it with a peer, the tutor or you. Now find a melody that can accommodate the sentences without distorting the rhythm of the language, and then polish the song.

That the tunes be old favorites is important. As Mr. Kind explains, "Familiar wrapping eases the resistance against the unknown." It is also important to render into song real-life situations, as he says, "to stimulate and activate more entrance channels into the mind." If the child learns how to say hello and ask someone's name and tell his, he can imagine himself in that situation in real life.

Sample Sing-lingual Songs

Here are some sample songs of the kind you might write:

Spanish: No comprendo. No comprendo.
Mas despacio, por favor.
Solo hablo un poquito
Mas despacio, por favor.
(Tune: "Clementine")

Come le va?
Muy bien. Muy bien.
Come le va?
Muy bien. Muy bien.
Come le va?
Muy bien, amigo.
Come le va?
Muy bien. Muy bien.
(Tune: "Oh When the Saints")

French: Comment allez-vous?
Très bien, merci!

Comment allez-vous?
Comme ci, comme ça!
(Tune: "Someone's in the kitchen with Dinah," from "I've Been Workin' on the Railroad")

Postscript

The plan was to fatten the family budget up a bit before returning to a francophone land. But was it irresponsible for a
family ever chinning themselves up into the middle class to do
what even the banker, lawyer and stockbroker cannot—i.e.,
take the children abroad each summer? All fall and winter I
scraped paint off wallpaper off paint, chased squirrels off the
eaves, bucketed leaks, wrote articles, minded my financial p's
and q's, and considered. Dissatisfaction with U.S.-based summers for my children was fomenting. It energized a longing to
see them at home in their other language and second, acquired
culture soon again.

Next summer could not honestly be decided until spring. In
the meantime I planned a fantasy trip. A French art-collector
friend, Claude Guintz, had spoken glowingly of Corsica as the
Côte d'Azur of 50 years past—unspoiled. It had its own island
culture, protected by precipitous mountains from resort over-
development. Moreover, I thought, the living—and interaction
with a local population—would be eased by a warm clime. And
Corsica even in off-season would be mild.

Emma's fascination with the Empress Josephine, and Burton's with *les guerres de Napoléon*, helped spur our study in picture French histories like Augustin Drouet's *Napoléon*, Paris:
Hachette (1979), the recording *Napoléon* (Hachette, #LAE 3308),
and Corsican travel brochures. Napoleon might have become
king of New Orleans had he made the trip in time; in the children's hearts, in Corsica, he was just that.

A map of Corsica went on the refrigerator, and, armchair travel being one of life's great joys, I trumpeted my romance with the unknown isle about, getting responses. People began volunteering information—which ferry to take; the name of a real estate agent; how to arrive in a village inconspicuously (so as not to be pegged as a tourist, you must come by bus); somebody's aunt rents her Bastian house the greater part of the year at a trivial housesitter's rate. I also heard about the Italian coloring to the Corsican character, about wild boar hunts and the rock-coasted sea. Emma decided that where there are boars, there must be fairy princesses!

But resorts, with few exceptions, bore me in season. So to Corsica I finally said: All in good time; some year or half-year I would like to take my children there for local French schooling. The project was set aside.

Then at eight one morning, EST, a Paris-based journalist and novelist, Jerry Dryansky, phoned. Mothers are supposed to be up and alert at that hour, right? I, of course, was unreachably groggy. It is unclear who had told Jerry our house was (perenially) available for summer house exchange; I nevertheless accepted his offer—1896 Bronxville house for 1896 Paris apartment—for the month of July. He painted a charming picture of the antique *meubles*, discarded by the Tuileries, that furnished his home, and the new addition of a clothes dryer—an ultimate luxury for a Parisian family—to their automatic washer. We agreed it would be fun to live in another writer's environment during the proposed exchange.

Next year I shall squire the twins to France again. More practiced at a migratory pattern, we are setting our mutual aims beforehand. We won't bother to pay homage to the Louvre and Notre Dame de Paris, *de rigueur* sights being too rigorous for young children. We'll frequent our favorite parks and edges of the Bois de Boulogne, and rendezvous with Professor Sibonie's children and with Suzie, the café proprietor's daughter, near our old hotel. We won't brook anything as touristy as the chateaux of the Loire in summer. Instead, we'll go to La Rochelle, the Atlantic seaport painted by Albert Marquet. I shall seek answers to questions about whether Renaissance youth swam in the rivers and oceans, how sixteenth-century roof gang hoodlums worked, and what good hunting drew François I to the southwest.

Emma and Burton are helping me research these matters, which will feed into a novel about France's last legal duel (July 10, 1547). The federation of over 200 *ateliers*, or workshops, in Paris (L'Association pour le Développement de l'Animation Culturelle [ADAC], 27 quai de la Tourelle, Paris 75005) has classes in fencing; Burton will enroll in an *atelier* during our stay. Lessons will help me get into the mood of the chivalric code, too.

I'll take mine at the French military club, Le Cercle Militaire, that I scouted out in the summer of 1984. My revered teacher is Monsieur Jean Samson, a *maître d'armes* who fought in the French Resistance as a youth and was decorated by the American Legion. This year I am taking lessons—and Burton is observing—at Manhattan's Fencing Club. It has Olympic teachers—we will be *en plein forme* for Monsieur Samson!

It astounds me how much adventure and delight has followed from raising the twins bilingual. One of the parents I interviewed for this book was Judith Bastanelli, a nurse and sewing teacher in New Hampshire, who has kept up her daughters' French, inherited from Judith's ex-husband, the girls' Corsican father. (The how-to of the twins' bilingual upbringing was also an important part of my own divorce agreement.) Recently, Judith and I sat over tea at the Hotel Algonquin in New York, figuring out where in France to intersect when she takes her children touring and camping in the summer. A question came up: Do we raise our children bilingual, and by extension bicultural, for ourselves or for our children? We'll never know, Judith and I agreed. And the beauty of it, as we said that afternoon,, is that the answer is of no consequence. Bringing up baby bilingual *by choice* is a seamless story vis-à-vis the achievements and interests of each member of the family. It is, as I hope you have the experience of finding out, a stairway to exotic and wondrous, yet truly plausible dreams.

Afterword

The Nature and Significance of Bilingualism

Wallace E. Lambert
McGill University

One of the wonders of the social world is the capacity humans have for creating a variety of languages. Even more wonderful, in my thinking, are the potential linkups we have between and among languages because of people who are bilingual. And, as we have seen in this book, there are many intriguing ways people can become bilingual.

Suppose for a moment that we had no modern communication systems and that an important message had to be circulated throughout the world by person-to-person methods. Let's suppose that the message is a socially significant one—for instance, "eating acorns protects one from cancer"—and suppose that the discovery took place in the toe of Italy and the news was to be relayed up to the Swiss, Yugoslav and French borders and from there out around the world. Although the message would certainly have a bumpy transmission through numerous dialect communities in Italy itself (Hall, 1980) and through various language groups in multilingual Yugoslavia, it would ultimately penetrate all language barriers.

The most important elements in the relay, of course, would be bidialectic or bilingual people, and they would be found in high concentrations at the borders of each linguistic community. They would have developed their bidialectic or bilingual skills through communication experiences in the region of overlap of the two codes, or they might have migrated from one region to another, meaning that they brought their old-community code along with them. Chances are that they would be less versed in the written form of the second language than in the spoken form.

Of course, some bona fide residents of each community could also be bilingual if they had the interest and inquisitiveness (like that of an anthropologist) to get to know another community's language, literature and culture. This more educated subgroup would likely be better versed in the written than the spoken form of the other language. This example may not seem that important, but as we will see, the ways people become bilingual can make very important differences.

At certain relay points, only a few people would be bilingual enough to translate the message, whereas at other points many bilinguals would be available. An English version of the message, for instance, might pass without need of translation among large numbers of educated Danes or Swedes, whereas a Danish or Swedish version would stop abruptly at the ports of England or France before a Danish-to-English or Swedish-to-French bilingual could be found. Thus, certain languages at certain times in history place high on a hierarchy of language status or usefulness, while others have little usefulness outside a restricted community. Where a particular language falls in this hierarchy influences one's attitude toward learning another language; those with a high-status language wonder why they need to know any other, whereas those with a low-status language realize they must.

Conceptions of Bilingualism: Old versus New

What is it like to be one of these critical message relayers? More generally, what is the social significance of being bilingual? First of all, bilinguals are people who, because of ancestry, place of residence or interests of parents, have social and emotional connections with some "other" place and some "other" group. The demarcation between one's "own" group and an "other" group is emphasized more by monolinguals than bilinguals, for it is the monolingual person who is especially likely to wonder and ask questions about bilingualism, questions such as: Can one really depend upon the allegiances of those who are partly connected elsewhere? The monolingual, who is shut out of the communication flow in a bilingual's other language, often becomes suspicious (sometimes even paranoid) about what's being communicated in the unknown code.

It is just a short step, then, to where the monolingual would become frightened of social policies that seem to encourage either societal or individual forms of bilingualism. For a society, the argument goes, the more bilinguals there are, the less integrated and cohesive (and thus the less productive) the society must be. For individuals, the more bilingual they become, the less integrated their personalities must be. Of course, the argument continues, there will always be a need for a few bilinguals to translate and relay messages from one group to another, and that chore can be done best by those who are in transition—still bilingual but on the road to real integration in the new group. In any case, translating and message relaying might best be considered as mechanical, relatively low-status operations, because there is no sense in encouraging or aggrandizing bilingualism at any level. It is quite a different matter, however, when the better educated within one's own ethnolinguistic group learn other languages and learn about other people's ways of life. *Their* bilinguality and *their* allegiances are not questioned because they can prove that they have deep, unshakable roots in the home society.

Only recently has this traditional monolingual person's view of bilingualism been challenged, and the challenge has come mainly from new research findings in the behavioral sciences. Consequently, we now have a clearer picture of what bilingualism is and how it works. Rather than being a person divided between two linguistic and cultural groups and not belonging to either one fully, the bilingual actually has the potential to belong comfortably to *both* ethnolinguistic groups and to be a well-integrated person as a consequence. At the society level, there is also a new appreciation for the presence of bilinguals who, in the minds of perceptive people in both developed and developing nations, are beginning to be seen as precious national resources.

To arrive at this new perspective, researchers began by checking on the validity of some widespread beliefs about bilingualism—for example, the belief that being bilingual results in some type of mental confusion or retardation. Carefully conducted surveys of performance on intelligence and school achievement tests found that bilinguals, instead of being handicapped, were actually scoring higher than matched monolinguals on IQ tests and moving along as swiftly if not more swiftly in school (see Lambert, 1981, and Cummins, 1979, for reviews of the pertinent research studies). Earlier studies over a 50-year period had concluded strongly in favor of monolinguals because, it turns out, they had not matched bilingual and monolingual groups on factors such as social class background. Nor had they measured the bilinguality of those presumed to be bilingual.

Researchers then began to ask questions about the supposedly muddled mind of the bilingual. Does it function as well as the monolingual's mind? We now have several reasons to argue that it may be something more and something better than the monolingual mind. For one thing, the fully bilingual person manages to work effectively with two linguistic systems and to keep the two functionally separated (see Lambert, 1969). Bilinguals can listen to a long list of words read word by word, half presented in one language and half in the other in a mixed order, and remember as many as monolinguals can when the whole list comes in one language and do so while making hardly any translation errors in recall; that is, saying "grapefruit" when *pamplemousse* was the word actually presented. Furthermore, the two systems provide the bilingual with a cross-language and cross-cultural comparative perspective that the monolingual rarely experiences, a realization of the important differences that exist in shades of meaning across languages, not only in the meanings of words but also in the meanings of gestures, sounds and pitches.

This sensitivity to meaning that comes with bilingualism deepens one's understanding of concepts. Bilinguals realize that concepts have distinctive meanings in the context of each linguistic system, and this realization broadens their perspective on language and on reality. Through experience, bilinguals recognize that words are only arbitrarily attached to referents (for example, the things we sit on are called *chaises* in one system, *Stühle* in another). This awareness protects bilinguals from the traps of "reification"—believing that because names are assigned to entities like "mind" or "spirit" that such entities actually exist, or that names and referents are naturally linked and inseparable. As a consequence, bilinguals are better able to think beyond the bounds of linguistic systems and to play and create with words and abstract concepts. It is as though bilingualism provides people with a mental stereoscope, enabling them to see concepts in perspective. This is perhaps what Wilder Penfield, the famous neurosurgeon at McGill University, meant when on several occasions he expressed his view that "the bilingual brain is a better brain." (He did not talk about a better bilingual "mind.") Actually, current research indicates that bilinguals, compared to monolinguals, involve more of the right half of the brain when decoding or encoding verbal material, the right half being considered the site of cognitive restructuring and creative processing (see Vaid and Lambert, 1979).

A word of caution is called for, though, because not all bilinguals are able to maintain functional equivalence in their two languages, nor are all able to reap the advantages of bilinguality. Many are blocked in their progress toward full bilingualism because of attitudinal and motivational hang-ups (see Gardner and Lambert, 1972), and many, because of society's insensitivities, are forced to abandon their bilinguality (see Lambert, 1981).

As for the healthiness of the bilingual's personality, which was also called into question by earlier writers on bilingualism, the few research findings so far available reveal no signs of disturbance or maladjustment that can be attributed to bilingualism. For example, young people who become functionally bilingual through immersion programs in the elementary school years benefit by increased self-esteem and confidence because of the experience (see Lambert and Tucker, 1972), and those who are permitted to become bilingual and bicultural through early family experiences develop a deep appreciation for their parents and the roles parents play, at the same time benefitting from the cultural diversity represented by their parents (see Aellen and Lambert, 1969).

Recent research by sociolinguists has also forced a re-examination of the effects of linguistic and cultural pluralism on the economic and social development of societies. Stanley Lieberson and colleagues, for example, in their cross-national comparisons of mother-tongue diversity and national development find no substance to the belief that mother-tongue diversity hampers the economic or social development of nations (Lieberson and Hansen, 1974).

This new research has direct implications for developed nations like the United States and Canada, which receive large numbers of immigrants. There are signs that these nations are experimenting with changes in their social and educational policies so as to protect the languages and cultures of newcomers. Thus, there may be the beginnings of an appreciation for languages and cultures as precious societal resources. There are, of course, serious and cogent counterarguments to such changes, and much more research is called for before we can expect fundamental modifications in national policies on societal pluralism (see, for example, Rabushka and Shepsle, 1972).

It turns out, then, that many of the bilingual person's problems of adjusting and coping are determined primarily by the attitudes and reactions of society at large. Society is harsh and often merciless, picking up on the slightest signs of ethnicity— including the way a person uses language—and reading all sorts of negative things into them, often things that aren't really there, except in the minds of the "readers." Take the accents bilinguals often have in their speech. Accents reveal in an instant the whole experience of expatriation and migration that is sometimes a joyous affair but often a spirit-wrenching one. For many listeners, accents conjure up stereotypes about "foreigners" or "strangers in our midst," with all the attendent suspicions about bilingual/bicultural people, and their supposedly divided allegiances. Society thus makes up its collective mind about people on the basis of small things like accents and language styles.

Of course, the status hierarchy of languages works itself into these judgments, and thus bilinguals with humble backgrounds are singled out and hurt most. Research is now exploring this social judgment-making process. For instance, tape recordings are made of a series of speakers, each reading a standard passage. In the series, some speakers are bilingual, so that they give two renditions, one in one language, the other in their other language. In some other cases, the speakers are bidialectic, so that they present themselves once with a foreign accent and once without. These readings are presented to listeners who are asked to judge the personality makeup of each speaker. The listeners are kept ignorant of the fact that the same speakers sometimes appear more than once, at different places in the series. What is astonishing in such studies is the fact that so many listeners, from all walks of life, attribute biased, stereotyped traits to a speaker according to the language or accent guise the speaker momentarily adopts. Thus, the accent or the other language evokes in large proportions of listeners an image of a less dependable, less socially attractive, less likely to succeed person than is the case when the same person drops his accent and "speaks white" (see Lambert, 1967; Giles and Powesland, 1975).

There is, of course, no basis whatsoever for these attributions, but true or not, they are so crystallized and widespread in so many societies that they constitute a formidable barrier to interpersonal communication and understanding. Knowledge about this process through research paves the way for correctives, and these are now being tried out. For example, innovative approaches to learning other languages and learning about other cultures in the form of immersion classes, taught exclusively through a foreign language, are being introduced to children in school settings and those seem to have a corrective effect (see Lambert and Tucker, 1972). The evaluations of French immersion programs for English-speaking children in

Canada and the United States, measuring changes in pupils' attitudes and social perspectives, are very encouraging (see Lambert, 1984).

Additive versus Subtractive Forms of Bilingualism

These studies of reactions to speech style indicate that society puts great pressure on ethnolinguistic minority groups to shed the traces of old cultures, languages included, and to embrace the new. This pressure usually means that members of a less prestigious ethnolinguistic community are expected to accommodate to some vague but powerful norm about the expected and acceptable language of communication. They are induced to put aside their native or home language and even the accented traces associated with it. They are expected, in other words, to venture toward a bilingualism that essentially subtracts the home language by shifting the focus to the new, usually more prestigious, language of the host culture. We refer to this form of bilingualism, where the language of the new country comes to substitute for the original home language, as "subtractive" bilingualism, implying that in the long run the bilingualism is more apparent than real since one language is progressively put aside or subtracted.

Some now believe that this experience leaves ethnolinguistic minority group members—adults as well as children—in a psychological limbo and that it contributes to the incapacity they often have with both native and new-nation languages and the difficulties they have in achieving in school or in occupations (see Lambert, 1981). By way of contrast, "additive" bilingualism characterizes those who are at home and well rooted in their own language and culture, but who delve seriously into the mastery of a second or foreign language. Additive bilingualism provides opportunities for mainstreamers to "add" one or more languages to their repertoires and to enjoy a number of personal advantages—in self-confidence, openness of mind, intellectual enrichment—as a consequence of becoming bilingual (Lambert and Tucker, 1972; Genesee and Lambert, 1983).

The challenge for social planners and educators in this decade, then, is to help transform instances of subtractive bilingualism into additive ones. Some research on how such transformations take place is available (see Lambert, 1981; Lambert, Giles, and Picard, 1975). These transformations, it was found, involve radical changes in collective thinking. Instead of being pressured to accommodate and to put their home languages behind them, the ethnolinguistic minorities are given an opportunity to develop the home language fully by being schooled in the early years through that language so that it can be written and read as well as spoken and understood. The "rooting" of the home language in this fashion is coordinated with an independent program of study conducted through the national language, enabling the minority group young person to be at home in both languages and cultures.

As I see it, our best chance to meet this challenge is to recognize that there are two faces to bilingualism, a subtractive and an additive face, and to provide opportunities for *majority* group members—the mainstreamers in society—to embark on effective programs of language learning and bilingualism. Mainstreamers stand to profit a great deal from the addition of a new language. Society stands to profit even more because as soon as mainstreamers make the effort to develop real skill in other languages, they thereby demonstrate an appreciation of minority groups and minority languages. This appreciation then becomes the impetus minority group members need to master and be proud of the home languages and cultures they are now so often pressured to bypass and ignore. But most important of all, this suggested change permits the development of a genuine appreciation of bilinguals as national resources, and it permits as well the mainstreamer to become part of the same national enrichment.

How People Become Bilingual

Becoming bilingual depends mainly on the events and exigencies within families or communities or within a person's life experiences that make that person or those family members bilingual. Since one of the main themes of *Bringing Up Baby Bilingual* is how one can, even when the odds are low, become bilingual, it may be useful as a summary to explore typical ways the process starts. Bilingualism can start early or late. At its earliest, bilingualism can, as Merrill Swain (1972) so nicely put it, be the child's "first language." When both languages are given the chance to develop, these infant bilinguals show full command of the two (or more) codes, as though they were double monolinguals. And each of these double-language lives has its special fascination. My two children are a case in point. Some thirty-plus years ago, they were infant bilinguals with bilingualism as their first language. Born in Chapel Hill, North Carolina, of a French mother and an American father, they were a captive audience, in a sense. Actually, their bilingual experience was my wife's doing, because she didn't want to be a stranger to two American children, nor did she want to deprive them of the exciting, rich and unforgettable world of French stories, songs and points of view that she so cherished. We were shocked, in fact, to see so many other "mixed marriages" where the non-American partner's language and culture were put aside, purportedly to help their children cope and adjust to America. In this sense, then, our children had special treatment because we instigated their bilinguality, with French the within-the-home language and English the outside language. There was no trouble at all at the start, until graduate students specializing in French on the university campus began to recognize our children as amazing sounding-boards for oral practice, even though the children thought it was strange and wrong that these outsiders used our inside code. After all, the children never let friends their own age in on that secret. Complications arose also when it became clear that I was not a real speaker of French, that I was more comfortable in English and that they could join my wife in correcting my many errors. As they zoomed past me in French and caught up with me in English, a natural division of languages came into play even within the home; the rule became: Speak one way with Mother and the other way with Father. Family get-togethers ever since have been marked with this division. A sentence will start in French whenever my wife is involved and neatly turn English (at any point in the complex structure of the sentence) if the conversation is directed particularly to me. Otherwise, the within-family code still remains French, unless my wife slips out of the conversation even momentarily!

Not all mixed families in the same college town let their foreign language wither. The Dunn family was linguistically much richer and interesting than ours, especially for our daughter, who had a close friend among them. The Dunn girl's mother was of Russian background but had grown up in France; the father was an American. But Mrs. Dunn's father, who lived with them, was monolingual Russian. So the daughter had three full-blown strands to her multilingualism and that intrigued our children and put their bilinguality in proper perspective.

The switch of our residence to Montreal kept the two languages rolling, with education mainly in French-language schools. By the preteen years, two forms of French—Canadian versus European styles—were being perfected, and schooling in other languages was started, supplemented by work periods in the post-teen years in Germany for our son and Puerto Rico for our daughter. What amazes me is how large a role the language factor has played in their lives to date. My son, an economist and political scientist, lives in France, where his work demands that he be fluent in English as well as French, but where his special usefulness turned on his abilities in German and Italian (picked up, with perfection, at the college level). My daughter, an applied linguist, is a specialist in interpretation and translation in California and her teaching hinges on her skills in Spanish, French and English. Isn't it that what people mean when they say "The world is my oyster?"

But there are various ways in which infant bilingualism can be initiated. As Filstrup has illustrated, two languages can be introduced as family languages when a child is born, one language emanating from one parent, the second from the other parent, with no requirement that either parent be bilingual. In such a family, strong emotional attachments to each language are initiated. Both parents usually want to have a hand in the linguistic socialization so that their child is not a stranger to them. In this way, the child builds up parental associations with each language. In the process, the child becomes ethnolinguistically something more than either parent because he or she has a better opportunity to belong to both feed-in cultural groups than does either parent. To the extent that both parents keep up a socializing role, they can regulate and modulate the bilingualism and the biculturalism of the child, making it either balanced or lopsided. The child also has the means, through ethnic and linguistic ploys, to control the parents and the ethnic and linguistic atmosphere of the whole family.

By was of contrast, if both parents know the two relevant languages when a child is born, different emotional and identity demands are placed on the child. Their shared bilinguality usually reflects common background experiences for the parents and suggests that in some previous generation, some other set of parents had initiated the bilinguality. The more the child in this type of family becomes bilingual, the more he or she becomes similar in important respects to both parents.

Bilingualism that starts after infancy also can take various forms. A monolingual child can encounter a second language as a community or commerce language outside the home, as when the family lives in a foreign country. Or a second language can be the medium of schooling for an otherwise monolingual child, as is the case for many children in immigrant families. The shifting of residences through emigration can delay the start of bilingualism to even later age levels. And one can develop full bilingualism at any age through the intensive study of the second language. The current popularity of early immersion programs is an interesting case in point. In many Canadian schools and certain American ones, mainstream anglophone children can start immersion training—in which a monolingual French (or Spanish or Russian or whatever) teacher uses only the foreign language as the medium of instruction from kindergarten on, with English introduced only at grades 2 or 3 in small doses by a separate English-speaking teacher—and develop a rich form of functional bilingualism by the end of elementary school, with no retardation at all in their English-language development (see Lambert and Tucker, 1972). More exciting still is the "double immersion" experience, wherein anglophone youngsters can be introduced to two languages by two different immersion teachers (the example is Hebrew and French for Jewish children who speak only English). The amazing trilingual progress of children in these programs opens up all sorts of possibilities for educators and parents (see Genesee and Lambert, 1983).

Interestingly, current research indicates that these differences in starting point of bilingualism have significant effects on the linguistic, cognitive and emotional development of a child. Apparently the ultimate form of bilingualism is shaped in important ways by the age of inception. For instance, McGill studies show that early versus late bilingualism appears to affect how much the right half of the brain is brought into play in the control of language, and, surprisingly, the later development, as in the teen years, seems to initiate most right-side involvement (see Vaid and Lambert, 1979).

There are other ways to become bilingual as well, but to me the most heartening way is the one described in this book. It is a story, almost magical at points, of twins who are given the chance to become bilingual, starting in their second year of life, by parents who had relatively little linguistic means to support the process but who through interest, affection and ingenuity manufactured a comfortable bilingual environment in a suburb of New York City. These parents did it the hard way but in doing so and describing the fun they had in carrying it out, they leave few excuses to other parents who might look enviously on those mixed-language households who seem to have everything going for them linguistically. But even more than that, the story told here will have the greatest impact on ethnolinguistic minority families who may have started questioning the value of their ethnic and linguistic background. The message to them is clear: If some parents work so hard and have so much fun in engineering their children's bilinguality, why should ethnolinguistic minority groups think of shortchanging their children?

July 1984

References to Lambert

Aellen, C., and Lambert, W.E. 1969. "Ethnic identification and personality adjustments of Canadian adolescents of mixed

English-French parentage." *Canadian Journal of Behavioral Science*. I: 69-86.

Cummins, J. 1979. "Linguistic interdependence and the educational development of bilingual children." *Review of Educational Research*. 49: 222-51.

Gardner, R.C., and Lambert, W.E. 1972. *Attitudes and Motivation in Second-language Learning*. Rowley, Mass.: Newbury House.

Genesee, F., and Lambert, W.E. 1983. "Trilingual education for majority language children." *Child Development*. 54: 105-14.

Giles, H., and Powesland, P.F. 1975. *Speech Style and Social Evaluation*. London: Academic Press.

Hall, R.A., Jr. 1980. "Language, dialect and 'regional' Italian." *International Journal of the Sociology of Language*. 25: 95-106.

_____. 1967. "A social psychology of bilingualism." *Journal of Social Issues*. 23: 91-109.

Lambert, W.E. 1969. "Psychological studies of the interdependencies of the bilingual's two languages." In J. Puhvel (ed.), *Substance and Structure of Language*. Los Angeles: University of California Press.

_____. 1981. "Bilingualism and language acquisition." In H. Winitz (ed.), *Native Language and Foreign Language Acquisition*. New York, N.Y.: The New York Academy of Sciences, 9-22.

_____. 1984. "An overview of issues in immersion education." In *Studies on Immersion Education*. Sacramento: California State Department of Education, 8-30.

Lambert, W.E., and Tucker, G.R. 1972. *Bilingual Education of Children: The St. Lambert Experiment*. Rowley, Mass.: Newbury House.

Lambert, W.E., Giles, H., and Picard, O. 1975. "Language attitudes in a French-American community." *International Journal of the Sociology of Language*. 4: 127-52.

Lieberson, S., and Hansen, L.K. 1974. "National development, mother tongue diversity, and the comparative study of nations." *American Sociological Review*. 39: 523-41.

Rabushka, A., and Shepsle, K.A. 1972. *Politics in Plural Societies: A Theory of Democratic Instability.* Columbus, Ohio: C.E. Merrill.

Swain, M.K. 1972. *Bilingualism as a First Language.* Doctoral dissertation, University of California, Irvine, California.

Vaid, J., and Lambert, W.E. 1979. "Differential cerebral involvement in the cognitive functioning of bilinguals." *Brain and Language.* 8: 92-110.

INDEX